Management Accounting in Public Service Decision Making

Radical changes to public service delivery have swept across many regions of the world. Management accounting methods are vital to support operational and strategic decision making in public services internationally. This book provides a comprehensive and "leading-edge" guide to the topic.

Written by an expert scholar with practical experience of public service delivery, this book takes account of key trends such as increased demand for public services, financial austerity, technological change and enhanced performance management.

A globally relevant book, informed by cutting edge academic research and benefitting from integrated case studies, this is essential reading for both students and practitioners involved with the financial aspects of public services management.

Malcolm J. Prowle is currently a professor at the Gloucestershire Business School who has extensive experience of public services finance, in the UK and overseas.

What the experts say

"This book comes when public services face three major challenges: the austerity legacy, the pandemic and climate change. These require new strategic thinking and make unprecedented demands on decision makers. Without sound information, through good management accounting, decisions are made in ignorance. With its emphasis on strategic issues, it should be essential reading for public sector managers and accountants alike."

—Roger Latham, CPFA, Former Chief Executive and County
Treasurer, Nottinghamshire County Council, Past President
of CIPFA, UK

"This book offers an interesting and complete analysis of the crucial role Management Accounting should play in public services. It is written in a format for international relevance, both for students and public managers. Its contribution is very necessary in the current economic context of countries like Spain that are facing the challenge of optimizing their public spending."

—Dr Carolina Pontones Rosa, Associate Professor, Public
Sector Accounting, University of Castilla-La Mancha, Spain

"Professor Prowle utilises his wealth of practitioner and scholarly experience, advanced methods and applied case studies to explore and bring alive the impact of high quality management accounting on decision-making across the public sector. Traditionalist to contemporary, operations to strategic, performance to risk; this book compares and contrasts through expert-informed, well-researched and lived insight."

—Dr Peter Cross, CPFA, Chief Financial Officer, De Montfort
University, Leicester, Former NHS Finance Director, UK

"An excellent book that covers wide areas of management accounting in public sector organisations. It is one of a few books that address the context of the public sector in which management accounting operates at the international level. With its practical applications, the book will be useful for both managers and students in my country."

—Dr Ali Alyamoor, Senior Lecturer in Management
Accounting, University of Mosul, Iraq

"Malcolm Prowle puts management accounting into the context of public services, and from there goes on to elucidate how best to apply state-of-the-art approaches at a practical level. This involves considering the various strategic and operational decisions that face public services and examining the potential relevance and applicability of management accounting methods in each case."

—Rob Whiteman, CPFA, Chief Executive, CIPFA, UK

"An easily accessible and informative book for anyone keen to develop knowledge and understanding of the role of management accounting in public sector decision making. A vitally useful source for all public service managers grappling with a plethora of financial and practical challenges, resulting from increased demand and supply-chain pressures, made more complex in our post-Covid 19 world."

—Lynne Barrow, CPFA, Assistant Dean (International),
Hull University Business School, UK

"The title of Professor Prowle's book does scant justice to its relevance. Consistent with the premise that management accounting is a vital tool for decision making across a broad range of public sector organisations and functions, the text itself is much more than an arid accounting textbook. Using straightforward language, and drawing on numerous examples from the author's extensive practical experience, it is as much about management as it is about accounting. While undoubtedly an invaluable resource for members of the management accounting profession, this book is also essential reading for anyone who is, or aspires to become, a financially literate public sector manager.

Professor Prowle's book is also highly relevant for those who are tasked with leading public services in the developing world. Without undue reliance on specialist language, it provides a clear explanation of key concepts in public sector management, describes the vital role that information can play in guiding both operational and strategic decision making, and explores the contributions that management accounting can make in support of efforts to improve or reform public services. As such, the book occupies an important 'sweet spot' between generic management textbooks and more technical material."

—Philip Davies, Former Permanent Secretary, Fiji Government Ministry of Health & Medical Services, Former Deputy Secretary, Australian Government Department of Health & Ageing, Former Vice-Chair, WHO Executive Board

Management Accounting in Public Service Decision Making

MALCOLM J. PROWLE

The Chartered Institute of
Public Finance & Accountancy

Routledge
Taylor & Francis Group
LONDON AND NEW YORK

First published 2021
by Routledge
2 Park Square, Milton Park, Abingdon, Oxon OX14 4RN

and by Routledge
52 Vanderbilt Avenue, New York, NY 10017

Routledge is an imprint of the Taylor & Francis Group, an informa business

British Library Cataloguing-in-Publication Data
A catalogue record for this book is available from the British Library

Library of Congress Cataloging-in-Publication Data
Names: Prowle, Malcolm J., author.
Title: Management accounting in public service decision making / Malcolm J. Prowle.
Description: 1 Edition. | New York: Routledge, 2020. |
Series: Mastering public finance and accountancy |
Includes bibliographical references and index.
Identifiers: LCCN 2020035962 (print) | LCCN 2020035963 (ebook)
Subjects: LCSH: Managerial accounting. | Public administration. | Decision making.
Classification: LCC HF5657.4 .P768 2020 (print) |
LCC HF5657.4 (ebook) | DDC 352.3/3—dc23
LC record available at https://lccn.loc.gov/2020035962
LC ebook record available at https://lccn.loc.gov/2020035963

ISBN: 978-1-138-36616-9 (hbk)
ISBN: 978-1-138-36617-6 (pbk)
ISBN: 978-0-429-43046-6 (ebk)

Typeset in Sabon
by codeMantra

CONTENTS

PART A   Context of management accounting in public services

CHAPTER 1   Public service organisations and the public sector   3

CHAPTER 2   Operations management of public services   19

CHAPTER 3   The importance of strategy in public services   29

CHAPTER 4   Public service reforms   49

FIGURES

TABLES

CASE STUDIES

FOREWORD

Public services across the world face the twin pressures of increasing demand for services coupled with tight constraints on the level of financial resources available. Major policy challenges, such as climate change and the impact of disruptive events, including the recent Covid-19 pandemic, only add to these pressures.

In these economic and social conditions, public service organisations, wherever they may be located, require effective decision making about service delivery and the use of resources. Such decision making requires high-quality financial input using state-of-the-art management accounting practices. CIPFA is at the forefront promoting such practice improvements, worldwide, and indeed management accounting is a key building block in our Professional Qualification and our International Public Financial Management qualifications.

Management accounting has been in existence for more than 100 years and is applied in business and public services, but the role of the management accountant is continually changing. The management accountant of the future, as well as having first-class technical skills, requires expertise in both information management and organisational change management. The core of management accounting practice is also continually evolving to deal with changes in management practices and external forces such as environmental sustainability. Also important is the ongoing impact of new technology on management accounting practice.

CIPFA is one of the leading professional accountancy bodies and the only professional body, in the world that specialises in public service finance and accounting. Part of CIPFA's mission is to promote improvements in management accounting practice, in public services, through a variety of means such as education, training, thought leadership and the development of guidance. This book aims to be an advanced guide for practising managers and finance managers in public services across the world, and to students studying for professional accountancy qualifications including the CIPFA qualification.

As I've noted, management accounting is a core foundation of CIPFA's qualification suite, but I firmly believe public service organisations could be making more out of the potential the practice offers. That's where this book comes in. It provides a comprehensive and insightful guide that will allow you to grasp, fully, the opportunities and gains that management accounting offers.

A long-standing CIPFA member, Professor Malcolm Prowle is ideally placed to write this book. He has held management accounting posts in many parts of the public sector and has many years' experience as a consultant working on the financial analysis of public service projects. As well as UK experience, he has worked extensively in the public services of several other countries. In addition to his practical experience, Malcolm has held academic posts at a number of UK universities and has authored several books on management and financial management in public services, including publications for CIPFA on forecasting and the development of values-based cultures. He has also provided advice and evidence to select committees of the House of Commons, worked as a financial consultant to the World Health Organisation and lectured and spoken extensively at academic and professional conferences, addressing everyone from senior government officials to business and industry leaders. In the chapters that follow, Malcolm puts management accounting into the context of public services, and from there goes on to elucidate how best to apply state-of-the-art approaches at a practical level. This involves considering the various strategic and operational decisions that face public services and examining the potential relevance and applicability of management accounting methods in each case. This book is full of real-life case studies about various issues.

It's my firm wish that both managers and students in public service organisations put this book to good use.

Rob Whiteman
Chief Executive
CIPFA
June 2020

PREFACE

In all parts of the world, public services, today, face a daunting set of challenges. These challenges are fully discussed in this book but in summary they involve the tension between growing demands for public services (consequent on population ageing, technological development, etc.) and limitations on the amount of financial resources that can be committed to the financing of public services. While resources for public services have always been limited, over the last decade we have also seen the existence of what is now termed "austerity". This term came to prominence as a consequence of the Great Recession of 2007/09 and implies a strong downward pressure on the level of resources being devoted to public services as a consequence of the state of the public finances. While the details of this situation will vary between countries, austerity exists to some extent almost everywhere.

Add to the above, the pressures on all governments of other factors, which are either on the horizon or already with us, and the picture is even more complex and difficult. For example:

- The climate change issue is well known, and dealing with climate change is something likely to impact on the workload and resources of governments, everywhere, for decades to come.
- At the time of writing, the coronavirus pandemic is impacting around the globe and the precise impacts of this event are difficult to discern. However, we can be certain there will be serious implications for the economies of all countries as well as for the provision of public services, especially health services.
- For some years now, inward migration has been seen as a major political problem in many developed and developing countries around the world. The impact of climate change is likely to exacerbate this situation with parts of the world becoming uninhabitable. Thus, the scale of migration in years to come is likely to dwarf the current rates of migration and will have major impacts for public services and public funds.

In the light of the above, it can be seen that there are huge challenges facing governments and public servants everywhere. Consequently, effective and efficient decision making by governments and public service agencies will need to be a priority. Unfortunately, there is much evidence to suggest that such decision making in public services is far from being optimal. Failures of public policy development and policy implementation exist everywhere, both in developed and developing countries along with dissatisfaction with public services. Given that funds for public services will always be limited, the financial input into public service decision making must be of the highest quality. This is where effective management accounting comes in.

The practice of accounting is often divided into two types in both public and private sectors. Financial accounting, primarily, involves the preparation of annual financial statements for organisations, which are then released into the public domain, and which show the financial performance and financial position of the organisation for the year ended. Thus, they are a mechanism for accountability for the use of funds. On the other hand, management accounting involves the provision of information and analysis to managers in the organisation to facilitate decision making in the organisation particularly around strategic choices and operational practices. Quite often, the role of management accounting is often understated but good management accounting is vital if the organisation is to make good decisions.

This book aims to outline what good management accounting involves and how, if applied properly, it can be a major factor in achieving effective decision making and optimising public services. This is especially important in public services where an absence of good financial information (or any other relevant information) can lead to decisions being over-politicised. This book is aimed at two broad groups of people:

- Managers who make use of management accounting information and advice in making decisions in public services need to understand the nature of good practice in this area.
- Management accountants and other finance managers who need a better understanding of the nature of public service decision making and the role that management accounting should be playing in this arena. It also considers the way in which the role of management accountants is, in the near future, bound to change substantially, particularly as a consequence of technological (AI) and other developments taking place.

This book is written with an international perspective and will be of great relevance to managers and financial managers in public services in all countries.

Part A of this book describes the context of public services in which management accounting will operate. The configuration and operation of public services will vary from country to country, but these first six chapters attempt to describe the key contextual factors for management accounting practice which will be relevant everywhere.

Part B of this book will consider, in detail, the different aspects of management accounting practices and how they might be applied in public services in all countries. Case studies illustrate the practical applications of the various approaches involved.

I must record my thanks to a number of people. First, my wife Alison for her ongoing and unfailing support. Second, thanks are due to a number of colleagues, friends and family members who agreed to cast their expert eyes over the various draft chapters of this book. These were Lynne Barrow, Dr Peter Cross, Dr Simon Cox, Gillian Fawcett, Dr Don Harradine, Roger Latham, Dr Mike Lucas, Manj Kalar, Dr Henry Midgely, Mark Bowling, Fiona Bradley, Dr Vangelis Tsiligkiris, Alison Prowle and Caitlin Prowle. Finally, thanks are due to Drew Cullen and Rhiannon Price (CIPFA) and Kristina Abbots and Terry Claque (Routledge) for their help and encouragement. Also, to Rob Whiteman, chief executive of CIPFA, for writing the foreword. All errors are, of course, mine.

Professor Malcolm J. Prowle
June 2020

ABOUT THE AUTHOR

Professor Malcolm Prowle currently holds academic positions in several UK universities. He is an academically and professionally qualified accountant (CIPFA, ACCA) and has extensive experience of strategy, financial and economic analysis, and performance management in both private and public sectors.

This was gained by wide-ranging experience (in the UK and overseas) of senior financial management posts in several public sector organisations, management consultancy positions with two major international consulting firms (KPMG and PWC) and academic posts at the Universities of Warwick, Wolverhampton, Gloucestershire and Nottingham Trent.

He has worked at the highest levels of government and has advised Ministers, Ambassadors, senior civil servants and public service managers on various issues. He has been financial adviser to two House of Commons Select Committees, adviser to two Shadow Ministers and a consultant to the World Health Organisation. He has spoken and presented papers at a wide range of events and conferences including that of the Prime Ministers Policy Unit, the Government Accounting Service, the CBI, the World Health Organisation, Welsh Government as well as academic and professional conferences.

He has over 80 publications to his name. This includes seven full-length books, three book chapters, numerous research reports and papers in both academic peer-refereed and professional journals. He has co-published several published reports for CIPFA.

ABBREVIATIONS

3Es	Economy, effectiveness and efficiency
3PL	Third party logistics
3Rs	Reduce, reuse, recycle
3SOs	Third sector organisations
ABC	Activity-based costing
ACCA	Association of Chartered Certified accountants
AI	Artificial intelligence
ARR	Accounting rate of return
BDA	Big data analytics
CBA	Cost-Benefit Analysis
CIMA	Chartered Institute of Management Accounting
CIPFA	Chartered Institute of Public Finance and Accountancy
CUA	Cost Utility Analysis
DBABC	Driver-based activity-based costing
DCF	Discounted cash flow
DSM	Decision support modelling
DSO	Direct Service Organisation (of a local authority)
DSS	Decision support system
EMA	Environmental management accounting
FE	Further Education
GDP	Gross Domestic Product
GNI	Gross National Income
HE	Higher Education
HEI	Higher education institution
ICT	Information and Communications Technology
IOCM	Inter-organisational cost management
IS	Information system
IT	Information Technology
ITU	Intensive Therapy Unit
LCC	Life-cycle costing
MCS	Management control system
MIS	Management Information System
ML	Machine learning
NAO	National Audit Office
NHS	National Health Service
NPM	New Public Management
NPV	Net present value
PAB	Programme analysis and budgeting
PAC	Public Accounts Committee
PBB	Priority-based budgeting

PCT	Primary Care Trust (of the NHS)
PFI	Private Finance Initiative
PM	Performance management
PBB	Priority-based budgeting
PPP	Public-private partnerships
QUANGO	Quasi-autonomous non-governmental organisation
SCA	Strategic cost analysis
SCI	Strategic cost improvement
SLA	Service level agreement
SWOT	Strengths, weaknesses, opportunities, threats
TA	Throughput accounting
TDABC	Time-driven activity-based costing
TOC	Theory of constraints
VCA	Value chain analysis
VFM	Value for money
WACC	Weighted average cost of capital
ZBB	Zero-based budgeting

Context of management accounting in public services

Public service organisations and the public sector

INTRODUCTION

Over the last 30–40 years, public services in many countries have had to face an environment of continuous and sometimes radical change. Looking forward, a variety of political, societal, economic, technological and legal trends in the world suggest that public services will continue to undergo substantial pressure for change. This will be the case in both developed countries and developing countries although the precise nature of the changes will vary from case to case.

In this environment of ongoing and almost continual change, it is essential to ensure that public services are provided in such a way that they meet the needs of service users and are provided in a manner that makes the best use of the scarce public funds that are available.

In the last decade, public services in many countries have had to face what became known as "austerity", which is basically coping in an environment of increasing demand coupled with limited (or nil) growth in resources. Many will argue that this climate of austerity has involved a certain degree of "damage" to public services in terms of the impact on those who receive services and those front line staff who deliver services (Gray and Barford 2018). Now while effective financial management and decision making cannot resolve the issues of austerity, it can mitigate the impact by ensuring that the decisions made are making the best use of available resources. Published evidence and my own observations suggest that the standards of financial management and decision making vary within public services from the excellent to the adequate. Clearly, the aim must be to raise the standards in those organisations that would be seen as just "adequate". This requires service recipients, service professionals and managers, at all levels, in public service organisations to be aware that resources are always limited and to make decisions, strategic and operational, about the services they are responsible for. To undertake this role they will utilise a wide range of management tools and approaches.

An essential part of these management tools and approaches is the application of what we term "management accounting". There are many definitions of management accounting but one based on the work of the Institute of Management Accountants is as follows:

> Management accounting involves partnering in management decision-making, devising planning and performance management systems, and providing expertise in financial reporting and control to assist management in the formulation and implementation of an organisation's strategy and operations.
>
> (IMA 2008)

This will be further discussed in a later chapter but for the moment, it should just be noted that, as a key part of the management process, public service organisations will need to develop and apply effective approaches to management accounting. This is in order to ensure that the decisions made about those scarce resources are made in an optimal manner.

Before starting to consider specific aspects of management accounting practice, it is first necessary to consider various aspects of public services where management accounting will be applied. In this chapter we start by considering the following aspects of public service organisations and the management of public services:

- What are public services?
- What are the distinctive features of public services?
- Challenges facing public services
- Aims and structure of this book

WHAT ARE PUBLIC SERVICES?

Economic history shows us that in virtually all countries, as economies develop there are major shifts in the configuration of their economies. The first major shift concerns a shift from agriculture to manufacture and the second from manufacture to services. In developed countries, the shift from agriculture to manufacture started at the time of the industrial revolution. However, in the last 40–50 years or so we have seen major shifts in the economic output from manufacture to service industries to the extent that services dominate the economies of most developed countries. In developing countries, the shift from agriculture to manufacture has been more recent with a subsequent shift to services.

The economies of countries can be analysed into a series of sectors such as agriculture, construction, manufacture and services. The category of services can be provided by private sector organisations or public sector organisations (public services). However, service organisations are not homogeneous and show a large degree of variety including retail, transport, distribution, personal services. At this point, it is worth considering what exactly are the characteristics of services and service organisations and how they differ from the manufacture of goods. Services can be considered to have the following main characteristics.

1. **Intangibility.** When one purchases a car or a radio you can see it, feel it and even test it prior to purchase. In other words, goods have tangible qualities that provide information to consumers so they can easily compare one product to another. Services, on the other hand, are intangible. Most services cannot be experienced or consumed until the purchase is made.
2. **Inseparability.** To continue using the automobile analogy, cars are produced at one location, sold at another and used at yet another location. Services are unique because they are usually provided and consumed at the same time in the same location (e.g. a haircut or car tune-up). Because of the characteristic of inseparability, users have strong expectations about how a service will be provided, which can lead to disappointment if their expectations are not met.
3. **Perishability.** If a car does not sell today, it can be stored and sold the following day or at some other time in the future. Services, on the other hand, are often perishable, meaning that unused capacity cannot be stored for future use or sale. For example, a restaurant might be full one night and half empty the next. The spare capacity on the second night cannot be stored and used another time.
4. **Variability.** Once you have decided to buy a particular model of car then you know that there will be little or no variation in the quality of that model from one dealer to another. Manufactured goods tend to have automated processes and quality assurance procedures that result in a consistent product. However, the quality of a service can vary by many factors, including who provides it, where it is provided, when it is provided and how it is provided. The more an organisation relies on humans to provide services (instead of automation), the more susceptible it is to variability.

If we look more closely at public services, we find the following:

- Public services are (as the name suggests) usually concerned with the delivery of services. Today, in the UK, it is rare to find an example of a public service organisation that manufactures a product although this was not always the case in the past with such organisations as a nationalised steel industry. In many other countries, one will find state-owned companies which manufacture products, state utilities, etc., but the predominant role of the public sector will still be the delivery of public services.
- Public services are a large and vital part of an economy. However, this will vary from country to country.
- As public services involve services they will share the above characteristics and this will have implications for organisational management. However, the mix of characteristics will vary from service to service. This will become important when we discuss detailed aspects of management accounting since there are specific issues concerning management accounting which apply in service organisations (including public services) which differ from those in manufacturing organisations.

Looking beyond this we need to consider, further, the question of what exactly constitutes public services. There is no simple answer to this, and in the sections below, we try to address this question from four main standpoints:

- Statutory basis for existence
- Types of organisations
- Types of services
- Source of finance

Statutory basis

Generally public service organisations have been created on the basis of a specific piece of legislation passed by the country' legislature. This legislation defines a large range of issues concerning the public service organisations such as structures, duties, governance, financing and reporting.

Private sector organisations like charities and companies will also be set up under a statutory framework but a different framework to that for public service organisations. However, whereas private individuals can set up a company or charity within the approved statutory framework, it is only government which can establish public service organisations

Types of organisations

The opposite of a public sector organisation might be seen as private sector organisation but this of course is an over simplification. There are also a wide range of other organisations (e.g. charities, think tanks, churches, etc.) which are often described under the heading of third sector organisations. However, some might argue that, in reality, such third sector organisations are really just a particular type of private sector organisation and are not public sector organisations at all. Nevertheless, these third sector organisations are a key component of public service delivery in most countries.

Thus, the main public sector organisations might be classified as follows:

National Government

These are the government departments which operate at the national level and support the policies of the various Ministers. Some examples of such departments are as follows:

- Prime Minister
- Finance
- Foreign Affairs
- Defence
- Interior
- Health
- Education
- Environment
- Welfare
- Economy, etc.

TABLE 1.1

Executive agencies

Parent Government Department	Executive Agency	Operational Functions Undertaken
Department of the Environment	Highways Agency	Management and maintenance of major roads
Department of Work and Pensions	Job Centre Plus	Payment of welfare benefits and assistance with finding employment
Home Office	Passport Agency	Issue of passports
Home Office	National Offender Management Service	Management of prisons and probation service

In addition, a novel approach pioneered in the UK (but subsequently applied in other countries) was the creation of a series of executive agencies that operated at "arm's length" from their parent government department and might be referred to as arm's length management organisations (ALMO). As such, they undertook the various operational activities on behalf of the relevant department. Some UK examples of such executive agencies are shown in Table 1.1.

Although these agencies operate at arm's length from their sponsoring government department they are still a component of national government sector. However, the "arm's length" arrangement involves the creation of a contract between the government department and the executive agency concerning the services to be delivered and the funding to be provided. The contract performance will be monitored, and any failures may result in financial penalties being levied on the agency. Hence, the agency can be seen as operating on a quasi-trading basis.

Sub-national government

In many countries, there is often a tier of government that sits between the national government and local government. This might be referred to as regional government, provincial government, state government, etc. The nature of this sub-national tier in terms of its role, its power bases, whether it is elected or appointed, etc., will vary hugely between countries. In the UK, a form of devolved government has been created for certain parts of the country (e.g. Scotland) which might be referred to as a Parliament or an Assembly and which has responsibility for a range of services in the devolved areas.

Government agencies

These organisations are neither central government departments nor are they executive agencies. They might be seen as operating in semi-autonomous relationships but still ultimately accountable to central government. These types of organisation are sometimes referred to as *quasi-autonomous non-governmental organisations* (QUANGO).

Local government

In many, if not, most countries it is usual to find what might be termed local (or municipal) government comprising a number of what are described as local (or municipal) authorities. These local authorities might be subordinate to national or sub-national government depending on the country concerned. Local authorities are responsible, as the name suggests, for providing a wide range of what might be termed "local" services. Thus, they are those public services most visible to the general public. However, beyond that there will be significant variations between countries in the arrangements for local government:

- In some countries, there might be a single unitary local government structure involving just one type of local authority (e.g., Wales). In parts of England we see a binary system involving county and district councils, while in parts of India there could be three tiers of local authority.
- The range of services provided by local authorities will vary greatly. In the UK, local government is responsible for the provision of education and social care as well as what might be seen as the more mundane services of street cleaning and waste collection. By contrast, in Australia, the services provided by local authorities are more restricted to issues such as care of physical infrastructure and environmental management although this is an evolving situation. In Sweden, local authorities are responsible for the provision of health services.

Partnerships

These are not separate public service organisations but a series of organisations working together in a partnership arrangement to meet local service needs. At this point, we should distinguish between two types of partnerships:

Public-public partnerships Such partnerships often exist largely because the organisational boundaries between different public service organisations do not reflect the continuity of some services across those boundaries. Others exist because of the potential for obtaining economies of scale in public service provision. Partnerships can show great variety. Some may be formal in nature and others much more informal with several organisations working loosely together. Some may have a strong strategic focus, while others are more concerned with operational implementation of services. Examples of organisations working in partnership arrangements could include local government, health services, police, third sector, etc.

Public-private partnerships It should also be noted that there are also a wide range of partnerships in existence that involve public service organisations working in partnership with the private sector.

There are a variety of different forms of public-private partnerships (PPPs) including the following:

- The outsourcing of services (e.g. catering, security, maintenance, etc.) to the private sector as opposed to in-house delivery by public service employees

- Companies jointly owned by a public sector and private sector organisation
- The transfer of responsibility for delivery of a public service to a private sector organisation but paid for out of public funds. For example, a patient being treated in a private hospital but the treatment being paid for by the government health agency
- The Private Finance Initiative (PFI) – The PFI is probably the best known of these PPPs, and although the details of a PFI project will vary from case to case and from country to country, the process probably goes something like below:

  - The private sector (which could be a single company or a consortium) designs, finances and constructs a new building for the delivery of public services (e.g. a hospital, a school).
  - The private sector provides a range of services concerned with the building such as cleaning, security and maintenance.
  - The private sector charges the public service organisation an annual payment to cover the costs of using the building and the associated services.
  - The public sector organisation provides the core staff (e.g. doctors, nurses, teachers) needed for service delivery and manages the delivery of those services.

There are a number of possible reasons for having such PPPs including:

- Access to private sector capital funds for the purposes of developing public sector infrastructure
- Improved efficiency and value for money in the use of public funds
- Innovative ideas from the private sector about service delivery
- Access to private sector capacity at a time of high demand for public services

Overall, it is probably fair to say that the overall success of PPPs is debatable to say the least. Many will argue that it is really just a sleight of hand to privatise public services on ideological grounds.

Other public sector organisations

There are other organisations which may be regarded as being definitely public sector organisations, but in other cases there may be doubt as to whether they are really public or private sector. These include the following examples:

- Virtually all countries will have universities which in some cases might be seen as public, in other places private and sometimes the situation is unclear.
- Companies – some public sector organisations have formed companies for a specific purpose such as economic development where they are the sole shareholder.

Types of public services

Public services and the public sector are terms that we use every day to describe certain activities that affect our lives on a daily basis. Thus, for example, we see local authority services such as schools, waste collection, roads maintenance and health services in terms of hospitals, primary care, etc.

Clearly public services are numerous and varied, and many of them probably do not impinge on our consciousness to the same extent as others which are more visible. However, we can attempt a broad classification of public services of which the main groups would be as follows:

- *Defence and foreign relations* – this involves relations with other countries (diplomatic service) and defence of the country (armed forces).
- *Economic management* – this involves a wide range of economic issues including the promotion of economic growth, the management of public finances, public debt management, regional economic development and trade relations.
- *Law and order* – a key role of the state is to maintain law and order in society. Thus, in this group would be included such services as police, prisons, courts of law, probation services, etc.
- *Population welfare* – these are concerned with the basic well-being of the individuals and the society at large. Thus, they could include such services as education, health, social care, social protection etc. In many developing countries, such services may not be provided, formally, by governmental organisations but, informally, by family members, voluntary groups, etc.
- *Physical infrastructure* – the maintenance and development of the physical infrastructure of the country including roads, housing, airports, communications and power. This may be done by direct provision by government or the use of private companies regulated by government.
- *Environmental protection and management* – this has always been an important area of public policy in all countries, but in recent decades the increasing importance placed on the problems of global warming and climate change has significantly increased the emphasis placed on various aspects of the environment. This trend can be expected to continue in the future. A wide of variety of issues fall under this heading concerning waste disposal, energy, water supply, land management, pollution control, etc.
- *Health protection* – this is a term used to encompass a set of activities within the public health function. It involves such matters as the safety and quality of food, prevention of communicable diseases, managing outbreaks and the other incidents that threaten the public health. Health protection has both a domestic and an international dimension, and its importance has been greatly magnified in recent months because of the coronavirus pandemic.

We have seen above that, in any country, there can be a number of different public service organisations that provide a range of different services. The relationship between the organisation and the services provided is complex and will vary considerable from country to country. A complete sectoral analysis is difficult to produce, but some examples are shown in Table 1.2.

At this point, it is important to mention the importance of multi-agency provision of public services since this is a theme that will be, frequently, mentioned throughout this book. The reality is that many public services will not

TABLE 1.2

Public sector organisations and public services

Service Sector	Organisations Involved
Education	• Federal department/Ministry for Education • Sub-national Governments • Government agencies • Local government • Schools • Universities and colleges
Defence	• Ministry of Defence • Government agencies • Armed forces (army, navy, air force)
Health	• Federal department/Ministry for Health • Sub-national Governments • Government agencies • Hospitals • Local authorities (Environmental Health)
Economic development	• Federal finance ministry • Other federal government departments/ministries (e.g. trade) • Sub-national Governments • Government agencies • Universities/colleges • Local authorities (Economic Development Units)
Social welfare/employment	• Ministry of Social Security • Government agency • Local authorities
Law and order	• Federal department/Ministry of Interior • Police • Courts • Prisons

be provided by a single agency but will require the involvement of several public service agencies with the aim of providing a seamless service to the client. To do this requires close cooperation, at both strategic and operational levels, between the various agencies involved.

Source of finance

In the simplest terms, public services can be paid for from two main sources.

- From public funds either from locally levied or nationally levied taxation or government borrowing
- From private funds (individuals or organisations) through the levying of charges for services provided. In some cases the charge might be levied indirectly, in that the person has paid for a private insurance policy which pays for the public service when required

In reality, in most countries, the vast bulk of public services is financed from public funds although the mix between public and private funding will vary between countries and organisations.

WHAT ARE THE DISTINCTIVE FEATURES OF PUBLIC SERVICES?

There are a number of ways in which a degree of distinctiveness can be seen in public service organisations compared to other organisations. This section is not necessarily exhaustive but some examples of distinctiveness are given below.

Governance

Effective governance arrangements are important in the public sector as they are in the private sector, and there have been many instances of failed governance in public services to sit alongside those in the private sector. However, there are some key differences in governance arrangements that should be highlighted:

- **Agency.** One of the key concepts in corporate governance is that of agency. In a private company of larger size, the people who manage a business do not own it, and manage the business on behalf of the owners. Thus, it is said that management has an agency relationship with the principals (owners), in that they have a duty to help the principals achieve the objective they seek. Managers in the public sector have a similar agency role but the principals are more varied. While companies have shareholders as principals, public sector organisations have a number of stakeholders all of whom are interested in the performance of the organisation and the way in which it is managed. These include the following:
  - Those that fund the activity (e.g. taxpayers)
  - Those that use the services (e.g. hospital patients)
  - Voters in local or national elections
  - The general public at large
  - The media

Thus, the governance process in public services has greater diversity of focus.

- **Objectives.** Public sector organisations emphasise different types of objectives to the private sector. Whereas private companies may aim to increase their sales, maximise their profits, optimise their competitive positions, etc., public sector organisations tend to be concerned with social purposes and delivering their services in such a way as to meet the needs of users while delivering value for money in the use of public resources. Such objectives are far more wide ranging, complex and often difficult to demonstrate through the governance process.

Political influence

One distinct feature of public services which is often quoted is the inextricable link with politics. This is especially the case in countries with democratic forms of government where elected representatives at national, regional or local level take a keen interest in public services because the availability and quality of those public services can impact on voting intentions. Even in non-democratic societies, it is likely that the country's leaders will also take a strong interest in public services to avoid public dissatisfaction or even unrest.

Hence, it is inevitable that the activities of public sector organisations will be closely followed by a range of stakeholders, and changes to the pattern, location, etc., of public services can easily become a hot political issue both locally and/or nationally. Now it is true that commercial organisations can be influenced to change certain policies and practices through the views of its customers and other stakeholders. What makes things different in public services is that elected representatives, at local or national level, can directly involve themselves in decision making by public service organisations

Monopolistic tendencies

Monopolistic private sector businesses are usually regarded as a bad thing for the simple reason that monopolists can often exploit their customers and make large profits without any fear of competition. It is often argued that some public service organisations are also monopolists since they are the only organisation who can supply a service to a client, as there are no competitors. Examples here might be state telecommunications organisations, local government waste collection services, etc. In such a situation, public service monopolists can also abuse their position by being inefficient or not meeting client needs satisfactorily. For several decades, in some countries, the solution to this problem was seen to be the conversion of a number of monopolistic public sector organisations (e.g. telecommunications, energy, transport) into private sector companies. This is termed privatisation. However, these newly privatised companies might, in the absence of a government regulatory regime, be seen to be just converting public sector monopolies into private sector monopolies (Prowle 2008). Nevertheless, to a lesser or greater extent, public services in, probably, all countries display some monopolistic tendencies.

Free at point of consumption

The discussion of the ways of financing public services outlined that services can basically be financed by the taxpayer or by the service user by means of charges. Now this illustrates the point that no public service can be regarded as "free" for the simple reason that there is always someone who pays for them in one way or another. However, when we consider typical private sector goods such as cars, computers, houses and food it is usual that the consumer of those goods makes payment or them out of their own pocket. This contrasts greatly with the situation regarding public services. While a range of charges may be levied for certain public services the reality is that in **most** countries, **most** public services are provided to the user with no charge and are thus described as largely free at the point of consumption. Thus, public services such as health, schools, roads, defence and policing are provided with little or no charge to the user. Even where user charges are levied, it is likely to be the case that most charges do not reflect the full cost of the service and therefore involve a public subsidy.

CHALLENGES FACING PUBLIC SERVICES

In all countries, public services, today, face many challenges. These challenges will be discussed further in the chapter on public services reform but a brief description of the main challenges is outlined below.

Increasing demands for services

In many countries today, we see an ongoing and increasing demand for certain public services. There are probably four main issues that drive increasing demands for services.

- **Population growth** – the global population keeps expanding. In 1960, the global population was three billion while today it is seven billion. By 2050, it is expected to be ten billion. Nor is this just a phenomenon of the developing world. The UK Office for National Statistics (ONS) projections suggest that the population of the UK will increase from 62.3 million in 2010 to 67.2 million by 2020 and 73.2 million by 2035. Clearly, population growth of any kind will have implications for the demand for a range of public services such as health, education and housing. However, the other side of the coin is that such an increase in population may result in higher levels of economic growth and tax revenues to government but this is uncertain.

- **Ageing population** – this is the well-known phenomena, in both developed and developing countries, of the ageing population brought about by continuing declines in all-age all-cause mortality rates meaning that more and more people are living into their 80s, 90s and beyond. In addition, there is also the phenomenon of declining fertility rates (and new births) which means that populations are becoming skewed to the older end of the spectrum. It is well established that a growing proportion of elderly in the population has resource consequences for a range of public services, most notably health and social care.

- **Scientific and technological developments** – these have implications for the demand for public services, and two aspects of this should be noted. The first concerns medical science and technology. New developments create demand for services where none previously existed. Consider the following: artificial joint replacements, organ transplants, drug therapies and imaging techniques. Before such developments took place, the demand for such services was zero. However, the existence and supply of such treatments, in turn, creates and fuels the demand that previously was non-existent. This is expected to continue.

  In addition, the IT revolution is well known and understood. In the last 30 years, we have seen a wide range of technological developments such as personal computing, networks, e-mail and the Internet. Such developments have truly changed the world and have revolutionised many aspects of human life including the delivery of public services. These developments have resource implications for public authorities and are likely to do so in the future.

- **Societal trends** – this concerns broad societal trends such as family break-down, loss of the extended family and the number of persons living in one-person households. Such trends have, over the last few decades, had major implications for many public services and seem likely to do so in the future. Also to be noted are increased public expectations of what public services will deliver and an enhanced sense of "entitlement" which probably has its origins in the "choice" agenda of the 2000s.

Austerity

The term "austerity" in relation to public services was coined in the aftermath of the Great Recession of 2007–2009. This was called the Great Recession because of its exceptional depth and longevity. Furthermore, while, after most previous recessions, countries generally recovered back to previous growth levels fairly quickly, this proved difficult to achieve following the Great Recession with many countries having only very small amounts of economic growth.

One of the consequences of the Great Recession and the associated financial crash were high levels of indebtedness among governments and individuals that had to be resolved. Consequently, many countries implemented policies that are often referred to under the blanket term of "austerity". These policies often involved limited growth or even significant reductions in the levels of funding growth for public services to much lower levels than had been experienced in the past, or even real terms reductions in the levels of funding available.

At the time austerity commenced, the expectation was that it would only be a temporary phenomenon and the growth in funding for public services would soon return to historic levels. However, this did not prove to be the case, and in many countries coping with austerity is still a key challenge for public services.

Indeed, it is possible that public services will have to cope with managing and delivering public services on a resource base, which grows only very slowly as time goes on. Hence, this might be thought of as something of a "perfect storm" involving ongoing growth in public service demand coupled with stagnant growth in funding.

Climate change

Most people would accept the existence of climate change and the fact that it is one of the great challenges facing humanity. The causes and timing of climate change are debatable but its impacts are a cause of concern to all. Just a few examples of the potentially extensive impact of climate change are as follows:

- Increased incidence of extreme weather
- Increased flooding through rising sea levels or extensive rainfall
- Some parts of the world becoming uninhabitable
- Reduced security of food supply
- Lack of access to water in some countries
- Increased prevalence of some diseases (e.g. melanomas)
- Large-scale migration of people from uninhabitable areas, etc.

Now the above (and other) factors will undoubtedly have an impact on organisations of all types but especially public service organisations. These impacts can be considered as three categories:

- The need to take actions to reduce the rate of climate change (e.g. improved waste recycling, better insulation)
- The need to make preparations to mitigate the impacts of climate change (e.g. flood defences)
- The need to take actions to deal with the consequences of climate changes (e.g. extensive flooding, cliff erosion, etc.)

Many public services are already extensively involved in all three of the above categories. However, the main challenge is to recognise the wide range of climate change impacts referred to above and to realise that the situation is likely to worsen over the next few decades.

Pandemics

Pandemics might be seen as one of a number of catastrophic events which would have major impacts for the population of many countries in the world, but which are largely unpredictable. Other examples here would be extreme weather, volcanic eruptions, etc.

However, it could be argued that a global pandemic isn't unpredictable. The possibility of a major global health pandemic has been discussed as a possibility for many years, and indeed, there were a number of serious outbreaks of communicable diseases (e.g. SARS, avian flu, Ebola) which came close to being termed a pandemic. Nevertheless, little action appeared to be taken by governments across the globe, and the appearance of the coronavirus (Covid 19) outbreak that became a pandemic caught most governments unprepared. At the time of writing the coronavirus pandemic is causing hundreds of thousands of deaths worldwide and wreaking havoc on world economies. The final impact of this pandemic will not be known for some time, but the costs to governments of providing health services and support to their economies are likely to prove substantial. Another key issue is what actions governments might now take (and what will be the costs) to prevent future communicable disease outbreaks from spreading around the globe and for providing services to those who are infected. This will be a particular issue in developing countries who do just not have the resources to strengthen their health systems but whose people, through international travel, might cause such a disease to spread. This seems a situation whereby developed countries, for their own benefit, might see a need to finance the strengthening of health systems in developing countries.

Organisational inertia

Given the challenges, referred to above, of coping with increasing demand and limited growth in resources, there is clearly an imperative to think closely about the way public services are delivered and what sorts of changes should be made to cope with the pressures involved. Such changes could involve any combination of the following:

- The range of services offered
- The location of service provision
- The way in which the services are delivered
- The potential use of new technology in service delivery
- The need for improved inter-agency working, etc.

Unfortunately, the planning and making of such changes is often difficult to achieve because of what might be termed "organisational inertia" (Hannan and Freeman 1984). Organisational inertia is a term used to describe the tendency of bureaucratic organisations to perpetuate established procedures and modes of operation, even if they are counterproductive and/or diametrically opposed to current and established organisational goals. Public authorities are traditionally seen as bureaucracies (in a non-pejorative sense) with political and cultural constraints not found to the same extent in most private sector organisations. Consequently, overcoming such inertia in the light of austerity is often a major challenge for such organisations. There is often strong resistance to change in public services caused by the large number of vested interests in maintaining the status quo that comprises a wide range of groups including employees, trade unions, professional bodies, politicians, service users, charities, politicians and the media. Hence, overcoming such inertia is a key challenge for public services.

AIMS AND STRUCTURE OF THIS BOOK

This book can be divided into two parts.

Management accounting cannot be considered in a vacuum, and the application of management accounting in any organisation is shaped by what the organisation does and how it is done.

Part A, chapters 2–6, describes aspects of public services that impact on the shape of management accounting:

- Chapter 2 discusses the nature of operations management in public services and outlines the potential role of management accounting.
- Chapter 3 discusses the nature and importance and strategy in public services and outlines the potential role of management accounting.
- Chapter 4 outlines the various reforms to public services which have taken place, worldwide, in recent decades and their impact on public services.
- Chapter 5 considers the nature and importance of leadership, management and decision making in public services.
- Chapter 6 discusses, in general terms, the nature and importance of management accounting in the management of public services.

Part B turns to the practice of management accounting in public service organisations in the context set out in Part A. Thus, chapters 7–13 discuss various applications of management accounting practice that have application to public services. These are as follows:

- Chapter 7 covers costing and costing systems. Costing is often seen as the bedrock of management accounting, and this chapter covers various aspects of costing as they affect public services.

- Chapter 8 looks at the roles of management accounting in operational decision making in public services.
- Chapter 9 looks at the roles of management accounting in strategic decision making in public services.
- Chapter 10 discusses management control and the role of management accounting from an operational and strategic standpoint in public services.
- Chapter 11 discusses the role of management accounting in performance management and performance improvement in public services.
- Chapter 12 covers the topic of risk management in public services from an operational and strategic standpoint and the role of management accounting.
- Chapter 13 discusses some contemporary aspects of management accounting which have implications for public services.

Operations management of public services

INTRODUCTION

This chapter is concerned with operational aspects of the delivery and management of public services and the role to be played by management accounting in decision making at this level.

It is often the case that the topic of strategy is seen, in organisations, as being more important and more glamorous than operations management. Now while a comprehensive and achievable strategy is vitally important in both public and private sectors, the existence of poor operations management in an organisation is likely to lead to a failure to achieve its strategic objectives. This point can clearly be observed in the world of military where war strategies may fail because of poor tactical practices on the battlefield.

Thus, effective operations management is a key component of management in the commercial sector and in the public sector. Originally, the subject developed in the manufacturing industry but the principles of operations management are now also well established in the commercial services sector. The principles of operations management are also applicable to many public services but in many public service organisations, the concept of operations management is not always well developed or understood (Radnor et al. 2016). There is sometimes a feeling that what is applicable in the private service sector is not applicable in the public service sector. However, if one looked at (say) a hospital, one would see quite quickly that the operational principles are similar in both public and private sectors.

Basically, operations management is concerned with the ways in which public services are developed, organised and delivered to clients. It specifically deals with decisions about what is required from operations managers for the simultaneous production and consumption of what is, usually, an intangible product. These decisions concern the processes, people, information and systems that produce and deliver the services.

The chapter is as follows:

- Aspects of public service operations
- Operations management activities in public services
- Relevance of management accounting

ASPECTS OF PUBLIC SERVICE OPERATIONS

Operations management in services (including public services) differs markedly from operations management in general, since the operational processes of service organisations differ greatly from those of manufacturing organisations where operations management was born. Before looking at some aspects of operations management in public services, it is important to consider some specific aspects of service (including public service) operations.

We have already noted in Chapter 1 the following aspects of services:

- Unlike physical goods, services display the four characteristics of intangibility, inseparability, perishability and variability (Dilworth 1993). There are no stocks of services or work in progress.
- The umbrella term "services" is wide ranging and covers a number of different types of service including hospitality, transportation, media, construction, retail, healthcare, distribution, education, financial services and legal services. Although falling under the common heading of "services", organisations in the above groupings will differ greatly in terms of structures, methods, etc.

Many of the above comments about services will also apply to public services, but there are a number of other (public service specific) issues that need to be highlighted before considering operational issues in public service organisations.

- **Wide variety of public services** – under the umbrella of public services we have a wide variety of distinctive types of services carried out in various parts of the public sector by various agencies. Examples of these are as follows:
  - *Cash transfers* – these are made to individual citizens in the form of pensions, social benefits, housing subsidies, retirement pensions, etc.
  - *Public protection services* – these concern communities at large and could include defence forces, police, services, fire and rescue services, health protection and consumer protection
  - *Personal services* – these are a wide range of public services provided to individuals including health, care, social care, education and training
  - *Business services* – these are services provided to the business community and could include advisory services and funding sources
  - *Environmental services* – matters to do with the protection of the external environment
- **The range implementing agencies** – as noted in Chapter 1, there are many types of organisations who deliver public services including government departments, local authorities, government agencies, third sector organisations and private sector organisations.

- The existence of multi-agency working – in Chapter 1, we mentioned the importance of multi-agency working in many aspects of public services. This will involve close cooperation between the relevant public service agencies and private sector organisations not only at a strategic level but also at an operational level.
- The prevalence of complex service delivery systems – while some public service delivery systems might be seen as relatively simple in nature, it is often the case that many public services have complex systems of service delivery involving, possibly, several different organisations and a wide range of skilled, semi-skilled and unskilled staff utilising a range of technologically complex equipment. Just consider, for example, the complexity involved in the management of health services, education services, defence forces, police forces, etc. While there are complex systems in many parts of the commercial sector, many would argue that public sector delivery systems have far greater complexity. In fact, some might argue (Collinson 2012) that the public sector is too complex and simplification is needed.
- The roles of teams and professions – public services employ large numbers of front line staff with strong professional backgrounds such as doctors, nurses, teachers, social workers, police officers and engineers. These staff often belong to very influential professional bodies and often have a very strong influence over the nature of service provision. Whether this influence has a positive or negative impact on service provision is often a debatable point. Furthermore, another feature of public services is that these public service staff often work together in multi-professional teams to deliver public services. Examples here concern teams in hospitals, teams in children's services, etc. While this multi-disciplinarity can have a positive impact on service provision, different perspectives of different staff groups can sometimes inhibit matters.

OPERATIONS MANAGEMENT ACTIVITIES IN PUBLIC SERVICES

In this section, we consider briefly some of the main aspects of operations management in relation to public services. These can be considered in relation to the following:

- Service design
- Service delivery

Service design

Product design is vital in manufacturing industry (Slack et al. 2001). Likewise, it is important that there is a robust design stage for any public service, and it is not just allowed to develop haphazardly. Design costs of any service can be significant, and, as will be discussed later in this book, there are management accounting tools which can focus on reducing costs at the design stage without affecting service standards.

Service design begins with a robust organisational strategy and an associated service strategy. The organisational strategy defines what the organisation is trying to achieve overall, and following this is the service strategy and service concept that provides the rationale for why the client would want to receive the service. In other words it fulfils the important task of reconciling what the service organisation is providing and what the client is receiving – something that is not always done in public services. This may be thought to be obvious but it is sometimes clearly not the case.

After defining the service concept, operations can proceed to define the service package. It consists of five parts, and it is important to define, carefully, each of these elements so that operations managers can subsequently design and manage a service operation. The service package must come first, before operations decisions are made.

Examples of service package characteristics are as follows:

- **Service facility:** accessible by public transportation, sufficient parking, interior decorating, architecture, facility layout, etc.
- **Facilitating goods:** sufficient inventory, quality and selection of items needed to deliver the service
- **Information:** accurate, up-to-date, timely and useful to the client and service providers
- **Explicit service:** waiting time, training and expertise of personnel, staff physical appearance and attitudes, consistency
- **Implicit service:** sense of well-being, privacy and security, atmosphere

Service delivery

Once the service package is specified, operations is ready to make decisions concerning the factors of process, capacity, quality, inventory, supply chain and information systems. These are the six decision responsibilities of service operations.

Processes

A service delivery process consists of all the routines, tasks and steps that are used to deliver service to clients along with the jobs and training for service employees which are needed to deliver services appropriately. There are many ways to organise a process to provide client service in an effective and efficient manner to deliver the service.

The design (and re-design) of service delivery processes is an extremely important task in public services. It is human resources coupled with facilitating goods (see below) which are utilised in the defined process to deliver public services. Thus, process design will have major implications for service effectiveness, client satisfaction and resource efficiency. However, service processes in public service organisations may vary enormously between delivery organisations for the same service. While there may sometimes be good reasons for this, other times there may not be a justification. In some public service organisations, services processes may be reviewed and refined periodically, while in others they

Re-designing public services

Employment services

The Ministry of Employment was looking to reform and re-design a number of existing employment services with the aim of introducing radically new ways of dealing with long-term unemployment and vulnerable citizens. One of the main elements has been to create a shift from a focus on activity to a focus on outcomes for citizens.

This has been done by exploring how to invest in creating positive change in the citizens' situations through interdisciplinary collaboration and greater professional freedom in case processing. Initially, they began a process of merging development and implementation exploring how employment processes really worked for citizens, in job centres and in the everyday practice of frontline staff.

They then used this research to engage national decision-makers and local practitioners in collectively analysing insights, co-creating new ideas and co-designing a number of activities in order to productively put the new reforms into practice. The project has since evolved into a situation where human-centred design is being applied and experimented with in other phases of the policymaking cycle. This is resulting in various new ways of connecting policy and practice including mandatory placements for policymakers alongside local case workers, and practice-oriented preventive units focusing on quick adaptation of failing reforms.

Key to this process was a consideration of the costs of change and the ongoing costs of delivery to be compared with the benefits and outcomes to be derived from the changes.

Drawn from the work of Nesta Ideo:Design for Europe – Designing public services

---

may remain unchanged for years. In a time of austerity, the review and re-design of such processes may often be the key to improvements.

In undertaking process design (or re-design), it is important to consider the degree of client contact and how that contact should be facilitated. Chase and Tansik (1983) argued that high client contact processes should be designed and managed differently from low-contact processes. High-contact processes have the client in the system while providing the service. This can lead to difficulties in standardising the service or inefficiencies when the client makes demands or expects unique services. On the other hand, high-contact processes also provide the possibility of self-service where customers provide part of the service themselves (e.g. patient self-testing for some medical conditions, self-learning in schools and colleges). Low-contact services are performed away from the client in what is often called "the back room." In this case, the service process can be more standardised and efficient since the client is not in the system to request preferences, customisation or changes. An example here might be paying council tax online.

Lean thinking can also be applied to process design, the time taken for each step in a service flowchart can be recorded and/or a separate value-stream map can be constructed. Then the process can be analysed for time reductions to reduce waiting and non-value-added steps. Changes can be made to reduce time and waste in the process. Waste is anything that does not add value to the process including waiting time in line, unrequired steps, client confusion and defects in service. Leite and Vieira (2015) suggest that service managers must realise that the client will be happy if the service provided meets or exceeds expectations. In addition, the interaction between the client and the people providing the service is essential to achieve satisfied customers. Employee involvement is often emphasised as part of lean thinking to achieve high levels of commitment by service employees.

Capacity management

Public services, like all organisations, have limited physical and human capacity. While capacity may be increased in the longer term, it is often largely fixed in the short to medium term. Hence, the management of capacity is a key aspect of operations management in many public services.

Forecasting service demand is a prerequisite for managing capacity. In some cases, traditional time series methods can be used to predict trends and seasonality in client demand. Future demand is forecast based on past demand patterns. Many of the same time series and statistical methods for forecasting can be used for manufacturing or service operations including public services. Examples here might be forecasting the demand for hospital care in winter among elderly people or forecasting the likely prevalence of road accidents at different points in the year. These traditional forecasting techniques have limitations, and, in future, the forecasting of client demand may increasingly make use of big data analytics (BDA) to make forecasts. The use of BDA is discussed further in Chapter 13.

Capacity planning is quite different between manufacturing and services given that service cannot be stored or transported to another location. As a result, location of services often (but not always) has to be near the client. Customers are only willing to travel short distances to receive most public services. Exceptions might be healthcare when the illness requires a specialist and other services where local expertise is not available.

Services (including public services) show variations in client demand over time, and a major operational problem is how to meet peak demand at any point in time. Service capacity is perishable and cannot be stored and used later. However, it is completely uneconomic to provide resources (physical or human) to meet peak demand since for most of the time much of those resources will be under-utilised. Hence, two other approaches might be employed:

- Find mechanisms to try reduce peak demand by some form of mitigating activities

- Top up existing capacity by a combination of approaches such as
  - Use of agency staff
  - Overtime
  - Sub-contracting
  - Hire of equipment, etc.

While some of these same mechanisms are used in manufacturing, they are much more crucial in service operations. However, the current coronavirus pandemic illustrates the problems with this. The impact of the pandemic meant that the demand in hospitals for Intensive Therapy Unit (ITU) beds and ventilators exceeded normal operating requirements by many hundreds of percent. Urgent actions were taken to procure more capacity but once the pandemic subsides, much of this capacity may be redundant and have to be mothballed. The key task in future will be to reconsider what constitutes peak demand.

Scheduling also has some differences between manufacturing and service. In manufacturing, jobs are scheduled through a factory to sequence them in the best order to meet due dates and reduce costs. In services, clients are being scheduled. As a result, waiting time becomes much more critical. While manufacturing orders don't mind waiting in line or waiting in inventory, real life clients do mind. Some of the scheduling applications for services are scheduling of patients to operating rooms in hospitals and scheduling students to classes. Many scheduling problems have been solved by using operations research methods to optimise the schedule.

Quality management

Quality management practices for services have much in common with manufacturing, despite the fact that the product is intangible. Various approaches are available and are widely used for services. These approaches have several things in common. They begin with defining and measuring the client's needs. Any service that does not meet a client's need can be thought of as a defect. Then these approaches seek to reduce defects through statistical methods, cause-and-effect analysis, problem-solving teams and involvement of employees. They focus on improving the processes that underlie production of the service.

In addition to intangibility, two approaches about quality are unique to service operations management.

- *Service recovery.* For manufactured products, quality problems are handled through warranties, returns and repair after the product is delivered. In high-contact services there is no time to fix quality problems later; they must be handled by service recovery as the service is delivered. For example, if soup is spilled on the client in a restaurant, the waiter might apologise, offer to pay to have the suit cleaned and provide a free meal. If a hotel room is not ready when promised, the staff could apologise, offer to store the client's luggage or provide an upgraded room. Service recovery is intended to fix the problem on the spot and go even further to offer the client some form of consolation and compensation. The objective is to make the client satisfied with the situation, even though there was a service failure. Ideally, such arrangements are also needed in public services but may not always be provided. It is a debatable point as to how easy it would be to make an immediate recovery of such defects in public services but it should be considered.

- *Service guarantee.* A service guarantee is similar to a manufacturing guarantee, except the service cannot be returned. A service guarantee provides a specific reward for failure of service delivery. Some examples are as follows:
  - Your package will be delivered by the time promised or you will not pay.
  - We will fix your automobile or give you £100 if you must bring it back for repair.
  - Customers who are not satisfied with their haircut get the next haircut free.

Service guarantees serve to assure the client of quality, and they provide a way for the employees to know the cost of service failure. Again, such arrangements may not always be provided in public services, and it may be difficult to do so in all cases.

Inventory management

Although, as we have already seen, services do not have inventories of finished goods or work in progress in the same way as manufacturing, effective management and control of inventories of physical items used in the creation of services are needed in service operations. These items are often referred to as facilitating goods. Almost every service uses some amount of facilitating goods, and this is the case in public services. In fact, the presence of facilitating goods is often critical to the process of service delivery. Consider, for example, the role of drugs in hospitals, learning materials in education, vehicle fuel in emergency services, ammunition for the military, etc. Thus, effective inventory management is essential in public services to ensure that facilitating goods are available when required while inventory costs are kept as low as possible. Key operational decisions involve such matters as stock levels, re-order levels, etc.

Supply chains

Supply chains for public service operations are critical in order to supply the facilitating goods needed. A typical hospital supply chain is an example. A hospital will use many goods from suppliers to construct and furnish the building. During day-to-day operation of the hospital, inventories of supplies will be held for the operating rooms and throughout the building. The pharmacy will hold drugs, and the kitchen will need supplies of food. The supply chain of facilitating goods in hospitals is extensive.

Both manufacturing and service operations often purchase services from outside the organisation. Internal support services such as accounting, legal, human resources, call centres and information systems may also be outsourced in part or entirely. Logistics services may be outsourced to Third Party

Logistics (3PL) providers. These services include transportation, warehousing, order fulfilment, returns and tariffs. Supply chains need to be established for the various goods and services needed to deliver public services, and these should be periodically reviewed in relation to such matters as reliability, efficiency, resilience, etc.

Information systems and technology

The information technology (IT) revolution has dramatically changed the ways in which public services are delivered and further change can be expected. Some of the major aspects of this for public services are as follows:

1. Prior to the invention of the Internet, clients used a variety of sources for acquiring knowledge including libraries, phone calls, universities and personal contacts. Now information can be provided immediately as a service by searching the Internet.
2. Some services such as advice lines, financial queries etc. can be provided remotely.
3. Bookings or appointments can be made on the Internet to reserve capacity more easily than by telephone.
4. Facilitating goods can be ordered directly by the Internet and delivered without travelling to a retail store. The services provided include browsing for merchandise, order entry, order checking, payment, order confirmation, notification of delivery and return services.
5. Communications between clients and service providers can be done online.
6. Internal information systems now provide an array of management information to help managers make better decisions.

RELEVANCE OF MANAGEMENT ACCOUNTING

At the start of this book, we stated that the role of management accounting in any organisation was to assist and facilitate decision making and such decisions could be operational, tactical or strategic in nature. This chapter aims to provide an overview of the subject of operations management in public services. It can be seen that operations management involves the making of a large number of complex decisions concerning service design, process design, capacity planning, use of IT, etc. It has been argued that, in an era of financial austerity, there is an imperative to look at the way services are designed and implemented to identify improvements. All of these operational decisions will, in all probability, have both service implications and financial implications, and the management has a key role to play in such operational decision making.

In later chapters, we will discuss some of the management accounting approaches that may contribute towards operational decision making. Some of these are as follows:

- Relevant costing
- Activity-based costing

- Target costing
- Operational capital investment appraisal
- Marginal costing
- Value chain analysis
- Financial modelling
- Big data analytics, etc.

The importance of strategy in public services

INTRODUCTION

It is sometimes said that strategy is one of the mis-used words in the English language and that strategy often means different things to different people. A couple of quotations illustrate this view:

- *"Nobody really knows what strategy is"* *(Economist 1993).*
- *"Nobody really knows what a strategy is or how to develop a good one"* *(Costas Markides, Professor London Business School).*

Nevertheless, the reality is that having an effective strategy is a necessary (but not sufficient) requirement for success in any organisation, be it private or public sector. This is especially the case in an environment of financial austerity where there is a need for an enhanced strategic focus.

This chapter focuses on the important, and often under-developed, task of strategic management and the role that management accounting can and should play in strategic decision making in public service organisations. It addresses the following key issues:

- The nature of strategic management
- Strategic change in public services
- The strategic management process in public services
- Management accounting and strategic decision making

THE NATURE OF STRATEGIC MANAGEMENT

A variety of definitions of strategy can be seen including the following:

- Strategy is the art and science of planning and marshalling resources for their most efficient and effective use. The term is derived from the Greek word for generalship or leading an army (Ancient Greece).
- Strategy is the planning and conduct of the long-term objectives in a game (Oxford companion to chess).

- Strategy is about being different. It means deliberately choosing a different set of activities to deliver a unique mix of value (Porter 1996).
- Strategy is about competitive position, about differentiating yourself in the eyes of the customer, about adding value through a mix of activities different from those used by competitors (Porter 1985).

What, then, is strategy? Is it just a plan? Does it refer to how we will obtain the ends we seek? Is it a position taken or does strategy refer to perspective with regard to the view one takes of matters, and to the purposes, directions, decisions and actions stemming from this view? Lastly, does strategy refer to patterns in our decisions and actions?

Strategy is all these – it is perspective, ploy, position, plan and pattern (Mintzberg 1987). Strategy is the course we chart, the journey we imagine and, at the same time, the course we steer, the trip we actually make. Even when we are embarking on a voyage of discovery, with no particular destination in mind, the voyage has a purpose, an outcome and an end to be kept in view.

Strategy is the bridge between public policy and strategic longer-term goals in public service organisations, and provides the link to operations, tactics and concrete actions. Strategy and tactics together straddle the gap between ends and means. However, any idea that there is a clear delineation between what is strategic and what is operational is delusional. The distinction is often unclear, and, indeed, some will argue that there are really three dimensions to consider in relation to public services:

- **Strategic** – longer-term considerations regarding public service delivery (three plus years)
- **Tactical** – considerations about public service delivery in the medium term (one to three years)
- **Operational** – consideration of the issues surrounding public service delivery in the short term (days, weeks, months)

Strategy, then, is a framework that provides guidance for actions to be taken and, at the same time, is shaped by the actions actually taken. This means that the necessary precondition for formulating strategy is a clear and widespread understanding of the desired ends to be achieved. Without these ends in view, actions are purely tactical and can quickly degenerate into nothing more than a flailing about.

At the outset, it must be noted that, in this book, the term "strategy" is being used as shorthand for what is best described as strategic management. This latter term implies the overall management of the strategic process in an organisation.

It is suggested that the management of public services is concerned with three main objectives:

1. Delivering on service targets in relation to access, quality, timeliness, etc.
2. Managing its finances in such a way as to avoid large over or underspends against budget
3. Achieving items 1 and 2 while at the same time transforming the delivery of services in line with its strategic plan

The third item in this list concerns the management of strategic change in public services, and this is usually a complex task. Quite often, if the management of strategic change is not undertaken effectively then either the public service organisation fails to achieve its strategic objectives and/or it fails in its operational objectives of achieving service delivery targets or financial balance.

STRATEGIC CHANGE IN PUBLIC SERVICES

As already discussed, the application of strategy in public services was virtually non-existent 50 years ago and the increasing importance of strategy has come about because of the increasing pace of change in society. At this point, it is useful to have a brief discussion about some of the main types of strategic change that have taken place in public services in recent years. Just a few examples are given below.

Mergers of public service organisations

Over several decades, major strategic changes have taken place in public services that involved the merger of two (and sometimes more) public service organisations such as health service providers, colleges, universities, government departments and local authorities. The rationale for such mergers was usually concerned with the small size of some existing organisations and the diseconomies of scale they faced in undertaking some activities but also their inability to offer a sufficiently wide range of services to their local communities. In some cases, such mergers were almost forced since one of the organisations was close to financial collapse.

While some such mergers could be seen as positive, a number of mergers (Prowle 2018) often displayed certain weaknesses including the following:

- Merger was seen as an end rather than a means with little attempt being made to deliver improved outcomes.
- Merger being seen as, purely, an exercise in cost savings where such savings did not materialise.
- Mergers being politically motivated rather than service motivated.

Reconfiguration of public services

Many types of major strategic change have taken place in public service organisations that can be described under the umbrella term of public service reconfiguration or transformation. Sometimes this might have involved the reconfiguration of service activity within a single organisation such as a national government agency but in other situations, reconfiguration involving several organisations might have taken place.

Some examples of such reconfigurations include the following:

- *Reconfiguration of health services.* In some countries, the configuration of health services in a locality may have undergone significant and substantial change. There may have been a number of key drivers for such change including the following:
  - Changes in the need for health services possibly due to population changes (e.g. ageing population) or changes in disease trends

- A policy of trying to treat people in settings outside a main hospital (which is expensive) and in a community setting or at the patients home
- A policy of increasing the capacity of the local health system in order to facilitate greater patient choice
- A policy of encouraging greater specialisation between hospitals in the same locality
- A drive to improve the efficiency of resource use in the health system because of constraints on resources available

Because of such trends, within a particular locality, a number of changes in the configuration of health services may have been made over a number of years.

- *Merger and reconfiguration.* In the UK, prior to 1990, the Department of Work and Pensions operated two arm's lengths agencies. These were the Benefits Agencies responsible for payment of benefits and Job Centre responsible for getting people back into employment. A decision was taken to merge these two agencies into one agency named Job Centre+. Clearly, there are linkages between the tasks of getting people back into work and paying them benefits. Across the UK, there were many towns and cities where there were offices of both agencies. These offices had to be physically merged, and the working practices in the merged organisations reformed to reflect the new roles of the merged body.

Commercialisation of public services

Many examples can be quoted of where public service organisations (or a part of an organisation) traditionally funded from public revenues were required to be converted into organisations which operated on a (fully or partially) commercial basis. This meant that they no longer had guaranteed funding but had to earn revenues to cover their costs. Such changes had implications for several aspects of the organisation. For example, certain business processes needed to be developed and implemented such as marketing, product costing, billing and credit control, and there would be costs associated with acquiring the technology needed to do this. However, perhaps the most significant change involved the culture of the organisation and the attitude and working practices of staff. In such an environment, staff had to be focussed on the need to "sell" their services to potential clients and ensuring client satisfaction and these were areas where traditionally they had no experience.

Significant mission change

This concerns a significant degree of strategic change within an individual public service organisation that was required to address the challenges faced in delivering certain public services. Such changes could involve combinations of the following:

- Changes to the organisational arrangements
- Changes to the pattern of service delivery

Commercialisation of public services

The children's services department of a large local authority had set up a specialist unit which advised schools on how to improve behaviour in the classroom. The unit was funded directly by the local authority, and services were provided at zero cost to the schools. The services were enthusiastically received by the schools themselves, and demands for the unit's services were high.

In preparing for the annual budget setting process, the children's services department was reviewing the merits of its various activities in a search for cost reductions. The work of this specialist unit came under the spotlight. A view was expressed that if schools were so enthusiastic about the work of the unit then, perhaps, they ought to be required to contribute to the costs involved out of their own budgets. Indeed, why shouldn't schools be required to pay the full cost of the service and then the unit would become self-financing?

It was decided to explore this matter more fully, and some market research was undertaken with schools to establish if they would contribute to the costs of the unit's services given that schools said the service was valuable. The results of the market research were that many (but not all) schools were unwilling to pay more than a token sum for the services provided.

Hence, it was concluded that the only way the unit could be a viable self-financing unit would be if it could generate additional income from schools in other local authorities and even from other types of organisations with a need to control behaviour. It was recognised that this would have major implications for the organisation and operation of the unit in terms of such matters as its overall strategy, marketing, scheduling of work, client satisfaction, financial monitoring, etc. In addition, a financially sound business plan would need to be prepared. There was some scepticism about whether this could be done but the local authority agreed to investigate the possibilities.

- Changes to the mode of service delivery such as the enhanced use of digital technology

The above factors have strong inter-dependencies and need to be undertaken within a coherent strategy.

Enhanced public service partnership working

For many years now, there are many examples of where public service organisations have been encouraged to work together in some form of formal or informal partnership arrangement rather than working in isolation. The aim here was to improve coordination of service delivery and the efficiency with which resources are being used through the avoidance of duplication. It is probably fair to say that the success of such partnerships can be described as "mixed" with variations between different types of partnership and different parts of the country. This may be because the importance of the partnership having a strategic focus and a strategic plan was not always fully recognised.

The examples above involve mainly large-scale and well-known examples of strategic change in public services. In addition, there are of course many other examples of public service organisations that have undertaken smaller-scale strategic changes.

Financial aspects of strategic change in public services

The strategic changes to public services described above usually have significant financial implications. It is likely that many or all of the following might be encountered in the above strategic changes:

- Additional capital expenditure on buildings and/or equipment because of the change
- Part or all of existing sites might be disposed of thus generating a capital receipt
- Cost savings might be generated because of the changes made
- Additional running costs might be incurred in certain areas of activity
- Redundancy costs associated with reducing number of staff
- Incremental travel costs associated with staff who are relocated
- In some cases, additional income might be generated
- Significant costs associated with managing and implementing the change process (e.g. staff training)

Unfortunately, major strategic changes in public services are not always seen as successful and the following problems are often encountered:

- Planned timescales for the strategic change are exceeded
- The changes made do not deliver the outcomes anticipated
- Budgets for the strategic change are exceeded

The nature of these problems and the complex financial issues, which strategic changes involved, suggest a need for a stronger management accounting function in this area of activity.

THE STRATEGIC MANAGEMENT PROCESS IN PUBLIC SERVICES

Strategic management is a key element of the management process in public services today. One important point to emphasis is that strategic management is not synonymous with strategic planning, and there are other important aspects illustrated in Figure 3.1.

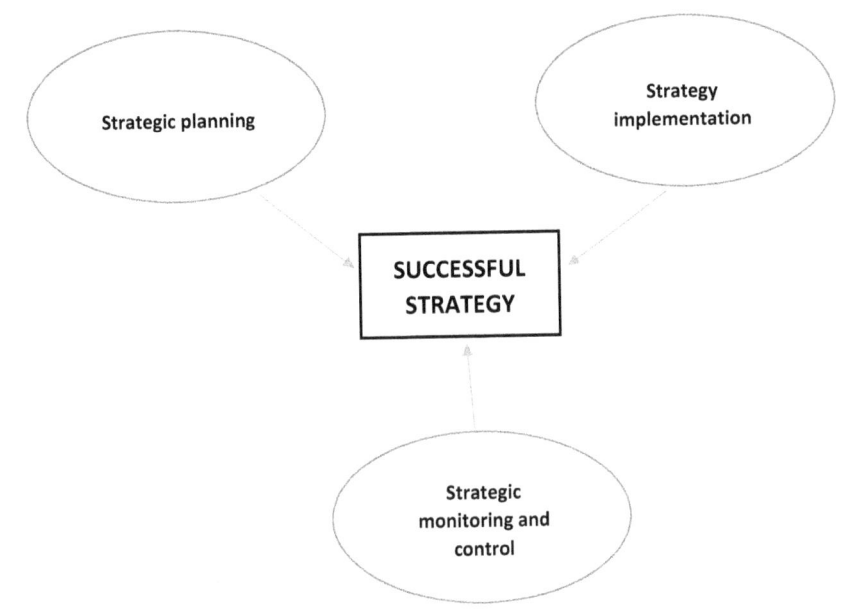

FIGURE 3.1
Aspects of strategic management.

Strategic planning

Like most aspects of management, the essence of developing a strategic plan for any organisation is very simple and is concerned with answering three main questions in relation to the organisation:-

1. Where are we now as an organisation?
2. Where do we wish to get to in the longer term?
3. How do we get where we want to be?

These three questions can be regarded as being in increasing order of difficulty to answer. It is **relatively** easy, although time-consuming, for an organisation to clarify the current situation and where it stands internally and in relation to its external working environment.

It is more difficult for it to establish where it wishes to be in the longer term in terms of its size, its range of activities, its priorities, its organisation, etc., and this is particularly difficult in public services because of the political environment in which it must function. However, perhaps, the most difficult aspect of strategy is establishing how to get from where we are now to where we want to be in the future. Achieving this can often require significant and radical change in an organisation, and the management of such change is often difficult particularly in the conservative culture of many public service organisations.

Some form of strategic planning is undertaken in most medium to large organisations in both public and private sectors. However, within public services, a broad distinction can be drawn between the following:

- Strategic planning in a service commissioner organisation
- Strategic planning in a service delivery organisation
- Strategic planning in multi-agency partnerships

Strategic planning in service commissioner organisation

The commissioner-provider separation was one of the most significant reforms that has taken place in public services over the last 30 years, in several countries. Under such arrangements, in theory at least, commissioner organisations should not be delivering services direct to service users (although this does sometimes happen in practice) but should use the financial resources at their disposal to commission and contract services to be delivered by other public sector, third sector or private sector delivery organisations. Unlike service providers who will have large amounts of physical, human and financial resources available to them to deliver services, the physical and human resources of the commissioner organisation will be relatively limited but they will have large amounts of financial resources available to them to commission services.

There are many depictions of the commissioning process in relation to public services but one approach is to see it as two distinct but related processes with different aims and different timescales:

- *The commissioning (or strategic commissioning) process.* This process is concerned with identifying the long-term pattern of services needed by the population and ensuring there is a sufficient range of providers to deliver those services.
- *The purchasing/contracting (or operational commissioning) process.* This is concerned with selecting specific providers and letting contracts for service delivery.

This chapter is concerned with strategy, and so we will focus on the strategic commissioning process and it will be seen that the process can be sub-divided into four phases as shown in Table 3.1.

Clearly, Table 3.1 shows an idealised view of the way strategic commissioning should operate but in practice, it will be much more "messy". Politics, vested interests, lack of evidence, etc., will all impinge on this idealised process.

However, a cursory consideration of the above will show that there will need to be a strong financial management involvement in the strategic commissioning process in order to make it a more rational process. Issues to be addressed are:

- Forecasting the likely level of resources available to the commissioner
- Identifying the costs of current service provision and the distribution of total resources over different services, client groups, etc. This would include services financed from earmarked sources and services financed from general sources

TABLE 3.1

Phases of strategic commissioning

Phase	Tasks
Analyse	• Identify the service needs of the client population using data which may already be available or may need to be collected • Analyse current service provision regarding volume, quality, access, etc., and the resources being used in delivering those services
Plan	• Identify gaps in current service provision and set strategic objectives as appropriate • Develop commissioning strategy based on desired outcomes and within the constraint of resources available • Identify the magnitude of changes required compared to current service provision and the resource consequences and challenges of effecting such changes
Do	• Based on the analysis of the current market for service provision, take action to encourage new service providers • Assist with capacity building, particularly in relation to third sector organisations • Develop a framework for managing provider relationships
Review	• Review achievement of strategic objectives • Review market performance and overall contract performance

- Evaluating the financial consequences of the commissioning strategy to ensure that it aligns with the likely levels of resources available. However, it may be the case that there are several possible strategic options for strategic commissioning and the financial consequences of each needs to be considered alongside the service impacts
- Assessing the financial viability and financial management expertise of potential providers, especially the smaller third (voluntary) sector organisations. It may also be appropriate to deliver some financial management training to such organisations to improve their managerial capacity
- Comparing the unit costs of service provision with that of other local providers (and providers in other areas) in order to assess value for money (VFM)
- Participate in the review of the commissioning strategy, in particular its VFM component

Strategic planning in a service delivery organisation

Unlike service commissioners, service delivery organisations have a wide range of resources including fixed assets, manpower and finance in order to deliver services to the public. Clearly, such organisations may be public sector, third sector or private sector in nature. In some ways, they are all partially analogous to private sector organisations who are involved in delivering services to customers in return for funding. Consequently, the type of strategic planning employed in such organisations is sometimes referred to as strategic business planning.

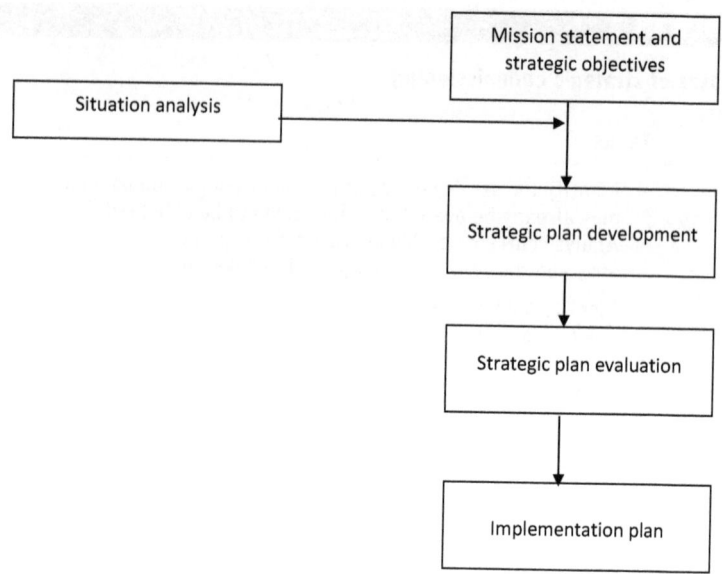

FIGURE 3.2
Stages of strategic business planning.

The classical approach to strategic business planning has a number of inter-related stages that are shown in Figure 3.2.

These various stages can be linked and summarised in terms of the three key questions already identified as shown in Table 3.2.

Briefly, we will consider each aspect of the strategic planning process:

Mission statement and strategic objectives

For a public service organisation, this involves defining the longer-term strategic aspirations of the organisation through the derivation of some form of

TABLE 3.2

Three key questions of strategy

Where are we now	Situation analysis incorporating: • an internal appraisal of the organisation itself and the services it provides • an appraisal of the external working environment (physical, social, economic, etc.) in which it operates
Where do we wish to get to in the longer term	This involves preparation of a mission statement and a series of strategic objectives for organisation
How do we get there	This involves the tasks of strategy development and evaluation, risk analysis, implementation planning and change management

mission or vision statement. However, mission/vision statements are sometimes described as banal, meaningless or *"motherhood and apple pie"* in nature. Hence, the development of strategic objectives will involve fleshing out the mission statement into some precise and quantifiable elements, and such objectives should provide the foundation for outlining what the organisation aims for in the longer term. In this context, the term SMART objectives is often used to cover objectives that are specific, measurable, achievable, relevant and time-based. A strategic plan should have a series of strategic objectives that will be service specific and concern the services it provides but also a number of over-arching objectives may also exist which should apply to the whole organisation and which should be incorporated into its plan.

Other key features of the strategic plan include:

- **Viability** – the plan needs to ensure viability, and particularly financial viability, for the organisation. It is not sufficient for the organisation to plan to, merely, break-even financially – or to make a small financial surplus since an unexpected event could endanger the viability of the organisation if it has no financial "cushion" to absorb the shock. Public service plans are often weak in consideration of financial viability.
- **Sustainability** – the plan needs to ensure that the organisation will be sustainable in the longer term. It will, therefore, have to plan to identify (and provide funds for) future investment in physical resources and human resources. The organisation that does not plan for such investment will, over time, probably become less viable, and this could endanger its sustainability.
- **Acceptability** – it is of vital importance that the strategic plan of the organisation is acceptable to service professionals, service users and the community at large. Looking externally, where a public service organisation has strong links to the local community or region then the strategic plan needs to be acceptable to local stakeholders such as other public services and the third sector.

Some possible strategic objectives in public services are shown in Table 3.3.

Situation analysis

Strategic planning must be undertaken with as full as possible an understanding of the current situation and what the future may hold. A key element is a SWOT (strengths, weaknesses, opportunities, threats) analysis that comprises two distinct but related parts:

- *Internal Appraisal: Strengths and Weaknesses.* It is essential that any internal assessment of the organisation is both systematic and honest. Experience has shown that many organisations overstate their strengths and understate their weaknesses because they find it uncomfortable to face up to reality. Examples of areas to be covered in this internal review include such matters as staff numbers and skills, range, capacity and quality of buildings and equipment, client satisfaction, service range and quality, unit costs of service provision and internal communications.

TABLE 3.3

Possible public service strategic objectives

Local Authority Leisure Services	Police Authority	Further Education College	Prisons
• Increased overall uptake of leisure activities • Greater diversity of participation in leisure services • Increased sporting excellence in the locality • Improved financial performance	• Reduced prevalence of crime • Improved crime detection rates • Improved support to victims of crime • Improved community cohesion • Increased investment in areas currently seen as weak • Improved use of resources and VFM	• Increased student numbers • Increased employability of students • Greater proportion of income from private sources • Reduced unit cost of teaching • Reduced staff turnover	• Improved safety in prisons • Reduced levels of re-offending • Increased employment levels among former prisoners • Improved use of resources

- *External Appraisal: Opportunities and Threats.* This aims to review the external environment in which the organisation operates in order to identify opportunities to seize and threats to avoid or negate. It is important to realise that some factors can represent an opportunity or a threat depending on circumstances. A number of opportunities and threats may present themselves to a public service organisation preparing a strategic plan, and these matters should be taken account of in the plan. One approach to this is termed the PESTLE approach where the review of the external environment would focus on six groups of factors, namely, Political, Economic, Social, Technological, Legal and Environmental.

Using this approach many specific trends might be identified including the following:
- Growth in the elderly population
- Increase in the number of competitor organisations
- Increasing local unemployment
- Likely political change
- New drug therapy coming on stream
- New regulatory mechanisms
- Many new housing units in the area due for completion
- Increasing number of single parent families
- New ring road being constructed
- Cost pressures on commissioners, etc.

Strategic plan development

Within a public service provider organisation a variety of different strategies might be identified as there are usually several different routes to any destination. In fact, it is important not to assume that there is only one approach. Such strategies can be viewed as a series of strands that meet to provide an overall corporate strategic plan for the organisation. This is illustrated in Figure 3.3.

In reality these separate strategies are best viewed as components of an overall and integrated strategic plan, hence the reference to them as strands. Thus within the overall strategic plan there will be a series of strands concerned with service activities or client groups and also a number of resource strands concerned with HR, buildings and equipment and IS/IT. Binding all of these together will be the financial strand. In the absence of a robust financial strand a public service organisation cannot be confident that its overall strategic plan can be afforded or that it will be able to meet its financial objectives concerning surplus/deficit, cash flow, capital financing, etc.

Regarding the service activity strands some examples of such strands might be as shown in Table 3.4 but each of these main strands can, of course, be broken down into smaller strands representing service sub-divisions, client groups, etc.

Thus, the formulation of strategy within a public service provider organisation will primarily be concerned with the following issues:

- **Strand continuation** – the organisation may come to a conclusion that some smaller strands may no longer be viable or effective and should be discontinued where this is legal and desirable. Equally, the organisation may decide to initiate some new strands.

FIGURE 3.3
Strategic development strands.

> **TABLE 3.4**
>
> **Possible service activity strands**
>
> | Local Authority Children's Services | University | NHS (National Health Services) Trust |
> |---|---|---|
> | • Primary education
• Secondary education
• Child protection
• Parenting
• Childcare development, etc. | • Teaching
• Research
• Consultancy
• Other | • Emergency services
• Elective services
• Mental health services
• Health promotion
• Primary, secondary and tertiary care |

- **Strand balance** – the overall balance between the various strands and whether this situation needs to change.
- **Strand configuration and diversity** – within each of the strands, the strategy will need to address the diversity of activities undertaken and the detailed configuration of those activities.

In public service organisations, it must be recognised that changes to any of the above can be very contentious and that there may be significant political concerns involved.

In developing a resource strategy, a large number of issues will need to be addressed including the following:

- What should be the balance between full-time, temporary and hourly paid staff?
- What staff remuneration mechanisms should be introduced?
- On how many sites should the organisation operate?
- What should be the balance between purchase and lease of equipment?
- What role should IS/IT play in operational activities?
- What is an appropriate balance between fixed costs and variable costs for the organisation?

Strategic plan evaluation

Having identified and developed possible strategies, each must be evaluated to establish the best way forward. There are two essential matters to consider:

- Is the strategy, strategically feasible – will it enable the strategic objectives to be achieved?
- Is the strategy, resource feasible in terms of the availability, to the organisation, of key resources?

Both of these are important and necessary conditions as it is possible to develop strategies that are feasible regarding strategic objectives but not feasible in resource terms. The opposite may also be true, and strategies that are resource feasible should not necessarily be followed. Commercial organisations frequently sell off profitable and well-resourced activities, simply because they do not fit in with the strategic objectives of the organisation.

Strategic feasibility

This involves identifying that strategy which has the best chance of success in terms of attaining the strategic objectives. Three different evaluation approaches considered are summarised below:

- *Identify competitive advantage*: this is a classic approach in the commercial sector. It is only relevant in public services where a public service organisation is in competition with other organisations (public, private or third sector) to provide some of all or its range of services. Evaluation of possible strategies will be in terms of whether they can give the organisation a competitive advantage over the other providers. This competitive advantage could be through lower costs, by differentiation (e.g. better quality) or by specialisation (niche market).
- *Strategic Appraisal*: this approach involves evaluating the various strategies proposed against the results of the SWOT analysis. If, for example, a particular strategy utilises one of the existing strengths of the organisation then this would be a plus point for that strategy. However, if the strategy required pursuit of an activity in an area where the organisation was weak (e.g. with poorly skilled staff) then it would have to choose between not pursuing that particular strategy, and/or taking action to reduce or eradicate the weakness, possibly through significant investment. Each of the strategies identified is judged as to whether it involves building on internal strengths or weaknesses or whether it involves building on areas identified as "opportunities" or "threats". Thus, for each strategy, a scorecard is compiled which assists the organisation in making an informed judgement about which is the best strategic option.
- *Risk Profile*: all organisations (public, private or third sector) face a variety of risks. Many of these risks involve the ongoing delivery of service activities but some may be strategic risks. Hence, in preparing strategic options, it is necessary for the public service organisation to assess the risks associated with the various services and resource strands. Clearly, it would be unwise to pursue many activities that have high degrees of risk but equally just undertaking the lowest risk activities may not be optimal. Hence, a balanced portfolio of activities is desirable.

It is important to emphasise that these three approaches to evaluating strategies are not mutually exclusive but are likely to be applied individually or in combination. The key issue is which strategic option is most likely to enable the organisation to attain its strategic objectives.

Resource feasibility

Strategies must be feasible both in terms of achieving strategic objectives and in resource terms, the latter including human resources, fixed assets, specialist supplies and finance. Some factors that may result in a strategy not being resource feasible are:

- Unavailability of certain human resources
- Fixed assets and specialist supplies are unobtainable
- The whole strategy is financially unsound
- Redundant resources cannot be disposed of

Although finance is not the only resource which must be considered it is perhaps the most critical.

Outline implementation plan

A strategic plan that pays no cognisance to issues of implementation is deeply flawed. Issues of implementation will be discussed in a later section but for the moment, it is important to note that the plan should contain some form of outline implementation plan that describes the challenges to be faced.

Strategy in partnerships

A considerable amount of the strategic commissioning of public services is now done through multi-agency partnerships rather than single commissioner organisations. Largely, it would appear that the processes of strategic commissioning will (at a basic level) be the same for the individual commissioner but the practice of developing and applying those processes will be much more complex. For example, with a multi-agency partnership:

- The assessment of population need will be more complex because of the different standpoints of the various agencies about what constitutes need and how it should be measured.
- The identification of the costs of current service provision and the distribution of total resources over client groups will be more difficult to undertake because it will mean integrating financial information from several agencies each with its own accounting and costing approaches.
- The assessment of the costs of future multi-agency initiatives to achieve the strategic objectives might prove to be more complex because of the different approaches involved.

However, none of these problems are insurmountable and, in time, will no doubt become routine.

On further point that needs to be noted is that although the commissioning strategy will be prepared on a multi-agency basis, to a large extent its implementation will be undertaken by individual agencies. This situation may change in time but, for the present, it does pose challenges in relation to strategy implementation.

Strategy implementation

Strategic plans do not implement themselves – they must be managed. A comprehensive implementation plan needs to be prepared to ensure that the planned events actually occur. In reality, the large size of many implementation plans is frequently due to the need to describe the large number of tasks that need to be undertaken to put the plan into action. Such a plan will have a number of key elements including the following:

- Tasks that need to be performed
- Individual responsibilities for ensuring they are performed
- Timetable for completing tasks
- Resources needed
- Barriers to be overcome

In addition, the plan may also identify critical success factors and possible bottlenecks in implementation and possible ways around them. The approach to these issues could adopt project management techniques.

Too often, the tasks of implementing a strategy are not properly addressed, and if things go wrong, there is sometimes the danger that a judgement is made that the strategy is flawed rather than the implementation has failed. As already noted above, a key component of strategy implementation is a comprehensive and robust implementation plan.

However, it is often thought that implementation of a strategic plan for change simply requires the construction of a series of operational plans, and their implementation will result in the implementation of the strategy and the achievement of strategic objectives. Thus, there is no concept of strategic implementation. This is an example of a theoretical model which does not fit the real world since there will be many real-life barriers to implementing the strategy. These will particularly concern the failure to address issues of cultural and organisational change.

An alternative model is shown in Figure 3.4.

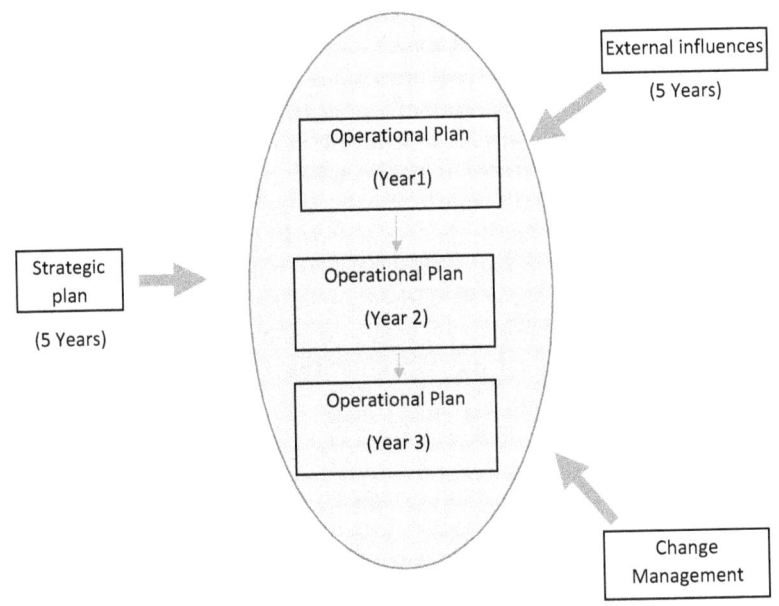

FIGURE 3.4
Strategic management implementation.

This model also shows organisations that operational plans should be derived from strategic plans. However, it also indicates the underlying reality that strategic plans do not implement themselves and too often, there is a tendency to assume that once a strategic plan has been created then little more needs to be other than to implement the operational plans. This is a huge mistake as the implementation of a strategic plan is a complex and difficult task. The implementation of operational, or short-term, plans is not always that difficult since it often requires little change in operational practices, in the organisation, from those currently undertaken. However, the implementation of a strategic plan often raises issues of resistance to organisational change, imperfect markets for services, inability to obtain resources, etc., and these issues must be addressed as part of a process of strategy implementation. The implementation of a strategic plan may require substantial changes in the organisational arrangements and operational practices. Such changes are often so radical that they may generate fierce opposition and resistance to change from many parts of the organisation and the successful implementation of the strategic plan rests on overcoming such resistance to change. Hence, the organisation needs to develop a suitable change management programme and commit sufficient resources to that programme.

From a financial management point of view, the key thing to recognise is that the process of change management has financial implications and is not cheap to apply. Thus in planning for strategic change, it is important to make financial provision for the process of change management, otherwise the success of the change process may be compromised.

Strategic monitoring and control

In implementing a programme of major strategic change, it is also important that the public service organisation undertakes some form of strategic monitoring. This is not the same as operational monitoring where one is monitoring the impact of annual operational plans. Strategic monitoring involves monitoring the impact of the strategy in terms of the achievement of strategic objectives. Furthermore, strategic monitoring may need to continue for some years after the strategic change has been fully implemented in order to judge its impact. Thus at the time as the strategic objectives are being set, organisations need to think about how, in future years, they are going to collect the information needed to assess whether those service objectives have been met. This may require the setting in train of various data collection or survey exercises to ensure such information will be available when it is needed. Again, there are often substantial resource implications of setting up systems and processes to collect this data.

The results of this strategic monitoring exercise will then inform future strategic plans. While such strategic monitoring is difficult to undertake in practice (since there may be problems of data collection and evaluation methodology) these difficulties should not constitute a reason for inaction and some strategic monitoring is better than none.

MANAGEMENT ACCOUNTING AND STRATEGIC DECISION MAKING

This book has continuously emphasised that the role of management accounting and management accountants is to assist decision making in public service organisations. Below are summarised a few of the ways in which management accounting can make this contribution to strategy, and these will be discussed in more detail in later chapters.

- Setting of strategic objectives
- Resource forecasting
- Analysis of existing activities
- Evaluation of strategic options
- Strategic capital investment appraisal
- Implementation of strategy
- Monitoring of strategic objectives

Setting of strategic objectives

Along with other planning objectives, public services need to have some clear strategic financial objectives. Just because we are dealing with public services doesn't mean that financial objectives can be ignored, and in the section on strategic objectives of service providers, we referred to the issues of viability and sustainability. Usually these financial objectives will be something to do with levels of financial surplus, debt ratios and returns on investment or liquidity positions. However, it is also possible to think in terms of financial objectives that are concerned with other matters such as the percentage of costs represented by staff costs, the percentage of costs represented by IT costs and the percentage of costs that might be regarded as truly fixed.

Resource forecasting

This task essentially involves forecasting the likely level of financial resources available to the organisation over a strategic period of several years. Given the level of uncertainty and risk involved, it will be necessary to prepare several different resource scenarios based on differing sets of assumptions and upon which different strategic planning scenarios can be built. Financial modelling is an essential tool and will be discussed later in this book.

Analysis of existing activities

The analysis of existing activities of the organisation is one of the bedrocks of strategy development. Part of this involves a financial analysis of the organisation, and as will be discussed in Chapter 7 an analysis can be provided of the costs and financial performance of existing service activities to identify the level of surplus/deficit being generated by each activity.

Evaluation of strategic options

In preparing strategic plans, public service organisations must develop and evaluate a number of different strategic options. This evaluation process must cover both strategic feasibility and resource feasibility, particularly financial feasibility. Hence, the organisation should undertake an evaluation of the financial implications of the various strategic options that have been identified. None of these changes can be achieved in one year, and thus, there must be a multi-year strategy. Longer-term financial plans will be needed to support strategic planning, and it is completely inadequate to rely on an annual financial plan.

Strategic capital investment appraisal

As already noted, one of the major features of strategic change in public services is the prevalence of major capital investment projects. Hence, it is vital to try to get the decision making around these projects as optimal as possible that is not always easy giving their multi-faceted nature. Good management accounting practices can guide decision makers to understand the financial complexities of different projects in a manner that can simplify their decision.

Implementing strategy

As already discussed, public service organisations have faced, and will continue to face, a situation of continuous and ongoing change and will need to prepare strategic plans and associated financial strategies to deal with and assist with the changes deemed necessary. However, it is one thing to prepare a strategic plan and another to implement that plan and situations have arisen where organisations have failed to implement the strategy they have prepared.

Monitoring of strategic objectives

Management accounting also has an important role to play in relation to monitoring the achievement of strategic objectives. This applies both to financial and non-financial objectives.

Public service reforms

INTRODUCTION

Public service reform has been a major theme in public services for many decades and has manifested itself in many different ways across different countries (Colgan et al. 2016). Moreover, it is reasonable to assume that the pressures of increased service demand and financial austerity mentioned in Chapter 1 means that public service reform should be seen as an ongoing process of evolution and not a series of past historic events. Thus, the process of public service reform will continue to pose challenges to public service management for the foreseeable future.

Effective management accounting has a strong role to play in this process of public service reform, and this role encompasses both:

- The planning (and subsequent evaluation) of the types of public service reform to be undertaken
- The implementation of the chosen path of reform to ensure the aims of the reform (both financial and non-financial) are met

Indeed, it could be that the absence of sufficient management accounting input is responsible, in part, for the limited levels of success being achieved by some such reforms in the past. This is a theme we will return to later in the chapter.

This chapter considers the following issues:

- Why does public service reform take place?
- What are the objectives of public service reform?
- What constitutes public service reform?
- Success and failure in public service reform
- What role should management accounting play in public service reform?

WHY DOES PUBLIC SERVICE REFORM TAKE PLACE?

Clearly, the precise reasons why certain countries underwent waves of public sector reform (PSR) will vary from case to case. However, a number of key themes can be identified as being important in stimulating the need for reform.

- **Increasing service demand** – as described in Chapter 1, we see the phenomenon of increasing demands for public services consequent on demographic, technological and societal pressures.
- **Inadequate standards of public service** – quite often the standard of certain public services may be seen as inadequate in terms of quality and/or access. This may be due, in part, to inadequate funding but may also be due to a range of other organisational and delivery factors.
- **Scarce resources** – as already noted in Chapter 1, austerity means there is a growing shortage of public resources, which forces a rethink about means of service delivery, the ways organisations function and the efficiency of the whole system. In some situations, where the availability of financial resources may <u>not</u> be a problem, the inability to recruit skilled labour to deliver those services is a problem.
- **Public dissatisfaction** – in some countries, there is a widespread perception of inefficiency and backwardness of the public sector as a whole (OECD 2019). This leads to high levels of public dissatisfaction with public services that need to be remedied. In turn, this can manifest itself into a reluctance to pay higher levels of taxation to fund the growth of public services. In turn again, this can have a profound effect on the electorate's decision making processes at election time, which, in turn, impacts the potentially changing underlying ideology of PSR. It is important to recognise, however, that public dissatisfaction does not necessarily align with inadequate standards of service. Sometimes dissatisfaction with services is a perception by those who haven't actually been recipients of that service while the actual recipients were satisfied.
- **Political ideologies** – these have always had a strong influence on attitudes towards public service reform. Between 1980 and 1990, political ideology in the Western world tended to be dominated by the views of Ronald Reagan and Margaret Thatcher, and this led to surge in public service reform based on marketisation, privatisation and the use of private finance to deliver public services. These trends spread well beyond the boundaries of the UK and USA and influenced public service reform in many countries and continued well beyond the period when Reagan and Thatcher were in office. At the time of writing, we see a decline in the influence of traditional political groupings and the growth of what is referred to a populist nationalism. It seems inevitable that this change will impact on public service reform in a way which cannot yet be delineated.
- **Risk and uncertainty** – for a variety of reasons, the environment in which governments operate has become increasingly unstable and uncertain. Uncertainty increases the risk of failure of an organisation's response. Hence, public service organisations need to be in a better position to cope with this uncertainty.

WHAT ARE THE OBJECTIVES OF PUBLIC SERVICE REFORM?

Before looking at detailed aspects of public service reform it is worth spending a little time considering what the reform process was intended to achieve (the objectives) in broad terms. An analysis of a variety of public service reforms suggests that the aims of PSR can be classified threefold: service aims, economic aims and political aims. These are discussed below under three main headings:

Service aims

These aims are concerned with the public services themselves, the way they are delivered and how well they are delivered. Thus, the aims could involve any combinations of the following:

- **Service outcomes** – the delivery of improved outcomes from service provision such as health outcomes and education outcomes
- **User satisfaction** – as already noted, there are often significant levels of dissatisfaction with some public services in some countries. Thus, the aim could be to deliver improved levels of satisfaction with public services from the users of such services
- **Choice** – the provision of increased choice to service users regarding the type and location of service they require
- **Access** – the provision of improved access to public services particularly in relation to the timing and ease of access
- **Flexibility** – greater flexibility in the delivery of public services and the improved tailoring of service provision rather than a "one size fits all" approach

Economic aims

The challenges faced by public services because of austerity have already been discussed in Chapter 1. While improvements in the financial and economic aspects of public services have always been an issue, the impact of austerity has strengthened this. Hence, public service reforms will always have a variety of aims including the financial and economic aspects of service provision. Some examples of such aims would include the following:

- **Cost reduction** – an important aim across virtually all public services has been that of reducing the costs of service provision without harming aspects such as service quality and service access
- **Resource efficiency** – improvements in the way in which public resources and public assets are utilised in the course of delivering service provision
- **Value for money (VFM)** – improvements in the overall value for money (economy, effectiveness and efficiency) being delivered through public services

Political aims

There are a number of aims that might be seen as more political or ideological in nature but this does not mean that they will not contribute towards the service and economic aims.

- **Eliminating public sector monopolies.** The issue of public sector monopolies was mentioned in Chapter 1. Many public service reforms undertaken in recent decades were concerned with breaking up such monopolies.

- **Reducing restrictive practices.** Many politicians were of the view that the public sector was rife with a large number of restrictive labour practices deriving from trade unions and/or professional bodies. Many of the reforms were concerned to loosen such restrictive practices as a means of delivering on the service and economic aims described above.
- **Altering the role of the state.** Clearly, the state (or the government) is an extremely important player in relation to public services but the state can play several roles in relation to such services including that of an enabler, a guarantor, a regulator, a financier or a direct provider. Thus, public service reform may concern changes in the roles that the state should undertake and the emphasis to be placed on each role.
- **Changes in the financing of public services.** Public service reforms often concern changing the balance between tax-based funding and charges to consumers of services.
- **Changes in patterns of decision making.** Much of what constitutes public service reform is concerned with changing the pattern of decision making within the public services. There are three aspects to this: first, greater decentralisation of decision making from the centre of government to the periphery; second, changes in the balance of power, with regard to decision making, between service professionals and generic managers; third, a greater involvement of the service user in decisions about what services should be provided. This is often termed co-production.

Overall, it is probably true to say that there is a constant argument about the extent to which the above political aims are purely ideological in nature and the extent to which they really contribute towards the service and economic aims.

WHAT CONSTITUTES PUBLIC SERVICE REFORM?

There has been much debate in trying to define exactly what constitutes public service reform. For example, a UN definition (UN ECOSOC 2006) stated that:

> Public sector reform consists of deliberate changes to the structures and processes of public sector organisations with the objective of getting them to run better. Structural change may include merging or splitting public sector organisations while process change may include redesigning systems, setting quality standards and focusing on capacity-building.

When we consider this further, we will find difficulty in obtaining a definition of public service reform that will meet all circumstances and eventualities. Terms like New Public Management (NPM) and post-NPM have been developed (Reiter and Klenk 2018) and are in common use but these terms are not comprehensive enough to describe the full range of reforms that have taken place in recent decades. For example, NPM seems primarily concerned with marketisation and competition while post-NPM seems to be about the development of holistic or joined-up government. Hence, we need to look a bit more deeply at this issue.

Perhaps it is not possible, or even helpful, to think in terms of over-arching theories about the causes and nature of public service reform. An alternative view is that public service reform is really concerned with dealing with a range of issues (some related and some not related) which have political implications. Thus, it is suggested that the vast majority of what is termed public service reform can be considered in relation to a number of key themes discussed later.

In any country, public services will have evolved over a long period of time. It is beyond the scope of this book to give a detailed history of public service reform in all countries but some of the themes involved are discussed below.

Clearly, the details of public service reforms that have taken place in many countries over the last 25–30 years will vary considerably between different parts of the public sector both in terms of their range and the detailed aspects of implementation. Set out below are some of the key themes of reforms which have taken place and which have been applied in many parts of the public services.

- Outright privatisation
- Mergers
- System reconfiguration and transformation
- Market testing, outsourcing and contestability
- Greater strategic focus
- Enhanced consumer orientation
- Regulatory changes
- Expansion of choice
- Emphasis on governance and accountability

Outright privatisation

In many countries, developed and developing, governments have embarked on a sustained programme of outright privatisation of state-owned activities. Although the pace of privatisation in the developed world has subsequently decreased from that in the 1980s and 1990s a number of smaller privatisations of state activities still take place and may continue to take place in the future. In other countries, particularly developing countries, programmes of privatisation are being pursued with vigour but not always with wisdom.

Mergers

Mergers of public service organisations are quite common in many different countries. These have involved, for example, the mergers of two or more health providers and in the education sector and the merger of several colleges or universities. The rationale for such mergers should be around achieving improvements in resource efficiency, the generation of savings or the creation of synergies whereby the merged organisation is able to undertake activities, which the individual units could not achieve. However, the success record of mergers in public services is mixed as a consequence of some mergers being seen as an end in their own right and with little thought being given to how the benefits of merger would be realised. Also, some mergers come about as a consequence of political opportunism.

Service reconfiguration and transformation

This broad-ranging reform has been applied in many public services in many different ways. As the title suggests it is concerned with reconfiguring different aspects of public services in such a way that they are "transformed" compared to what existed previously. The service reconfiguration can involve looking a range of aspects including the following:

- The range of services being provided
- The nature of the client base receiving services and their eligibility
- The different organisations that may be involved in service provision
- The physical location of service provision
- The timing of service provision
- The types of staff involved in service provision
- The process or system by means of which the service is delivered
- The equipment used to deliver services, etc.

The use of the term transformation implies that one is not talking about fairly minor changes to service provision but changes that radically affect service configuration and can deserve the use of the term transformation. Furthermore, the redesign and transformation exercise can apply to a single organisation or a group of organisations working together. Some examples of the latter might be the following:

- The reconfiguration of schools' education provision in an area involving all schools
- The reconfiguration of social care provision in an area involving hospitals, social care agencies and primary healthcare practitioners

Service reconfiguration and transformation is a complex and time-consuming process. It may involve the deployment of new digital technologies, the development of new staff skills and the creation of different systems and processes. Almost certainly, there will also be a strong change management aspect that needs to be addressed to ensure a successful transformation takes place. Consequently, there will almost always be significant financial implications.

Market testing, outsourcing and contestability

One of the key themes of public service reform (as exemplified in the term New Public Management) was that of exposing public services, which were traditionally provided in-house, to external competition via some form of market testing exercise. One possible outcome of such an exercise was that service provision might be outsourced to an external provider but there are also many examples of where in-house units improved their cost and quality performance to such an extent that they were successful in retaining the contract for service provision. There have been many examples of a wide variety of service provision being subject to market testing in many sectors and countries.

Contestability is not the same as market testing and competition. The concept of contestability was originally developed in the 1980s, by the American economist William Baumol in relation to industrial markets (Baumol 1982) and was concerned with the position and behaviour of monopolistic providers of goods and services in such markets. Baumol suggested that monopolistic providers did not need to be exposed to actual competition in order to make them responsive and competitive – the mere threat of competition might be sufficient to achieve these ends. Thus, contestability is not a synonym for competition but describes a situation where a provider faces a possible and credible threat of competition. In this context, contestability could involve, for example, the creation or encouragement of a credible alternative provider of goods or services. Contestability is fundamentally different to "market testing", as it does not require every individual service to be competed. Contestability has been subsequently extended to cover public monopolies and public service delivery (Prowle 2008). An example here would be the UK prison service which although largely publicly provided has some small element of private provision. The existence and operation of this private element provides a real and credible threat that, at some future date, and if deemed necessary, yet more of the prison service could be transferred to private provision. This inhibits the existing public provider from displaying strong monopolistic tendencies of inflexibility, resistance to change, etc.

Greater strategic focus

A number of important themes that have often been on the agenda of public service organisations are an emphasis on:

- The delivery of more effective service outcomes
- The achievement of high levels of customer satisfaction
- Improved access to services
- Improved resource efficiency

The achievement of these objectives is not always something that can be achieved in one year, and thus, public services had to start developing longer-term strategic plans setting out how they were going to make these achievements actually happen over several years. Consequently, they found it more and more necessary to produce strategic plans and associated implementation plans. Associated with the concept of strategic planning is also the broader concept of strategic management that also sets out how strategies will be delivered and monitored.

Enhanced consumer orientation

A strong theme in public service reform has been that of consulting and involving actual and prospective users of services about services. Such a consultation could be ex-ante in terms of consultation about changes to service provision or ex-post in terms of the degree of satisfaction with services received. Such consultation would take the form of consulting with individual citizens or with whole communities, and various techniques might be deployed such as questionnaire surveys, focus groups and citizen's juries.

A natural extension to consulting the users of services, about the services they receive, is to give them greater choice about the services they receive. A consideration of this idea of choice might lead one to conclude that individuals could exercise such choice in a number of dimensions:

- Choice of type of service required
- Choice of location of service
- Choice of timing of service
- Choice of means of delivery of service
- Choice of provider organisation

Regulatory changes

In recent decades, there was often a strengthened emphasis on the external regulation of certain public services. A variety of regulatory bodies might have been formed but they can probably be considered as being of two types:

- *Privatised public utilities* – these regulatory bodies are concerned with the public utilities that had been privatised. Since the process of privatisation often substituted a private monopoly for a public monopoly, regulatory bodies had key roles to play in ensuring private utilities did not misuse their monopolistic position.
- *Public services* – regulatory organisations may have been created to regulate the activities of certain key public services in order to protect the service user from poor quality services.

Emphasis on governance and accountability

During the 1990s, there were a number of high-profile "financial scandals" in the UK private sector (e.g. Maxwell, BCCI) which identified the lack of awareness and ineffectiveness of many non-executive directors of those companies. Similar scandals have also taken place in other countries. There were also a number of "scandals" in the public sector which caused adverse publicity and many critical reports. These events seem to suggest a certain ineffectiveness of non-executive directors, elected politicians, etc., in knowing what the public service organisation was actually doing. As a consequence there has been a greater emphasis on applying the principles of corporate governance to public service organisations, and this has led to such developments as:

- The formation of audit committees
- Strengthened internal and external audit to provide greater assurance to non-executives
- Codes of practice and training for non-executives, etc.

Whether these activities have really strengthened governance in public service organisations is a debatable point. Many people (including the author) would argue that the most important issue is the selection of non-executives and the importance of having people with the courage to raise issues and "rock the boat" where necessary.

SUCCESS AND FAILURE IN PUBLIC SERVICE REFORM

Failure of a PSR can probably be identified if there is a significant degree of any or all of the following characteristics associated with the reform:

1. The reform fails, significantly, to achieve the objectives set for it, at the outset, in terms of the impact on public services.
2. The costs associated with the reform go significantly over budget or cannot be assessed.
3. The project is significantly late in terms of being fully implemented.

Success or partial success would be the absence of the above.

Some might suggest that the generation of large-scale political embarrassment associated with a political reform might also mark the reform a failure but as this is a book on management, it is best to focus on the three characteristics of failure identified above.

Looking at public service reforms of various types and in various countries, it is probably fair to say that the results are mixed. There are successes, and there are failures. However, across the globe we can find many significant failures including the following examples shown in Case studies 4.1, 4.2 and 4.3.

In particular, the UK demonstrates a significant degree of public policy failure. A recent blog (Hudson 2019) by Professor Bob Hudson on the LSE website concluded,

> it has always been the case that the likelihood of policy failure is at least as high as policy success. But the currency of modern politics seems to be squarely that of failure – indeed major failure. The most prominent current British examples are Brexit, closely followed by Universal Credit, and now a new NHS Ten Year Plan that disavows the extensive reforms to the service introduced only six years previously.

CASE STUDY 4.1

Public service reform – Jamaica

In February 2012, the Government of Jamaica entered into a 27-month Stand-By Arrangement with the International Monetary Fund (IMF). This agreement was needed to buffer the economic challenges of the global financial crisis. To address these challenges, the IMF targeted the need for PSR as a key component. A subsequent report produced by the Caribbean Policy Research Institute (CaPRI 2015) noted that Jamaica's efforts at PSR had been a failure due to deep-rooted problems in the public sector and it called for changes to the implementation of the Public Sector Master Rationalisation Plan. According to the report, the impediments to successful reform include government's failure to clearly define its role, over-centralised decision making which creates implementation bottlenecks, lack of cooperation among public sector employees and lack of political will to make difficult decisions that may adversely affect its political support.

CASE STUDY 4.2

Public service reform – Bhutan

In a gathering of senior public officials of Bhutan in 2008, the Prime Minister declared that the Position Classification System (PCS) was a failure and had weakened the Bhutanese civil service. The PCS, a comprehensive set of PSRs, was the result of a set of recommendations made by the government in 2000 to improve the civil service in Bhutan. Although the reasons for this failure are complex, they seem to comprise a lack of understanding about the magnitude of the tasks being faced and matters such as having proper stakeholder analysis and change management strategies (Ugyel 2013).

CASE STUDY 4.3

Public service reform – United Kingdom

At the time of writing, a UK government reform which shows all the signs of a major public service reform failure is the policy of introducing Universal Credit as a replacement for six existing benefits payments. This approach to simplifying the benefits system had widespread support from many different areas of society including all the main political parties. However, the programme is six years behind schedule and has cost over £2 billion so far. A recent National Audit Office report (NAO 2018) on the programme has suggested that the new benefits system will fail to deliver promised financial savings or employment benefits, and leaves thousands of vulnerable claimants in hardship. The NAO suggests that the programme:

- May end up costing more than the benefit systems it replaces
- Cannot prove it helps more claimants into work
- Is unlikely to ever deliver value for money

Many more cases could be added to the list. In their popular exploration of "policy blunders", Anthony King and Ivor Crewe (King and Crewe 2013) identified 12 government policies that were said to have failed in their objectives, wasted large amounts of public money, 'wrecked the lives of ordinary people' and were foreseeable.

LESSONS AND CAUSES OF PAST REFORMS

Clearly, every case of failure in public service reform will a have a range of specific causes and no two cases will be identical. However, a number of themes can be identified which seem commonplace in such failures. These are discussed below:

- **Top down instead of bottom up** – much of public service reform works via a top-down approach whereby the reform approach is developed at the centre of government and promulgated throughout the public services sometimes with limited consultation. Not surprisingly, there is often little ownership of the reform's objectives within the public service itself and the reform is seen to fail. The alternative approach that is often advocated as likely to be more successful is termed the bottom-up approach. This approach involves innovations for improving public services being developed locally and not at the centre. If they prove successful they can then be replicated elsewhere in the sector.
- **Pilot projects** – a particular reform may be undertaken in a "big bang" fashion with the whole sector being reformed at the same time. If the reform fails, as it often does, this affects the whole sector and a huge amount of time and resource will have been wasted. The alternative might have been to test the reform with smaller pilot projects and to look for problems and complications. These could then be resolved by the time of a wider roll out of the reform. These pilot projects could be hosted by a combination of public service organisations, third sector organisations or private companies to see who performs the best and how success can be replicated.
- **Separation of design from implementation** – the process of formulating and designing a particular public service reform is divorced from the implementation of that reform. This often leads to implementation problems not foreseen in the design process. This is particularly the case where the two tasks of design and implementation are undertaken by different organisations.
- **Lack of management capacity** – implementing public service reform is an arduous and complex task that requires a sufficient level of management capacity to be successful. In some reforms, that capacity may just not be available leading to major implementation problems. This is particularly the case with regard to change management (a key aspect of public service reform) where the need for change management programmes is substantially under-estimated leading to capacity problems in this area.
- **Poor forecasting** – PSR often involves a large number of significant and inter-connected changes in organisation, process, resource use, etc. In making decisions about the type of reforms that could be undertaken it is important to try to make some sorts of reasonable forecasts of the consequences of such actions. Unfortunately, the standard of forecasting in public services is not always sufficiently robust and this can result impact on the degree of success of the reform.

THE ROLE OF MANAGEMENT ACCOUNTING IN PUBLIC SERVICE REFORM

From what has been said, above, it will be seen that the main causes of failure of PSR are varied. Some of these causes will be a consequence of a variety of political and managerial failures but, in this section, we give brief consideration to some areas where good quality management accounting practice could contribute to either improved design of PSRs or/and the implementation of those reforms:

- **Absence of data** – many people may think that public services are awash with data of a variety of types. While this may be true, it is often the case that the data is available is not what is required for analysing future reforms of public services. This is especially true of cost information, and it is often the case that decisions about public service reform are made with only limited, and not always accurate, cost information being available. Clearly, management accounting has a huge role to play here, and the tasks of obtaining and analysing cost information are discussed in Chapter 7.
- **Inadequate data analysis** – even where sufficient data is available, the approach to analysing that data is often inadequate. Historically, this might have been acceptable because of the complexities involved but in today's world, the use of big data analytics has revolutionised this task. This is discussed in Chapter 13.
- **Strategic options appraisal** – in undertaking public service reform, there is always likely to be a number of different approaches that need to be considered. These approaches will have differences in potential outcomes, resource use, risk, etc. Hence, some form of robust assessment of the various strategic options available should be a key element of the process but this is not always the case. The approach to strategic options appraisal is considered in Chapter 10.
- **Inadequate risk assessment and management** – activities as large and complex as the major reform of a public services should always be accompanied by a rigorous, objective and realistic assessment of the risks involved and the approach to be adopted if such risks should manifest themselves. It is important that the risk analysis should cover all of the risks involved and over-optimism should be avoided. Management accounting has a role to play here and the tasks of risk management are discussed in Chapter 12.

Leadership, management and decision making in public services

INTRODUCTION

An immense amount of research has been undertaken and written about the themes of leadership, management and decision making in organisations. In this chapter, it is not intended to repeat the findings of that research but to consider its application in public services. In particular, the aim is to provide context for discussing the role management accounting has to play in relation to leadership, management and decision making in public services. This chapter covers the following:

- Leadership and management in public services: distinctive features
- Decision making in public services
- Management accounting and decision making in public services

LEADERSHIP AND MANAGEMENT IN PUBLIC SERVICES: DISTINCTIVE FEATURES

No organisation, even the smallest and simplest, can manage itself, and every organisation needs some form of management to be effective. A simple definition of management concerns the deployment of resources (both human and physical resources) in a manner designed to achieve a defined set of objectives. However, this is far too simplistic a view to be of much use here. It gives no detail of how management should approach the organisation of the resources or how it should encourage or motivate staff.

Larger organisations today will often separate the different roles of management, appointing specialists for roles such as human resource management, while many smaller organisations may retain all management functions in one person. However it is structured, the task of managers is to guide the organisation towards achieving the goals set by the owners or sponsors of the organisation. But how do managers undertake this task? John Kotter's work on leadership is often quoted. Among other things Kotter strongly defended the view that management and leadership are different functions and that managers do not necessarily undertake the leadership functions. He argued that, instead, managers were responsible for ensuring order and efficiency in the organisation – they 'deal with complexity' – while leaders were responsible for having a vision of the future and then encouraging the organisation to adapt to that vision. Forcing through change would endanger the maintenance of order, efficiency, morale, etc. Kotter also put forward his famous eight-stage process of change (Kotter 2012) which is as follows:

1. Establish a sense of urgency
2. Create the guiding coalition
3. Develop a vision and strategy
4. Communicate the change vision
5. Empower employees for broad-based action
6. Generate short-term wins
7. Consolidate gains and produce more change
8. Anchor new approaches into the culture

At this point, it is important to note that earlier in this book it was mentioned that one of the key features of public services, compared to commercial organisations, was the involvement of politicians in public services. Consequently, in public services, one can think about leadership as coming from politicians (political leadership) and from managers (managerial leadership). In some cases, one or all of these types of leadership may be thought to be absent which can cause difficulties. Even worse would be a lack of coherence between political leadership messages and those from managers. Both should be "singing from the same hymn sheet".

Not everyone would agree entirely with Kotter's view but the distinction between management and leadership is helpful. The world is changing at an increasing pace, and the things we see today are very different from those even 20–30 years ago. In the commercial world, many companies that a generation ago were considered the bedrock of a country's infrastructure have disappeared. For example, ICI, once seen as the flagship firm of the chemical industry in the UK shrank in size until the remnants were purchased by other companies. Meanwhile, many of the new giants operate in sectors not even dreamed of a generation ago – Google, for example. In the field of public services, we observe similar levels of change. Government departments exist today, which were non-existent two or three decades ago. Similarly, organisations such as local authorities and NHS Trusts are considerably different in structure, activities and methods of working than they were over a similar period. While some of these changes might be questionable, some are undoubtedly due to changes in societies and changes in the required roles of public services. Also important is the societal context in which public services operate and that often changes substantially over time. Events that were seen as minor ten years ago might be looked at more seriously in today's climate.

Managers are charged with running the organisation and that is an essential role. But if they focus on this, there must be someone else who focuses on managing the dynamics of change, Kotter claims that this is the role of leaders. However, leadership has the following aspects:

- Leadership is about creating a vision of where the organisation needs to get to and facilitating the journey to that position. In other words it involves major strategic change.
- Leadership is not just a quality found in the chief executive. It needs to be identified and developed at all levels in the organisation from chief executive to first level supervisor.
- Leadership approaches need to be determined by the situation the organisation finds itself in. An organisation in crisis may need a different leadership approach compared to one which is well established and stable.
- While some people are born with good leadership skills, the skills can be developed in others.

In general terms, it is probably true to say that the principles of leadership and management in the public services are broadly similar to that in the private sector. However, certain significant differences can be delineated:

- **Value base** – it is sometimes argued that managers in public services have a different value base to those in private business. In the private sector, managers will probably be focused on such themes as sales, cost control, profitability, customer satisfaction, etc. Public management values are more oriented towards such things as public interest, public needs and political compromise. As a public service manager, the primary concern is the overall well-being of the people you serve. However, this can be overstated because, clearly, managers in (say) the private health sector, while concerned with revenues and profits, will also be concerned with professional standards and customer satisfaction.
- **Objectives** – public service organisations tend to have different and more complex objectives compared to the private sector. For the private sector manager, setting goals and measuring success is relatively straightforward, because objectives can usually be clearly defined and measured in financial terms such as revenues, profits and return on assets. The broader implications for competitors, customers and suppliers are not considered in the narrow equation for business efficiency. For the public sector manager, objectives are often abstract, over-arching, somewhat undefined and sometimes exceptionally difficult to measure. That is because in the public sector, goals apply to a much broader jurisdiction than a single business. They encompass multiple programmes, and their success is measured by the overall betterment of society. Moreover, in the business world it is the case that objectives are set by the business organisation itself. However, in many parts of the public sector it is the case that the organisation has to accept goals that are from outside the organisation most notably by national government.

- **The role of service professionals** – in simple terms, we can consider public service organisations as being staffed by a combination of people who might be referred to as managers (e.g. operational managers, financial managers, HR managers, etc.) and people who might be referred to as service professionals who have specific technical skills at delivering public services (e.g. teachers, doctors, nurses, firefighters). This distinction is not absolute because many service professionals also have a management role in their job and many people holding fully managerial posts were formerly service professionals. Similar situations can occur in the private sector where a company will also employ people who are specialist managers but also people who are technical experts (e.g. scientists, engineers, lawyers) concerned with the delivery of a product.

- **The role of politics** – as noted above, the reality is that the delivery of public services is inextricably linked with politics. Consequently, it is inevitable that public service managers always need to keep an eye on political trends when undertaking their roles and pursuing their objectives. Sometimes, objectives which have been agreed in the past will be over-turned or amended because of the state of national or local politics at the time. It will be the responsibility of public service managers to deal with those changes. While managers in the private sector will sometimes have to respond to political issues of the day, they do not have political masters and the extent of this will not be as great.

- **Public accountability** – accountability differs largely between public and private organisations. Managers in public organisations are accountable to a much larger group of people – everyone in the governed area – and are always under public scrutiny. Such a strong and palpable public influence plays a significant role in their decisions. Ultimately, a public service manager will attempt to appease as many people as possible while achieving results, adding to the complexity of their position. The private sector operates without the degree of checks and balances of the public sector but while business executives may not escape public scrutiny completely, they remain primarily accountable to a small group of shareholders. Their focus can therefore remain on maximising the bottom-line. Public service organisations are also far more transparent than private ones. In a free society, transparency is government's obligation to share information with citizens. It is at the heart of how citizens hold their public officials accountable.

- **Stability and leadership** – leadership is important in any organisation as is managerial stability. Now while there are examples of chief executives and senior managers in the private sector leaving their company after short periods of time in post, the situation does seem worse in public services with average times in post being shorter. Not too long ago, the average tenure of an NHS chief executive was just 18 months. Equally on the political front there are stability problems in relation to public services. Governments might change after a few years, and Government Ministers often only stay in post for a couple of years before moving on to another department or the back benches.

DECISION MAKING IN PUBLIC SERVICES

Public service organisations make innumerable numbers of decisions every week of the year. Before considering the role of management accounting in public service decision making, it is first necessary to consider the nature of decision making.

Decision making can be explored from a number of different standpoints according to different parameters.

- Decision types
- Decision makers
- Decision formats
- Decision focus
- Decision approaches

Decision types

As already noted, public service organisations and their employees will take innumerable decisions, every day, every week and every month of the year. It is probably true, but not particularly helpful, to state that all decisions will be unique. To make sense of decision making we have to have some approach to categorising decisions into a number of discrete types. One such approach is to categorise decisions as follows:

- **Policy and Implementation Decisions** – as the name suggests, policy decisions concern what policy directions the organisation should follow. Implementation decisions concern the way in which the chosen policy is implemented. Policy decisions are likely to be the province of politicians and top management while implementation decisions will be, largely, taken by lower level managers.
- **Tactical and Strategic Decisions** – operational decisions are those which a manager makes over and over again adhering to certain established rules, policies and procedures. They are often repetitive in nature and related to general functioning. Authority for taking tactical decisions is usually delegated to middle management levels in the organisation. Strategic decisions, on the other hand, are relatively more difficult. They influence the future of the organisation and involve the entire organisation.
- **Programmed and Non-programmed Decisions** – management scientist Herbert Simon used computer language in classifying decisions. Programmed decisions are basically of a routine type for which systematic procedures have been devised so that the problem may not be treated as a unique case each time it crops up. Non-programmed decisions are complex and deserve a specific treatment. It represents a problem which requires a thorough study of the causes of such a situation, and after analysing all factors a solution can be found through problem-solving processes.
- **Basic and Routine Decisions** – basic decisions are those which require a good deal of deliberation and are of crucial importance. These decisions often require the formulation of new norms through deliberate thought-provoking processes. Examples of basic decisions are service delivery

locations, access times, etc. On the other hand, routine decisions are of a repetitive nature and hence require relatively little consideration. It may be seen that basic decisions generally relate to strategic aspects, while routine decisions are related to operational/tactical aspects of an organisation.

- **Organisational and Personal Decisions** – organisational decisions are those which a manager takes in his official capacity and which can, if necessary, be delegated to others. On the other hand, personal decisions are those which a manager takes in his individual capacity. However, such decisions may have organisational implications. Examples might be choosing dates for annual leave or deciding to apply for another job. It is clearly important for there to be a clear dividing line between these two types of decision.

- **Reactive and Planned Decisions** – as its name suggests, reactive decisions are responses to a new situation which requires urgent action. On the other hand, planned decisions are linked to the objectives of organisation. An examples might be the distinction between fault repair and planned maintenance of equipment.

It is not necessary to agree with the above classifications and, in any case, there are clear overlaps between the different categories. However, it is important to note that there are distinctive types of decision which occur at different levels in the organisation.

Decision makers

Many different types of people might be involved in decision making, in different ways in public service organisations. It is not possible or helpful to try and name every sort of decision maker but is useful to consider different groups who might have different perceptions about how decisions are made in their organisation. The following groups might be considered:

- *Professional/Technical Staff* – public services employ a large number of varied and highly skilled staff who might be described as professional or technical and who work in front line service provision. Examples might be doctors and nurses in the NHS, teachers in schools, emergency service personnel, scientists and engineer in many organisations, etc. These employees are experts in their respective fields, and many decisions will be technical in nature which will require specialist expertise to make them.

- *Managers* – all public service organisations will have people who work in managerial roles, and such managers might be broadly classified as operational managers, middle managers or senior managers. Now many of these managers might be qualified public service professionals who no longer work in such roles but now occupy a managerial role in the organisation. In such a role, they may no longer get involved in detailed professional/ technical decisions but are involved in a wide range of managerial decisions. However, some of them may combine a part-time managerial role with some direct service provision (e.g. a practising doctor who also manages a clinical division). With regard to managerial roles, clearly, the types of decisions that managers will be involved in will vary according to their position in the hierarchy.

- *Politicians* – at local level, sub-national level and national level, politics is a key component of public services. Thus, it is inevitable and important that politicians are involved in some aspects of decision making. Without their involvement, the democratic process would be a sham. However, caution is needed here. Political decisions cannot be taken in a vacuum. They have to be considered in the context of predetermined strategies about what an acceptable service standard is and the level of resources required to achieve it. Hence, politicians need to be briefed about these matters. It goes without saying that political decisions should be avoided by managers and left to the politicians. However, managers also need to navigate the boundary between what is and is not political – what the politician needs to know and what is purely managerial.

- *Service users* – there are some situations in public services where decisions about services and resources are made by people who are current or prospective service users. Arguably, these approaches are often used when it is perceived that users are better able to understand their own needs than managers or professionals are? One example of this concerns personal social care budgets. With these, service users are allocated a sum of money with which to acquire the social care they feel they need. Consequently, they have to make decisions about their needs and what care to purchase. Another example might be that of participatory budgeting which has been advanced as an important tool for inclusive and accountable governance and has been implemented in various forms in countries around the globe. Through participatory budgeting, service users have the opportunity to gain first-hand knowledge of public service operations, influence policies and hold public service organisations to account. However, participatory processes also run the risk of capture by interest groups. Such captured processes may continue to bias government decision making and unintendedly promote elitism in government decision making.

Decision formats

Decision making can take place in three main levels: individual, group and organisational. It is possible to theorise about what sorts of decisions should be made at what level (Boettke and Leeson 2002), but the reality is that variations in organisational structures and cultures will mean that decision making will function in different ways in different organisations.

- **Individual** – evidence suggests that most individuals do not examine every possible alternative or collect mountains of information and data when making choices. Instead, most draw on personal experience, apply rules of thumb and use other heuristics when making decisions. Sometimes, that leads to trouble. Most individuals are susceptible to what psychologists call cognitive biases – decision traps that cause them to make certain systematic mistakes when making choices. However, examination of intuitive processes in great depth can show that intuition is more than a gut instinct. Intuition represents a powerful pattern-recognition capability that individuals have, drawing from their wealth of past experience. However, it must also be recognised that intuition can lead us astray, especially when the use of flawed analogies is involved.

- **Group** – while some decisions are made by individuals, decisions are often made in groups where there are complex choices to consider. Although there is no precision about this, a group can probably be thought of as comprising three to six people. Groups may often be seen as "smarter" than individuals but, in practice, this is not always the case. In many cases groups do not employ the diverse talents and knowledge of the members effectively. Groups may also experience a lack of synergy among the members. Problems may arise such as groupthink, which is the tendency for groups to experience powerful pressures for conformity. These may suppress dissenting views and lead to clouded judgements. Similarly, groups may also be dominated by powerful individuals, and their decisions therefore collapse back into individual decision making but with the added legitimacy of the perception that the decision was made by a group. However, when properly used, groups can stimulate constructive conflict, as well as achieve consensus and timely closure, so that they can overcome these problems and make better decisions.

- **Organisational** – decisions may often be made at the organisational level perhaps by the Board or some top-level committee of the organisation. The reality is that many (perhaps) most decisions at this level are correctly made and the decision achieves the aims intended. However, at this level of decision making the type of decision is often important, wide ranging and of great public interest. Consequently, any failures of decision making are well publicised. In public services, there are many well-known examples of major organisational failure caused by flawed decision making. Some examples could include the Stafford Hospitals scandal in the UK and the Columbia space shuttle accident in the USA. Other less dramatic organisational failures also take place in both public and private sectors but are sometimes less well published. These major failures of decision making cannot be attributed to one faulty decision, or to one poor leader. Instead, they relate to how the structure, systems and culture of the organisation shape the behaviour of many individuals and teams in the organisation. In these cases, we often see large-scale failures resulting from multiple small decision failures that form a chain of events leading to a catastrophe. However, if we look closely, we can also see examples of how many organisations have discovered ways to encourage vigilant decision making in the face of high risks, such that they perform with remarkable reliability. An example here is the air traffic control industry which abides by the principles of high reliability organisations.

Decision focus

It could be argued that decisions in public services could have a number of different foci:

- *Services focus* – the main thrust of these decisions concerns the provision of public services – the range, the volume, the standards, the location, etc. Such decisions could involve dealing with responses to serious problems or more gradual changes to enhance services. Clearly, the resource implications of changes in services would have to be (or should be) considered but the main thrust of the decision concerns the services themselves.
- *Resources focus* – the main thrust of these decisions concerns the resources of the organisation be that physical resources, human resources or finance. Again this could be in the context of some form of crisis such as shortages of specialist staff or major overspends. Alternatively, the decisions could involve changes to services to improve the use of resources, avoidance of duplication, etc. Again, while the main focus of decisions is on the use of resources it would also be important to consider the impact of such decisions on the public services themselves.
- *Balanced focus* – the above two cases perhaps represent extreme situations. Many perhaps most public service decisions require a focus on both service issues and resource issues at the same time. Examples can be quoted, in public services of where too strong a focus on one of the issues has led to flawed decision making which had to be rectified at a later date. An example here is the Mid-staffs hospital scandal (Holmes 2013). Similarly, consequent on a political scandal associated with an incident such as child abuse, managers can sometimes be forced to over-react to a set of risks in a way they would otherwise not have done.

Decision approach

Most people would probably expect decision making in public services to be a thoroughly rationale process but evidence suggests this is not always the case as will be discussed later.

What we term rational decision making is a multi-step process for making choices between alternatives which uses a rational model of decision making (Uzonwanne, 2016). The process of using a rational model of decision making favours logic, objectivity and analysis over subjectivity and insight. The word "rational" in this context does not mean sane or clear-headed as it does in the colloquial sense. The rationale approach is one which follows a sequential and formal path of decision making activities. This path includes the following:

- Formulating a goal(s)
- Identifying the criteria for making the decision
- Identifying alternatives
- Performing an analysis
- Making a final decision

In line with basic economic theory, the rational model of decision making assumes that people will make choices that maximise benefits and minimise any costs. For example, when shopping most people want to get the most useful products at the lowest price; because of this, they will judge the benefits of a certain object (for example, how useful is it or how attractive is it) compared to those of similar objects. They will then compare prices (or costs). Under the rational decision making approach, people will choose the object that provides the greatest reward at the lowest cost. In addition, the rational model also assumes the following:

- An individual has full and perfect information on which to base a choice.
- Measurable criteria exist for which data can be collected and analysed.

An individual has the cognitive ability, time and resources to evaluate each alternative against the others. The rational decision making model does not necessarily consider factors that cannot be quantified easily, such as ethical concerns or the value of altruism. It also leaves out consideration of personal feelings, loyalties or sense of obligation. It may also exclude things which cannot be measured because people don't know of their existence even though it might in principle be measurable. The rational model in its objectivity creates a bias toward the preference for facts, data and analysis over intuition or desires.

However, there are many criticisms of rational choice theory (or the rational model of decision making) which claim that this model makes unrealistic and over-simplified assumptions. Their objections to the rational model include the following:

- Decision makers rarely have full (or perfect) information. For example, the information might not be available, the person might not be able to access it or it might take too much time or too many resources to acquire. More complex models rely on probability in order to describe outcomes rather than the assumption that a person will always know all outcomes.
- Individual rationality is limited by their ability to conduct analysis and think through competing alternatives. The more complex a decision, the greater the limits are to making completely rational choices. Even these more complex models are subject to critique though as the probabilities do not necessarily factor in issues which may be unquantifiable.
- Decisions may also be influenced by factors which may force managers to decide less rationally. Governments are often criticised for setting up programmes too quickly because that is what the political timetable requires when actually if you were taking those decisions rationally you would have spent a lot more time on programme set up than actually happened. Also, in some situations there may be government incentives or disincentives which lead managers to choose an option which is not necessarily the optimal one. This is illustrated in Case study 5.1.

Rather than always seeking to optimise benefits while minimising costs, managers are often willing to choose an acceptable option rather than the optimal one. This is especially true when it is difficult to precisely **measure** and assess factors among the selection criteria.

CASE STUDY 5.1

Public-private partnerships and decision making

The emergency services sector in a country employs a wide range of skilled personnel working in various aspects of emergency services. The sector has to undertake a wide range of training activities, on a national basis, for new recruits to emergency services and experienced members of staff who require their skills to be kept up to date.

Currently training facilities are piecemeal and of poor quality, and this is having a deleterious effect on the level and quality of training. Indeed, a number of published reports have indicated failures of training which have led to deaths following incidents. Consequently, the senior management of the training department have prepared a business case for the construction and equipping of a bespoke training unit which, in the country's own currency, is the equivalent of several millions of US dollars.

The government of the country is aware of the pressing need for this development and has approved the business case. However, because of economic problems, they have difficulties in identifying a source of funds for the project. Hence, they have encouraged the senior management to look at a public-private solution using the Private Finance Initiative (PFI) model.

The senior management has developed a PFI proposal involving a construction company, a service company and a bank, and has prepared the required financial forecasts. They are also required to undertake the same level of analysis for a publicly funded approach to the project and to compare the publicly funded and PFI models to see which is most appropriate.

A first cut of the financial analysis suggests that the publicly financed model would be the preferred approach, but the senior management is aware that no government capital funds are available. Hence, if the PFI route is not chosen the project will not proceed. Hence, they agree to make some changes to the forecasts in order to suggest that the PFI route is the best option.

They make these changes in the knowledge that the project specification is likely to change during the course of the project, and the final project may look significantly different from the original planning version. Hence, no real ex-post comparison of the PFI version of the final project can ever be made against the publicly financed version of the original project.

The term non-rational decision making should not be read as someone being stupid, careless, unthinking, etc., although in some cases that might be true. Non-rational decision making is more to do with limitations of the decision making process. Non-rational models of managerial decision making are likely to be applied where there is a lack of information which may be completely unavailable or unavailable within a reasonable time and/or reasonable cost. Equally the time available to decision makers to make a rational decision may be insufficient for a variety of reasons. These sorts of limitations make it difficult for managers to make optimal decisions.

Some non-rational decision making models include the following:

- **Bounded rationality** – developed by Herbert Simon (Simon 1991), this approach holds that managers seek alternatives only until they find one that looks satisfactory, rather than seeking the optimal decision. Bounded rationality means that the ability of managers to be perfectly rational in making decisions is limited by such factors as cognitive capacity and time constraints. As already noted, actual decision making is not perfectly rational because of inadequate information, inadequate time, limited human memory and limited human data-processing abilities or the decision maker's own misperceptions or prejudices. Thus, satisficing can be appropriate when the cost of delaying a decision or searching for a better alternative outweighs the likely payoff from such a course.

- **Incremental model** – this holds that managers make the smallest response possible that will reduce the problem to, at least, a tolerable level. In these situations, managers can make decisions without processing a great deal of information. Such incremental strategies are usually more effective in the short run than in the long run.

- **Garbage-can model** – this model of decision making holds that managers behave in virtually a random pattern in making non-programmed decisions. Factors that determine decisions include the particular individuals involved, their interests and favourite solutions to problems, as well as any opportunities they stumble upon. The garbage-can approach is often used in the absence of solid strategic management and can lead to severe problems.

- **Negotiated Order** – this is a sociological approach that is interested in how meaning is created and maintained in organisations with a particular focus on human interactions. Negotiated order in an organisation concerns the pattern of activities that has emerged over time as an outcome of the interplay of the variety of interests, understandings, reactions and initiatives of the individuals and groups involved in the organisation. To examine negotiated orders in any given organisation is to turn away from the more traditional way of looking at organisations that give primacy of attention to the pattern or ordering of activities chosen (or "designed") by those officially in charge of the organisation. Studies in public service organisations suggests that, at least, some decision making at the organisational level is often a process of negotiated order (Cox 2019) rather than evidence based. Where there is an absence or paucity of data and evidence, decision making often involves an interplay and trade-offs between individuals in the decision making forum who have a variety of opinions, experiences, skills, prejudices, etc.

Returning to our earlier point about the expectation that decision making in public services would be rational, a moment's reflection will show that this is just not the case. From our own experiences of public service organisations, most of us will, probably, have observed decisions which have utilised some or all of the non-rational models at various points in time. In fact, the completely rational decision making process is probably a rarity as a consequence of the real-life constraints outlined. This does not mean that we shouldn't strive for greater rationality. Case study 5.2 outlines a possible non-rationale model of public service decision making based around negotiated order.

CASE STUDY 5.2

Health sector decision making and negotiated order

Negotiated order is a theoretical perspective which argues that virtually all social order is negotiated order. To accomplish tasks and to make decisions people chiefly negotiate with each other. It argues that management scholars seeking to understand decision making in organisations should focus on the characteristics of the negotiation context, as well as social and structural contexts in which the decision is taken.

In the UK NHS, clinical commissioning groups (CCGs) are the organisations who decide what health services are needed in an area and then enter into contracts with service providers to deliver those services. Thus, Longlinks CCG is responsible for the commissioning the bulk of health service in its area.

The CCG was undertaking a major review of its community health service activities which were seen to be in need of a reconfiguration to reflect changing population needs. The task facing the CCG was that of deciding what to do with this group of services essential to it achieving its strategic objectives. To achieve the necessary changes to service configuration they identified two main strategic options:

- To work with existing providers to reconfigure services
- To undertake an open market procurement exercise to identify a suitable provider of services according to a new service specification

(continued)

This was a major strategic decision for the organisation and in making such a decision there were a wide range of factors to be taken into account including the following:

- Public and stakeholder expectations
- Clinical Evidence
- National Health Policy
- Environmental factors
- Health Needs
- Financial constraints
- Cost data
- Risks, etc.

For many years, the term "*evidence based policy making*" has been something of a mantra in the NHS, and there is an expectation that major decisions such as this one will be primarily based on evidence. Unfortunately, there are still many situations where sufficient reliable evidence is lacking. This was such a situation.

In-depth research in the CCG suggested that in a situation such as this where evidence is lacking, decision making becomes a process of <u>negotiated order</u> between the participants in the decision making process. Each participant will have their own knowledge base, experiences, prejudices, etc., and this will factor into the decision making process. The participants in the decision making will involve general medical practitioners, other clinicians including a nurse and a secondary care consultant, and lay members and thus will have varied backgrounds.

Now this strategic decision, clearly, does not meet the criteria for a rational decision making model. However, the rational model is really a normative approach which can be regarded as an ideal situation. Now this is not to suggest that the decision made was bad or incorrect. However, it does suggest that the decision is a non-rational in the technical sense and is also subject to bounded rationality. However, the thrust of this book is that with better financial information and advice one can push the actual decision making closer to the normative model without ever actually getting there. Clearly, financial information is not the only issue or even the most important issue, and other data and information is also important in making decision making more rational.

MANAGEMENT ACCOUNTING AND DECISION MAKING IN PUBLIC SERVICES

In this chapter we have considered the themes of leadership, management and decision making in public services. We now look at the role of management accounting in this context which, after all, is the thrust of this book. This is summarised in Figure 5.1

Figure 5.1 indicates the factors impacting on the organisation and the contribution that management accounting makes to the decision making in terms of

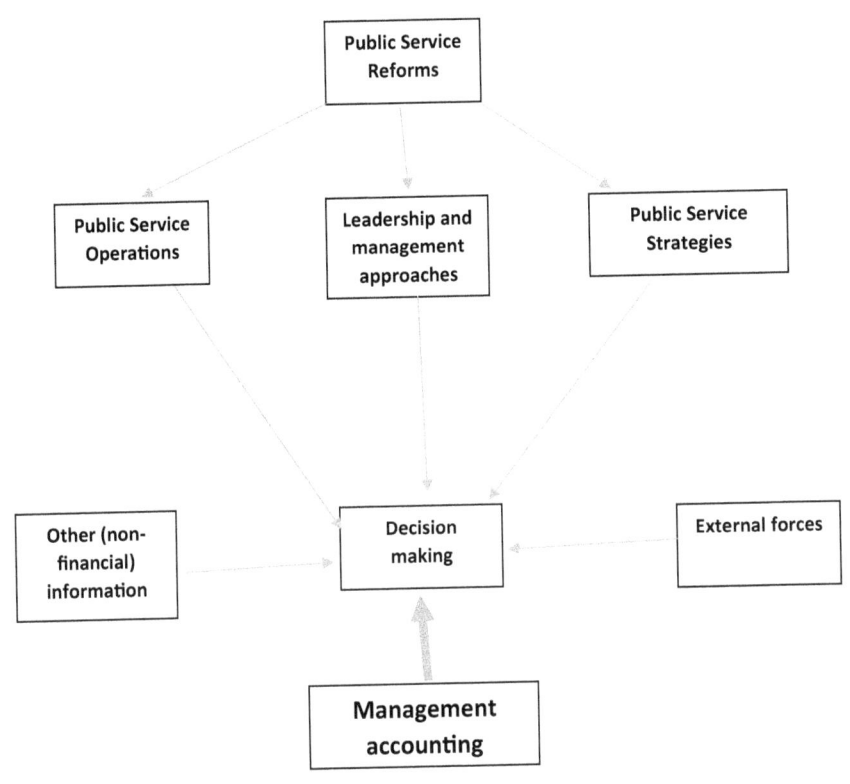

FIGURE 5.1
Management accounting and decision making.

information provision, analysis, communication, option development, etc. This will be discussed further in the next chapter.

However, the key points to note here are the following:

- **Complexity** – the complexity of the decision making process with a number of different types, makers, formats, foci and approaches. Of particular note is the tendency of decision making to veer away from the fully rationale model for a variety of reasons already discussed.
- **Leadership/management features** – these decisions have to be taken in an understanding of the leadership and management features described above which may differ substantially from those in the private sector.

Enter the management accountant. The management accountant has a key role in assisting with the making of decisions but also trying to ensure that the decision is made as close to the rational model as possible. Producing standard financial reports with limited analysis will not be good enough, and management accountants need to tailor their approach to the exigencies of the situation. This means the effective management accountant having

- A full understanding of the leadership and management features of the public service organisations

- Knowledge of the complexities and nuances of the decision situation in public services
- An understanding of the limitations of what the available data can tell one about a particular service in question

In the light of this, public sector management accountants must tailor their input accordingly. This is a particular issue for the management accountant who joins public services from the private sector who will need a fast learning curve to fully understand these issues.

In the next chapter, we consider, in more depth, the role of the management accountant in public services.

The relevance of management accounting in public services

INTRODUCTION

Before moving on to look at specific aspects of management accounting as they apply to public services, this chapter looks at the general nature of management accounting and its importance to public services management. This chapter follows on from the previous chapter which concerned leadership, management and decision making in public services.

The chapter covers the following:

- The nature and purpose of management accounting
- The modern roles of management accounting in relation to public services
- Behavioural aspects of management accounting
- Financial analysis and economic analysis in public services: the distinction
- The management accountant in modern public services
- Factors that drive the configuration of management accounting in public service organisations

THE NATURE AND PURPOSE OF MANAGEMENT ACCOUNTING

The nature of accounting is not always easy to define with any precision. The American Accounting Association defines accounting as follows:

> The process of identifying, measuring and communicating economic information to permit informed judgements and decisions by users of the information!
>
> (Valix et al. 2009)

Considering the key words in the above definition shows the following:

- **Decisions** – accounting is about informing judgements and decisions made by users.
- **Information** – it suggests that accounting is about providing information to others. Accounting information is economic information – it relates to the financial or economic activities of the organisation.
- **Identification and measurement** – accounting information needs to be identified and measured. This is done by way of a "set of accounts", based on a system of accounting known as double-entry bookkeeping. The accounting system identifies and records "accounting transactions". The "measurement" of accounting information is not always a straightforward process. It involves making judgements about the value of assets owned by the organisation or liabilities owed. It is also about accurately measuring the financial performance of the organisation over a particular period. As will be seen, the measurement of accounting information often requires subjective judgements to come to a conclusion.
- **Communication** – the definition identifies the need for accounting information to be communicated. The way in which this communication is achieved may vary. There are several forms of accounting communication (e.g. annual report and accounts, management accounting reports), each of which serves a slightly different purpose. The communication need is about understanding who needs the accounting information, and what they need to know!

Thus, accounting is basically about the provision of information to users (or potential users) in order to discharge accountability and enable the decisions to be made about the use of resources in the organisation. If one considers who are the people who examine and make use of accounting information it is possible to divide these users into two groups:

- **External users** – people external to the organisation such as suppliers, clients and lenders
- **Internal users** – people or groups internal to the organisation such as directors, senior managers and operational managers.

Consequently, in relation to public and private sector organisations, accounting practice is also usually considered as being of two types – financial accounting and management accounting. This is illustrated in Figure 6.1.

Both types of accounting utilise the same raw financial data but the distinction between management accounting and financial accounting is exemplified in Table 6.1.

If we turn now to management accounting, many definitions exist. One older and fairly simple definition states that management accounting is:

The process of preparing management reports and accounts that provide accurate and timely financial and statistical information required by managers to make day-to-day and short-term decisions.

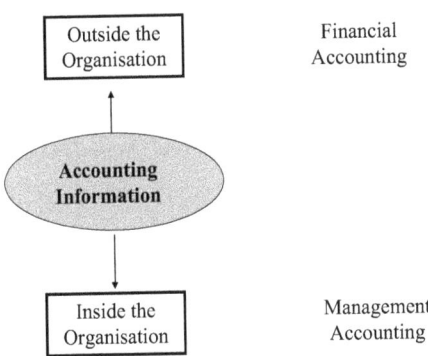

FIGURE 6.1
Financial and management accounting.

These days, such a definition as the above might be seen outmoded, in that it portrays the role of management accountant as being somewhat limited and confined to a passive mode of being the collector and giver of information to managers in order for them to make decisions. Other definitions of management accounting now exist, which are more broadly based and which, perhaps, give a better picture of management accounting in the modern world. These include the following:

Management accounting is the process of identification, measurement, accumulation, analysis, preparation, <u>interpretation, and communication</u> of financial information that is used by management to plan, evaluate, and control within an organisation. It is the information used for the planning, control, and decision-making activities of an organisation.

(AllBusiness)

TABLE 6.1

Distinction between financial and management accounting

Theme	Financial Accounting	Management Accounting
Focus	External to organisation	Internal to organisation
Period covered	Annual	Any period but typically much more frequently than annually (e.g. monthly, weekly)
Framework for production	Legislative/professional framework	User determined
Orientation	Mainly historically oriented	Historical and future orientation
Disclosure of information	Limited disclosure of information but enhancements being made	Wide and detailed range of information and external comparators

Management accounting is a profession that involves <u>partnering</u> in management decision making, devising planning and performance management systems, and providing expertise in financial reporting and control to assist management in the formulation and implementation of an organisation's strategy.

(Institute of Management Accountants in the USA)

the process of identification, measurement, accumulation, analysis, preparation, interpretation and communication of information used by management to plan, evaluate and control within an entity and to assure appropriate use of and accountability for its resources....

(CIMA Official Terminology)

These definitions suggest a management accountant who is much more of an active player in the organisation and who acts as a partner, with others, in making decisions concerning the organisation and its use of resources. This concept of a "business partner" is something returned to later.

When we turn from broad definitions and consider the specific roles played by management accounting in an organisation there are a number of ways of looking at this. One approach is to define the roles of management accounting as being concerned with contributing to decision making in the organisation in relation to:

- Planning
- Control
- Evaluation

A different approach to defining the roles of management accounting concerns what might be seen as the three questions any organisation will be concerned with, namely:

- **Scorekeeping: Are we doing well or badly?** – this involves the accumulation and classification of data which enables the assessment of organisational performance. However, the management accountant's role as a business partner means that this role shifts more into assisting line managers in interpreting a mass of complex information in order to assess performance rather than the somewhat mechanical tasks of accumulation and classification of data which, these days, are undertaken by technology.
- **Attention directing: Which problems should we look into?** – attention directing means reporting and interpreting information that helps managers to focus on operational problems, imperfections, inefficiencies and opportunities. This aspect of management accounting helps managers to concentrate on important areas of operations promptly enough for effective action to be taken.
- **Problem-solving** – the problem-solving aspect of management accounting brings the modern management accountant to the forefront of decision making in the organisation rather than being a passive observer. It involves assisting with the development of alternative courses of action and then undertaking a robust evaluation of the likely results of those possible courses of action – and often to recommend the best course to follow.

Problem-solving is commonly associated with non-recurring, non-routine decisions and situations that require special reports rather than the routine provision of information.

Finally, in relation to public services, CIPFA's Financial Management (FM) Model is structured around the three themes:

- Securing stewardship
- Supporting performance
- Enabling transformation

The examples quoted above look at management accounting in slightly different ways but the thrust of this book is to consider how management accounting in public services can, and should, contribute towards decision making in public service organisations at the strategic, tactical and operational level in relation to public service delivery. This will be continued in the next section.

THE MODERN ROLES OF MANAGEMENT ACCOUNTING IN RELATION TO PUBLIC SERVICES

To consider the roles of management accounting in public services, we must first consider the nature of leadership and management in such organisations. One approach is to consider this at three levels in the organisation as shown in Figure 6.2.

Thus, three levels of management in the organisation are identified:

- *Strategic level management* – this concerns the direction in which the organisation wishes to move in the longer term (say three to five years

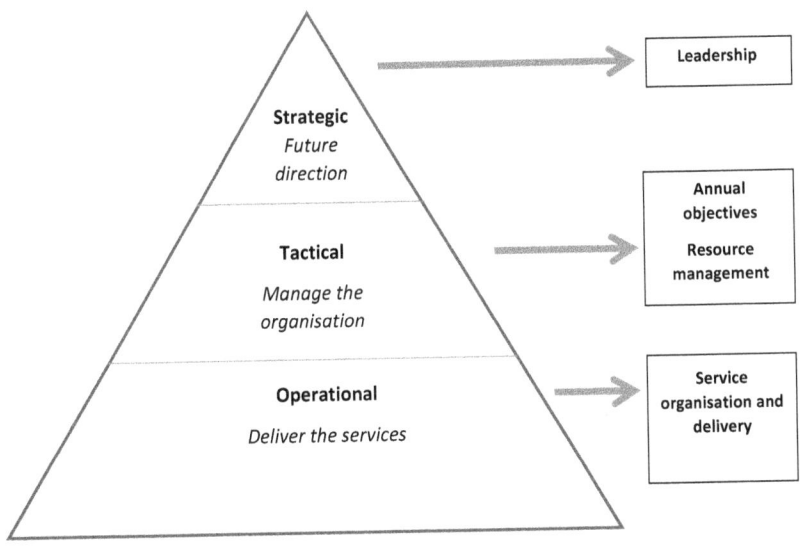

FIGURE 6.2
Management accounting and levels of management.

ahead). It concerns changes in the range of services being provided in the future, to whom they are provided and the way they are provided to users. The need for this to be addressed was emphasised in Chapter 1 when looking at the implications of increasing demand and austerity.

- *Tactical level management* – this sits between the strategic and the operational. It implies shorter range planning (perhaps one year or less) emphasising the current operations of various parts of the organisation. Tactical management involves emphasising what the various parts of the organisation must do for it to be successful in the year ahead in delivering public services.
- *Operational level management* – this concerns the way in which public services are provided to users on a day-to-day basis, in a timely and appropriate manner, by a variety of public service professionals.

In practice, it is not always easy to distinguish precisely between these three aspects of management and the precise situation will vary considerably between different organisations. Nevertheless, this framework is useful for thinking about organisational management. A further analysis of these aspects is shown in Table 6.2.

The historic development of management accounting practice broadly reflects this management hierarchy. Initially management accounting was traditionally concerned with aspects of tactical/operational management focusing on such matters as costing, budgeting, cash flow management, etc. Over time, management accounting started to become more involved in strategic management issues in organisations but perhaps not to the optimal extent possible. It cannot be emphasised too strongly that an enhanced role for management accounting in the strategic management of the public service organisation is vital for dealing with the twin challenges of increasing demand and austerity.

Shown in Table 6.3 are various management accounting techniques that could be used at different levels although, as we emphasise in a later section, techniques are not the be-all and end-all of management accounting. It could be

TABLE 6.2

Aspects of management accounting at different levels

	Strategic Management	Tactical Management	Operational Management
Done by	Senior managers	Middle managers	Supervisors
Timescales	Long (3+ years)	Medium (one year)	Short (days, weeks)
Type of information needed to manage at this level	Internal and external	Mainly internal but some external	Internal to organisation
Scope	Broad based covering a wide range of themes	Intermediate covering a limited number of themes	Narrow, relevant to particular service or client

TABLE 6.3

Management accounting techniques

Strategic Techniques	Tactical Techniques	Operational Techniques
• Activity-based costing • Life-cycle costing • Strategic management control systems • Target costing • Strategic cost analysis • Strategic capital investment appraisal • Economic analysis • VFM analysis • Data analytics • Environmental management accounting • Performance management – balanced scorecard • Benchmarking • Financial forecasting • Financial modelling • Budgetary planning	• Unit costing • Marginal costing • Budgetary planning and control • Responsibility accounting • Working capital controls • Relevant costing • Tactical capital investment appraisal • Techniques for dealing with risk and uncertainty in decision making • Short-term financial forecasting	• Activity data analysis • Cost recording and analysis • Limited budgetary management • Unit costs of activities • Relevant costing

argued, of course, that several of these techniques could appear in more than one column.

The application of management accounting to strategic issues is a relatively recent development and is often described as strategic management accounting. This differentiates it from the more traditional use of management accounting techniques in the tactical and operational arenas.

BEHAVIOURAL ASPECTS OF MANAGEMENT ACCOUNTING

No discussion of management accounting would be complete without a discussion of its behavioural impacts.

Basically, distributing management accounting information (or any information for that matter) within an organisation does not necessarily have a neutral impact. The provision of such information can have an effect on the behaviour of the recipients and that effect can be positive or negative for the organisation. The underlying issue here is what is termed "goal congruence". This is defined as consistency or harmonisation of individual goals with organisational goals. In other words, everyone in the organisation needs to be "rowing in the same direction". This is illustrated in Figure 6.3.

Basically, the extent to which the individuals goals can overlap with the organisations goals then the greater the chances of the organisation being successful.

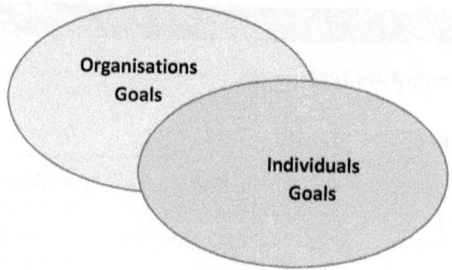

FIGURE 6.3
Organisational and individual goals.

The problem is that the wrong type of management accounting can fail to encourage or can even disrupt goal congruence which is damaging for the organisation. This is particularly the case when:

- An employee's performance is assessed by reference to certain management accounting indicators.
- This performance information is seen throughout the organisation.

There are lots of examples of goal incongruence which can be quoted:

- The procurement manager whose performance is strongly focused on the avoidance of stock-outs. This manager over buys commodities beyond the economic order quantity at a cost to the organisation.
- The manager who forgoes maintenance on equipment or vehicles because it would exceed his budget. The equipment breaks down and has to be replaced at high cost from someone else's budget.
- The school whose performance is assessed by the proportion of pupils achieving a minimum grade. Consequently, the school focuses on getting most pupils to minimum grade level and pays little attention to very high performing pupils or very low performing pupils. It just concentrates on those in the middle ground.
- Multi-agency partnerships working at a local level have their performance inhibited because the partner organisations (understandably) have a greater focus on their own internal performance measures (imposed nationally) rather than those of the local partnership which end up being understated.

Many more examples can be quoted.

There is a huge amount of research evidence on these issues. In the 1960s and 1970s, researchers like Hofstede (1976) and Birnberg and Nath (1967) attempted to draw preliminary results from studies of behavioural accounting research concerning the behavioural impacts of budgeting processes and control systems. Colville (1981) also offered a detailed look at the connection between accounting and organisations, and attempted to predict what the implications of a behavioural view of accounting would be for the organisational aspects of society.

FINANCIAL ANALYSIS AND ECONOMIC ANALYSIS IN PUBLIC SERVICES: THE DISTINCTION

In the business world, many of the objectives of a company will have a financial orientation such as profitability, sales growth, return on assets and gross margin. Consequently, it is inevitable that much of the work of the management accounting will concern financial analysis which will look at matters like revenues, financial costs, asset values and use of assets.

In public services, things are different. Although public service organisations will have some financial objectives, they will also have other objectives which might be seen as more important. These objectives will concern the public services delivered, the resources used and the impacts they have made on individuals and society. Basically, public service organisations face the following issues:

- Public resources are finite and they have limited (land, money, labour, equipment, etc.).
- Choices have to be made between competing public service activities for the use of those resources.
- Undertaking a particular activity means that there will be an opportunity cost associated with other activities which are foregone.
- Public service activities competing for public funds need to be assessed in relation to their <u>economic</u> efficiency. Economic efficiency is not the same as financial efficiency. Economic efficiency means assessing the overall net benefits (benefits minus costs) associated with each activity as an indicator of which activities should be pursued. This is termed economic analysis.

Thus in summary, we can say that financial analysis is just concerned with the financial costs and revenues associated with an activity while economic analysis is concerned with the financial and social costs and financial and social benefits associated with that activity.

In some situations, it is possible that the management accountant in the private sector will be faced with issues which require some economic analysis. However, in the public sector, economic analysis of activities will be, frequently, required, particularly in relation to strategic decisions about public services. Thus, the management accountant in public service needs, at least, a good working knowledge of the principles of economic analysis. We will return to this in later chapters.

THE MANAGEMENT ACCOUNTANT IN PUBLIC SERVICES

In Part B of this book, aspects of management accounting which can be utilised in various ways in public services are discussed in some detail. Consequently, it is tempting to think that management accounting just consists of a collection of tools/techniques and that all the management accountant needs to do is to apply these tools and techniques. Indeed, many well-known academic books on management accounting (e.g. Kaplan and Atkinson 1998) seem to reinforce this perception by largely concerning themselves with a discussion of these techniques.

However, management accountants, today and in the future, need to be more than just technicians and the professional management accountant requires a wide range of skills and competencies which are outlined below.

Technical competence

At the outset, having the knowledge and skills to use management accounting tools and techniques correctly is an essential attribute and pre-requisite of the professional management accountant, as is the ability to explain them to non-financial managers in the organisation. The techniques which might be used at the strategic, tactical and operational levels have already been listed and will be discussed further.

Sector knowledge

The application of management accounting tools and techniques is affected by the environment in which they are used. For example, while the principles of marginal costing are the same everywhere, the application of this technique is very different in organisations such as a hospital, a government agency and an army unit. Hence, it is imperative that the public service management accountant has a good understanding of the nature of public services in general and of the specific sector in which they are working. This knowledge must cover both the operational, and tactical and strategic levels.

Behavioural understanding

In a previous section we discussed, briefly, the behavioural aspects of management accounting. When producing and disseminating management accounting information in an organisation, care must be taken to consider how such information may influence the behaviour of those receiving it and whether this may have a positive or negative impact on the performance of the organisation. Hence, the management accountant needs to have a working knowledge of these behavioural aspects and must always keep in mind these behavioural issues and their potential negative impact on goal congruence. This goes beyond the purely technical aspects of management accounting.

Interpretive skills

Expertise in the analysis and interpretation of data is an essential skill for management accountants. Data analysis and interpretation are the process of assigning meaning to the data collected and determining the conclusions, significance and implications of the findings. Thus, the purpose of the data analysis and interpretation phase is to transform the data collected into credible evidence about the organisation and its activities.

However, it is important to realise that data does not always come in neat packages, which can be organised to provide input into decisions. Often, particularly in relation to strategic issues, data comes in messy and unstructured formats and the task of interpretation is increasingly difficult.

Data analysis and interpretation usually include the following steps:

- Organising the data for analysis
- Describing the data
- Interpreting the data

The steps involved in data analysis are a function of the type of information collected. Where quantitative data have been collected, statistical analysis can help measure the degree of change that has taken place and allow an assessment to be made about the consistency of data. However, it is often the case that much of the data available is qualitative (or soft) in nature and then interpretation is more difficult. In such cases, it is important to group similar responses into categories and identify common patterns that can help derive meaning from what may seem unrelated and diffuse responses.

We live in an age where the volume of (mainly) digital data has grown enormously and will continue to grow. Thus, the management accountant now needs a working knowledge of big data analytics (BDA) which analyses huge volumes of data and identifies findings and conclusions which may be important to the organisation. BDA is further discussed in Chapter 13.

In line with the "business partnering" role for management accounting discussed earlier, it is important to emphasise that it is not sufficient for the management accounting to merely produce data and leave it to others to interpret. The management accountant has a key role in the interpretation itself.

Communication skills

Effective communication skills are fundamental to success in many aspects of life. Many jobs require strong communication skills, and people with effective communication skills usually enjoy better interpersonal relationships and are seen as more effective. The management accountant has the role of communicating financial and non-financial information about the organisation (which is often voluminous and complex) to a range of internal and external stakeholders. Thus, effective communication is a key interpersonal skill in this situation. Even the most technically competent management accountant will have limited organisational effectiveness in the absence of effective communication skills.

Communication is a complex issue but some of the key themes to be emphasised are the following:

- Learning to listen
- Being aware of other people's emotions and agendas
- Empathising with others
- Learning to communicate effectively
- Use humour where appropriate
- Treating people equally
- Attempting to resolve conflict
- Maintaining a positive attitude where appropriate and possible

In practice, few of us will have all of these skills but this does not mean we shouldn't try to improve.

Creativity

Creativity has been defined as the ability to transcend traditional ideas, rules, patterns, relationships or the like, and to create meaningful new ideas, forms, methods, interpretations, etc. Even those not involved in explicitly creative fields must come up with new ideas and insights in order to enable the organisation to develop and improve what it does. This is especially true in relation to public services where creative approaches to dealing with the challenges of increasing service demand and austerity are urgently needed.

Management accountants are not usually thought of as being especially creative people but the effective management accountant must have strong elements of creativity. It is not sufficient to collect, interpret and communicate data about the organisation in a passive manner. The management accountant, as a business partner, must actively be involved in the search for solutions to problems and needs to bring a creative dimension to the organisation. Like many things in life, creativity is probably something which is innate to certain types of individuals but equally there are approaches to developing one's creative outlook.

Working relationships

A key issue for the management accountant concerns working relationships with other people in the organisation. The traditional view of the management accountant is, often, someone who spends all the time in the office looking at spreadsheets and responding to requests for information. This is an outmoded view which must not be seen as the epitome of high-quality management accounting practice. Instead, the management accountant must be seen as a visible and active professional getting pro-actively involved in a wide range of issues, strategic, tactical and operational, which concern the organisation.

As well as working alongside professional managers from various disciplines, management accountants in public services will find themselves working with a wide range of highly skilled and experienced service professionals such as doctors, nurses, teachers, engineers, social workers, soldiers and police officers. These service professionals may have a limited knowledge of financial matters and may often have a jaundiced view of the finance profession. To facilitate improved decision making the management accountant has to have a good understanding of the service manager's terrain and the challenges they face. They also need the ability to present their insights in a way which the line manager will find useful, stimulating and interesting.

FACTORS THAT DRIVE THE CONFIGURATION OF MANAGEMENT ACCOUNTING IN PUBLIC SERVICE ORGANISATIONS

One of the myths often perpetuated in the public sector is that it is possible to have some standard form of management accounting which is applicable to all public service organisations or all organisations in a particular sector (e.g. hospitals, colleges, etc.). Such a view displays a lack of understanding about the way organisations work and the impacts this will have on the design of management systems including management accounting. Management accounting systems must be built around the organisation, not the organisation built around some standard accounting system.

The reality is that there are a number of factors which will impact strongly on the design of management accounting systems in public services, and each organisation needs to consider its requirements for management accounting in the light of these factors.

- **Service and activity type** – organisations in different parts of the public sector differ considerably. Just consider the following: a mental illness hospital, a fire service division, a college, a local authority roads maintenance unit, an army unit, etc. A moments thought will show that these organisations will have significant differences in what they do, how they do it and the mix of resources they use. This will have implications for the management accounting systems they require to manage the organisation effectively.
- **Organisational structure** – different organisations (even those of the same type) will show considerable differences in their organisational and management structures. This implies different number of managers, budget holders, etc., with differing information needs which will have implications for the design of management accounting systems.
- **Strategic direction** – the strategic direction of the organisation will have implications for all aspects of management. Some organisations may anticipate only limited changes in what they do while others may aspire to more radical changes.
- **Operational processes** – the operational processes in the organisation, by means of which public services are delivered, will vary enormously between different parts of the public sector. However, as noted in Chapter 2, they may also vary considerably even between similar organisations in the same sector. Whether it be undertaking a hospital patient scan, admitting a new college student, collecting household refuse, awarding a grant, etc., the detailed operational processes may vary, for the same task, between organisations. This will have implications for the design of management accounting systems.
- **Organisational culture** – lastly, we come to organisational culture (which may be simply defined as the underlying basic shared assumptions that govern the way people behave in organisations). Clearly, the organisational culture in a hospital will be different from that in a central government department and different from that in a school. Differences in culture can be manifested in a number of ways. For example, within the same sector, some organisations will have a very centralised approach to management while others will have a more decentralised approach. Also, some organisations will be very much "open" in character with people feeling free to express opinions and make suggestions. Others will be much more "closed" to such matters. The point is that such differences in culture will

have implications for the design of management accounting systems and the roles of the management accountant.

- **Leadership** – the style of leadership in the organisation will also impact on the design of management accounting in the organisation.

This chapter brings to an end Part A of this book which was concerned with setting the context for a discussion of management accounting in public services. This chapter aims to provide an overview of the role, purpose and application of management accounting, and Part B will now consider detailed themes.

Management accounting practice in public services

Costing and cost information for decision making in public services

INTRODUCTION

The leading management thinker Peter Drucker is often quoted as saying that *"if you can't measure it then you can't manage it"*. This implies the needs for some form of information and measurement about the activities of an organisation in order to inform the management process and management decision making. By extension, it seems reasonable to also say *"if you can't measure your costs then you can't manage your costs"*. This is the focus of this chapter in relation to public services.

In any organisation, an understanding of the cost structure of the organisation and its activities and the way in which its costs might change in response to internal or external stimuli is critical to the effective management of the organisation. This is why costing can be seen as the bedrock of management accounting.

Historically, public service organisations have not been very good at identifying and measuring the costs of what they do but great improvements are being made in various sectors. Cost information can be used for a variety of reasons in any type of organisation and over a period of years the topic of costing has become increasingly topical within the public services. In this chapter we consider costing approaches in public services and the application of costing systems to produce that information.

This chapter considers the following main themes:

- How cost information can be used to manage public services
- Approaches to the classification of costs
- Costing systems and cost models in public services
- Traditional overhead costing and Activity Based Costing (ABC)
- Identifying and estimating costs in public services

- Difficulties and complexities of costing in modern public services
- Developing costing systems in public services

HOW COST INFORMATION CAN BE USED TO MANAGE PUBLIC SERVICES

Cost information has many actual or potential managerial uses in public services. Some of the main examples of these are discussed briefly below and will be considered, further, in later sections.

Activity cost analysis

In public service organisations, routine information may be produced on the overall costs incurred (and income received) by the various departments or units in the organisation. This information can be used to produce unit cost information of a department/unit such as:

- Cost per patient in medical imaging departments of a hospital
- Cost per student in a modern language department of a university
- Cost per mile of maintaining roads in a local authority
- Cost per client payment in a government social welfare department

However, there are usually limitations as to the level of detail of information available within the individual department or unit. The reality is that each such department or unit often undertakes a wide range of service or support activities and/or delivers a range of public services. However, the cost information currently available is often not always sufficiently granular to enable an analysis to be undertaken of the financial performance of the individual activities and services within the department. The following examples illustrate the need for such information:

- The costs incurred by a sub-unit of the department (e.g. the payroll section of a finance department)
- The costs incurred in undertaking specific activities, within a department/unit, which comprise service delivery (e.g. a client assessment of a social care client, a diagnostic examination of a hospital patient)
- The costs incurred by discrete services delivered within the department (e.g. domiciliary social care for the elderly)
- The costs incurred in delivering services to particular client groups (e.g. the elderly, women) or geographic areas

Such cost information is often needed for a number of reasons. First, it will be of particular importance if the department or unit involved is currently generating an overall financial deficit or overspend but is unaware of which particular activities or services are responsible for that deficit. For example, the modern languages department of a university may be generating a financial deficit but may not have information on the financial performance of the various languages being taught in order to identify the source of the deficit. Second, a department having compared its overall unit costs with that of other comparable departments may wish to establish why its unit costs are (say) 10% greater than its comparators. To do this, it will need a more detailed analysis of the costs of the various activities and services which make up the department. Third, a department may wish to know the impact on its costs of making changes in the (client) activity levels in the department. Again, to do this, an analysis will be needed of the costs (and income) attributed to the discrete activities of the department.

Budget reporting

In a later chapter, budget management and budgetary control is discussed in-depth. It will be clear that a key component of budgetary control is the availability of actual cost information to be compared with budgeted cost. This involves the provision of cost information, which shows an analysis of the income, and expenditure of each department or unit for a particular month in question and the cumulative for the year.

Pricing

Some public services levy charges (in full or in part) on clients for the services received. Clearly, costs are an important input into pricing decisions but are not the sole, or even the most important input. However, to make robust pricing decisions it is essential to have a minimal level of cost information concerning the activity or service to be priced. We will return to this in a later chapter.

Performance improvement and benchmarking

The issue of improving performance, at both operational and strategic levels, is a key theme in all public service organisations given the pressures on public funding. The process of improving performance will focus on value for money or VFM (or the 3Es of economy, effectiveness and efficiency), and financial management will have a key role to play.

A key aspect of this will be the availability of information about the current costs of activities and services, and how such costs may have changed over time or may compare with other similar organisations. It is common practice in public services to try and compare their performance against that of other comparable organisations as a means of identifying potential improvements in performance. Thus, it is quite common to compare its financial performance (e.g. cost per pupil, course, cost per mile of road maintained, cost per book issued, cost per invoice paid, etc.) against that of other organisations, and to do this, it is necessary to have cost information about the costs of one's own organisation. Benchmarking will be discussed more fully in a later chapter.

Strategic financial planning

As will be discussed in a later chapter, it is inevitable that over a period of time public services will undergo some degree of strategic change in relation to organisational structures, methods of working, staffing levels, remuneration structures, etc. Some examples might be as follows:

- Reducing the number of campuses in a college
- Merging several departments into one in a local authority

- Reconfiguring school education in an area
- Reconfiguring the health service provision in a particular area
- Restructuring the activities of an army regiment

Such changes may be large or small but whatever the case they are likely to have significant financial implications, and it will be necessary to undertake some degree of strategic financial analysis to assess the financial implications of such changes at each stage. It would be very difficult to undertake any robust strategic financial planning in the absence of information about the existing costs of the organisation and its activities. Thus, adequate and robust cost information is a pre-requisite of effective strategic financial planning in public services.

Capital investment appraisal

The appraisal of potential capital investments is important in any organisation including public service organisations. However, such investments can be considered twofold:

- *Strategic capital investments* – as part of the strategic planning process, within public services, new project developments may be under consideration often including new types of service and new locations. These will often require major capital investments amounting to tens, hundreds of even thousands of millions of pounds.
- *Operational capital investments* – public authorities will also need to invest in smaller and more operational capital projects such as new equipment or vehicles to maintain operational capacity. These will cost relatively lower amounts of money but will still involve significant sums.

The distinction between these two types of capital investments is not clear-cut but before any of these projects are initiated, good practice will require a full project appraisal and cost information will be needed to undertake the financial aspects of that appraisal. This will be further discussed in Chapters 8 and 9.

APPROACHES TO THE CLASSIFICATION OF COSTS

There are many different ways in which the costs of public service organisations (or any organisation for that matter) can be classified and described. This is not just a matter of jargon, and each classification approach represents a different perspective on costs. The main approaches are shown below and subsequently summarised:

- Financial costs and economic costs
- Resource costs
- Period costs and "product" costs
- Direct costs and indirect costs
- Fixed costs and variable costs
- Total costs and marginal costs
- Relevant costs and non-relevant costs

- Actual costs and forecast costs
- Absolute costs and comparative costs

Financial costs and economic costs

Financial costs can be considered to be those costs which have a direct financial impact on the organisation. Thus, they will include such costs as labour costs, consumables costs, overhead costs and costs of investment in fixed assets such as buildings. Economic costs include financial costs but also have a much broader remit. Thus, economic costs will incorporate the opportunity costs of undertaking a particular course of action. They will also incorporate the social costs of particular courses of action. For example, building a new airport will bring about social costs associated with noise, pollution, traffic congestion, etc. However, alongside economic costs there will, of course, be economic benefits.

It is probably true to say that economic costs are only of limited interest in the commercial sector since the main issues concern the financial viability of particular courses of action. However, in public services, economic costs (- and benefits) are very important in assessing the merits of different courses of action. However, it is sometimes the case that there is something of a tension between financial costs and economic costs. It is easy to see projects or courses of action which are beneficial in terms of net benefits to society, but which are unaffordable in financial terms. Hence, it is vitally important to be clear about what economic costs are and what financial costs are.

Type of resource costs

Financial costs can be classified according to the type of resource being utilised. Different classifications are available but the following examples illustrate the point:

- Staff costs
- Raw materials costs
- Consumables costs
- Energy costs
- Maintenance costs
- Office supplies costs, etc.

In most public services it is usually the case that a broadly standard approach to cost analysis would be applied, within the same sector, in order to facilitate comparisons between organisations in the same sector. In this way, for example, hospitals or schools could compare themselves with each other.

Period costs and "product" costs

These two approaches to classifying costs need to be clearly distinguished:

- "Period costs are those costs that arise as a result of the passage of time (e.g. staff salaries, maintenance costs) not as the result of providing particular products or services".
- "Product costs, on the other hand, arise as a result of providing a particular product or service (e.g. rewiring a building, treating a patient)".

While "product" is a common and understandable term in relation to commercial organisations, the term is not so clearly understood in the public services and needs to be discussed further. In public services, the term "product" cost information would imply information about the costs of the various public services delivered by the organisation. Just a few examples of "products" in public services might include the following:

- Cost of treating specific clinical conditions in a hospital
- Cost of delivering certain specific courses in a college or university
- Costs of undertaking crime prevention activities in the police
- Costs of delivering domiciliary social care services to the elderly
- Costs of responding to a factory fire incident

The relationship between product costs and period costs is illustrated in Figure 7.1 using a university as an example.

Traditionally, product costing in public services was limited but, for various reasons, has become more sophisticated in the approach over time. This will necessarily involve the following:

- Identify the main discrete service activities
- Identify the main cost elements associated with the delivery of each of those service activities
- Develop suitable approaches to attribute each cost element to each service activity

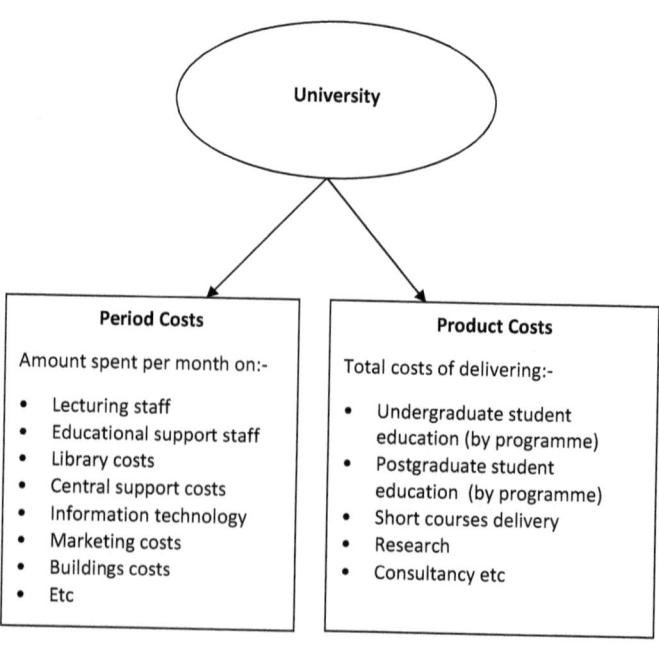

FIGURE 7.1
Period costs and product costs.

Direct costs and indirect costs

There is sometimes a view that the cost of a particular product or service activity is a unique and precise figure. This is not the case. Cost data is derived by means of a series of costing approaches and assumptions, and different approaches and assumptions will give different costs for the same activity or product. Thus, when examining the costs associated with a particular product or activity it is vital to understand the costing approaches applied to establish that cost and the assumptions underlying the approach adopted. It is therefore essential to understand the concepts of <u>cost centres</u>, and <u>direct and indirect costs</u> associated with those cost centres.

The differentiation between direct costs and indirect costs is fundamental to cost accounting practice but is frequently misunderstood, even by some accountants. Often the direct/indirect distinction is confused with the variable/-fixed distinction (see below) with direct costs being seen as synonymous with variable costs and indirect costs being seen as synonymous with fixed costs. This is a mis-understanding since the two types of cost classification are based on different economic principles. The distinction between direct and indirect costs relates to the different ways in which costs are recorded against "cost centres or cost units".

Within any organisation there will be a requirement to identify and track each and every income or expenditure transaction. This requires the use of cost centres. CIMA defines a cost centre as *"a production or service, function, activity or item of equipment whose costs may be attributed to cost units. A cost centre is the smallest organisational sub-unit for which separate cost allocation is attempted"*. Thus, a cost centre is essentially a form of conceptual "bucket" where costs can be collected. Some examples of cost centres in a factory would be a department, a machine or a product line: In public services a cost centre could be the following:-

- A front line service unit (e.g. a care home, a hospital ward, a school)
- A support department (e.g. a finance department, a maintenance department)
- A specific service (e.g. cardiac surgery, vocational college courses, social care of the elderly)
- A geographic area of service delivery
- A client group (e.g. children, the disabled)
- An individual client (e.g. an individual patient)

The costing system will enable costs to be classified against each individual cost centre via the expenditure coding system. Each cost centre will have a discrete code, and each item of expenditure will be attached to the appropriate cost centre code. In this way an analysis of expenditure by cost centre can be undertaken. Thus, the key issue is to develop a structure of cost centres that will facilitate production of the cost information needs of the organisation. Having cost centres at a high level of aggregation will mean that there are limitations to the granularity of cost information that can be produced while having cost centres at a low level in the organisation can be administratively cumbersome. A balance must be struck.

The next stages is to consider whether costs are attributed to cost centres by direct "allocation" or indirect "apportionment". The basic distinction is as follows:

- **Direct allocation** – a particular cost is allocated to a cost centre where there is information available to track that cost to a cost centre. These are termed direct costs.
- **Indirect apportionment** – where there is no information available to track a particular cost to a cost centre then costs will be attributed to cost centres by some form of apportionment or sharing, on some suitable basis. These are termed indirect costs.

Let us illustrate this issue using a simplified example of costing in a hospital environment as shown in Figure 7.2.

Situation A: cost centre = individual hospital ward

In a hospital ward two (of the many) items of expenditure would be medical and surgical supplies (MSS) which include dressings, syringes and electricity. MSS would be easily attributed to an individual ward cost centre through available supplies information systems. Hence, this cost can be regarded as a direct cost and is allocated to the ward. Electricity costs are also a cost of running the ward but usually the only information available concerns the electricity costs of the hospital as a whole. Hence, to obtain the total running costs of the ward it would be necessary to apportion the total hospital electricity costs over wards using an appropriate method, which might, for example, be related to the floor area or volume of each ward involved. Thus, the figure for the total running costs of the ward will depend on the apportionment bases chosen for indirect costs such as electricity. Similar situations will arise for many other costs.

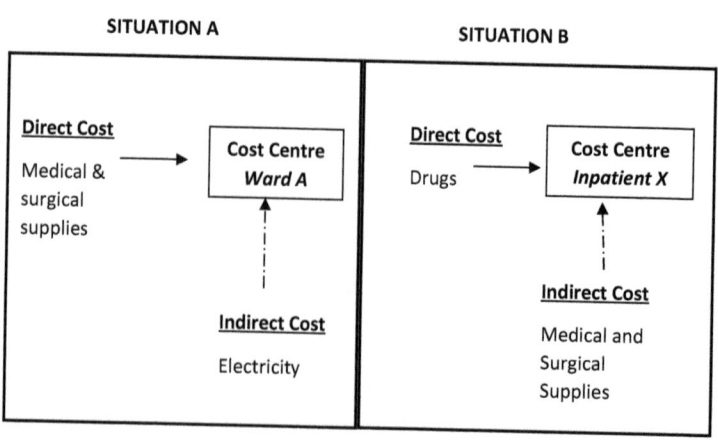

FIGURE 7.2
Direct and indirect costs: hospital example.

Situation B: cost centre = individual hospital inpatient

The cost centre used is now an individual patient residing in the ward, and the two items of cost considered are drug costs and, again, MSS. Drug costs are easily attributed to an individual patient through the patient's prescription record which is mandatory for clinical purposes. Hence, this drug cost can be regarded as a direct cost and allocated to the individual patient. However, it is unlikely that the ward has a system which records issues of MSS to an individual patient but since MSS are also a cost of caring for the patient an element of such cost must be included in the total patient cost. Hence, to obtain the total costs of caring for the patient it is necessary to apportion the total ward MSS costs over all patients in the ward using an appropriate method, which might, for example, be length of stay (in days).

A number of points should be emphasised regarding the above examples:

- *Determinants of direct and indirect cost* – it will be noted that MSS was a direct cost to the ward cost centre but an indirect cost to the patient cost centre. Thus, it is not the inherent nature of a cost type which determines whether it is direct or indirect. In general terms what determines whether a cost can be directly allocated or indirectly apportioned is the sophistication of the organisation's information systems. If, in the above example, the hospital had decided to install electric meters on each ward then the electricity consumed by each ward would be known exactly and electricity costs would become a direct cost of the ward instead of an indirect cost. A similar situation would occur if the hospital installed an information system which recorded MSS issues to patients.
- *Basis of apportionment* – where cost apportionment is applied it is important to realise that there is not necessarily a single correct basis of cost apportionment. As long as a particular basis of apportionment is "reasonable" and based on assumptions concerning the main factor determining the level of the particular cost incurred (the 'cost driver'), then it may be used to derive total costs.
- *Mix of allocation and apportionment* – total costs are derived from a combination of direct costs which are directly allocated and indirect costs which are apportioned in some way or another. Different approaches and assumptions will give different results.

Thus, there is no single "correct" or "accurate" cost. The end result of a costing exercise is dependent upon the balance between allocation and apportionment of costs and the method of cost apportionment actually used. A number of important managerial issues flow from this.

First, the degree of costing accuracy needed by the organisation will depend on issues such as the type of organisation, its geographic location, its current efficiency level and the degree of competition it faces in the market. Thus, in designing a costing system there is always a balance to be struck between the need for accuracy of cost information and the costs of obtaining that information. Hence, an organisation must evaluate both the benefits of better cost information and the "costs of costing". Second, although some commonality of structure is possible no standard costing system can be defined for all public services since organisations vary considerably in their needs for financial information, the degree of accuracy required and the resources they can devote to providing that information. Hence, each organisation must make its own judgement on this matter.

Fixed costs and variable costs

The distinction between a fixed cost and a variable cost is simple in principle but difficult to draw in practice. It is essentially concerned with the way in which the magnitude of a particular cost varies in relation to the activity or throughput level of the organisation. In simple terms, three different types of cost behaviour can be identified. These are illustrated graphically in Figure 7.3.

- *Variable costs* – the level of cost varies directly with the level of activity in the organisation.
- *Fixed costs* – the magnitude of cost is unaffected by the level of activity in the organisation.
- *Semi-fixed costs* – the above two examples are basically extremes and in practice other cost types may be found which are neither totally fixed nor completely variable.

Shown in Table 7.1 are some possible public service examples with suggestions as to the likely cost behaviour in each case.

However, a word of warning about such a simplified approach to cost classification is needed. The classification of costs into variable, fixed and semivariable is a simplification, and between the totally fixed and totally variable costs a wide range of cost profiles may be found. The type of cost behaviour encountered may not always be clear and may depend on the way in which the organisation procures goods and services. For example, as suggested in table 7.1, catering can be regarded as a semi-fixed cost in relation to student numbers in a college. This is a because small changes in student numbers will not result in

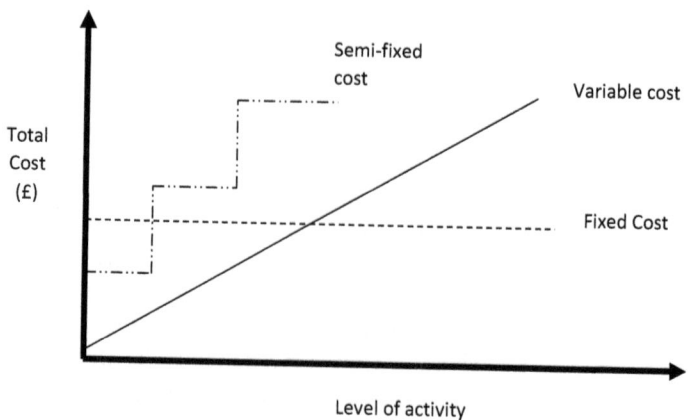

FIGURE 7.3
Cost behaviours.

TABLE 7.1

Cost behaviours in public services

Organisation	Type of Cost	Activity Measure	Variable	Fixed	Semi-Fixed	Comments
Hospital	Drugs	Number of patients	*			Roughly speaking drugs costs will vary with patient numbers
School	Teachers pay	Number of pupils			*	Costs will not change for a certain change in pupil numbers but ultimately a step-change will occur
University	Buildings maintenance	Number of students		*	*	Unlikely levels of planned maintenance will be affected by student numbers. Fault repairs may be affected
College	Catering	Number of students		*	*	Consumable costs will vary but staffing costs may be fixed
Ambulance service	Fuel costs	Number of miles run	*			Roughly speaking fuel costs will vary with mileage run
Hospital	Nursing pay	Number of patients			*	Costs will not change for a certain change in patient activity but ultimately a step-change will occur
Fire authority	Equipment Leasing	Number of fire incidents		*		This cost will be unchanged irrespective of the number of fire incidents

changes to catering staff numbers (and hence pay) but will increase catering consumable costs. However, if the college procured catering services from a private contractor on the basis of cost per meal delivered then catering would become increasingly a variable cost since increases or decreases in student meals would lead to an immediate increase/decrease in the costs.

Total costs and marginal costs

Total cost implies the inclusion of a proportion of all the costs of the organisation associated with a particular activity. This will incorporate both the direct costs of an activity and a share of the indirect costs apportioned to that activity. The marginal costs are the incremental costs of producing additional units of activity and will differ from the total cost because of the issues of fixed and variable costs referred to the above. If activity levels are increased, some costs will increase while others will remain unchanged.

This distinction between total and marginal costs is an important one and must be fully appreciated, particularly in relation to the following:

- *Pricing decisions* – the distinction between marginal and total costs is important for pricing purposes. Although the general rule is that prices should be set by reference to total costs circumstances can arise where they can be set by reference to marginal costs. This is discussed in a later chapter under marginal cost pricing.
- *Financial forecasting* – there will often be a need to forecast the financial effect of changes in future activity levels, and to do so, one will need to distinguish between fixed costs, variable costs and semi-fixed costs. For example, a local authority children's centre is planning to increase the size of its intake by estimating the incremental costs using total average costs, which would result in an overestimate since the total average cost would include a proportion of costs such as buildings maintenance, heat and light that would not increase if the child intake was higher. Furthermore, in terms of staffing there may be some existing slack capacity and increased workload can be absorbed without any cost increases. This situation is further exemplified in the Case study 7.1.

Relevant and non-relevant costs

The basic principle here is that decisions should be based only on those costs which are relevant to that decision. The principle is that decisions should be based only on those costs that change as a result of the particular course of action chosen. This is the principle of "relevant costs" for decision making. The more complex a decision, the more difficult it may be to establish which costs are relevant and which are not but an attempt must be made. A relevant cost is defined as a future cash flow that differs between the alternative courses of action being considered.

Examples of relevant and non-relevant costs are shown in Table 7.2.

Actual costs and forecast costs

Actual costs are clearly concerned with establishing the costs actually incurred by an organisation or its operating departments in delivering goods and services to users. These costs are established using various costing methods. Forecast costs look to the future and are estimates of the costs which are likely to be incurred in the next, week, month, year, etc. For comparability purposes it is best if forecast costs are calculated in a similar manner to actual costs although

> ### TABLE 7.2
>
> **Relevant and non-relevant costs**
>
> | Relevant Costs | Non-Relevant Costs |
> | --- | --- |
> | • Variable/marginal costs. As discussed above, a variable cost is a cost that changes automatically in direct proportion to the number of units produced. As such it will be a relevant cost with respect to decisions involving the production of additional or fewer units of output
• Incremental fixed costs. Incremental fixed costs are costs which, although they do not change automatically in direct proportion to changes in output (as variable costs do), are nevertheless incurred as a result of the decision in hand. For example, a decision might involve, among other things, the purchase of a particular piece of equipment. Once acquired, this cost is independent of the number of units produced (i.e. it is "fixed" rather than "variable"). The cost, nevertheless, arises as result of the particular decision. As such, any incremental fixed costs are relevant to the decision
• Opportunity costs. An opportunity cost is a cost in terms of the benefit foregone by not taking an alternative course of action. Where they arise, opportunity costs will always be relevant to a particular decision | • Sunk costs. A sunk cost is a cost that has already been incurred and, whatever action is now taken, cannot be recovered. Such a cost is therefore <u>not relevant</u> to the decision concerned
• Committed costs. A committed cost is a cost that will be incurred in future, regardless of which decision option is taken now. As such, it is <u>not relevant</u> to the decision concerned
• Notional costs. A notional cost is an imputed cost (for example management charges from head office to operating divisions within a company), for which no actual cash flow ever takes place; they are 'accounting costs'. Such costs, as they do not result in future cash flows as the result of a particular decision, are <u>not relevant</u> to the decision |

there will inevitably be differences between forecasts and actuals because of uncertainties about the future.

Absolute costs and comparative costs

Absolute costs are the costs incurred by a public service organisation or its constituent units or activities for a particular time period. However, it is often the case that absolute costs are of limited use in isolation and what is needed are useful comparators. Such comparators can come in two types:

• Costs from other similar and comparable organisations or activities
• Costs from the same organisation but from previous time periods

Comparing absolute costs against comparators can often provide more information than the absolute costs alone.

Table 7.3 provides a summary of the different approaches to cost classification.

TABLE 7.3

Summary of different approaches to cost classification

Classification	Distinction
Financial/ economic	Financial costs = financial costs Economic costs = financial costs + opportunity costs +social costs
Resource type	Costs classified by type of resource being used (e.g. labour, consumable, maintenance, etc.)
Period/product	• Period costs – costs incurred as result of the passage of time • "Product" costs – cost incurred on specific "products" or services provided by the organisation
Direct/indirect	• Direct costs – costs directly attributable to a particular cost centre • Indirect costs – costs **not** directly attributable to a particular cost centre and therefore apportioned over several cost centres on a suitable basis
Fixed/variable	• Fixed costs – cost levels which remain unchanged with regard to changes in activity levels • Variable costs – cost levels which change with regard to changes in activity levels
Total/marginal	• Total cost includes a proportion of all the costs associated with a particular activity • Marginal costs are the incremental costs of producing additional units of activity
Relevant/ non-relevant	Relevant costs are those costs that will be incurred as the result of a specific decision. Non-relevant costs have no role in the decision making
Actual/forecast	• Costs actually incurred by the organisation • Costs forecast to be incurred by the organisation in future time periods
Absolute/ comparative	Costs compared against other comparable organisations/activities or previous time periods

COSTING SYSTEMS AND COST MODELS IN PUBLIC SERVICES

In this section we consider the nature of costing systems in public services and how they can be used in relation to financial decision making. A costing system can be regarded as a system comprising a set of processes, controls, data flows and reports that are designed to aggregate data and report to management about the revenues and costs of the organisation. The system should be designed in such a way that it delivers the cost information needed by management to monitor what is happening in the organisation and to make the required decisions.

Since costing systems should be focused on the decision making needs of the organisation, it follows that the idea of establishing some form of standardised costing approach for all organisations in a particular sector is a mistake. While

CASE STUDY 7.1

Financial forecasting in public services

The orthopaedics speciality of a hospital has the following cost and activity information for a year

Cost Type	Total Cost (£)	Unit Cost per Patient (£)
Medical	475,520	320
Nursing	1,367,120	920
Pharmacy	326,920	220
Other direct patient costs	371,500	250
Theatre costs	1,114,500	750
Laboratory costs	297,200	200
Support costs	1,753,480	1,180
Overheads	460,660	310
Total costs	6,166,900	4,150

These costs related to the treatment of 1,486 completed cases during the year. The hospital board is considering expanding the throughput of patients by a further 75 patients per annum which is about a 5% increase.

Using the total costs of treating a patient (£4,150) a further 75 cases would cost £311,250. However, this calculation fails to take account of the fact that some costs will not change at all, or change very little, in response to fairly limited increase in workload. The finance director has estimated that the variability of different types of cost is as shown below:

Cost Type	Unit cost per patient (£)	Marginal element of unit cost	Marginal cost per additional patient(£)
Medical	320	20%	64
Nursing	920	30%	276
Pharmacy	220	100%	220
Other direct costs	250	50%	125
Theatre costs	750	70%	525
Laboratory costs	200	20%	40
Support costs	1,180	30%	354
Overheads	310	0%	0
Total costs	4,150		1,604

Thus, the marginal costs of treating an extra 75 patients is forecast to be 75 × £1,604 = £120,300 which is substantially less than the total cost calculation.

some form of harmonisation is appropriate for the purpose of making comparisons, it should be left to managers in each individual organisation to decide how to manage their organisation and the format of their costing systems based on the strategic and operational challenges they face.

The reports of a costing system are intended, primarily for internal use, and so are not subject to the reporting requirements of any of the accounting frameworks, such as GAAP or IFRS. Instead, management can decide what types of information it prefers to see, which information to ignore and how the results are to be formatted and distributed for its consumption.

In considering the design of a costing system, there are two over-arching matters to consider:

- **Need** – the cost information that the organisation (and its managers) needs to enable it to make effective decisions, concerning the strategic and operational challenges it faces, in such a way to optimise its use of resources available. Now public service organisations will vary in the challenges they face (even in the same sector) and the organisational and management arrangements they have in place to manage the organisation. Hence, the cost information needs will vary between organisations.
- **Cost** – inevitably, the more complex and sophisticated a costing system becomes, the more it costs to develop and operate the system (i.e. the cost of costing). This may, particularly, be the case in relation to capturing the data needed to populate the system.

There is clearly a tension between these two factors, and it is easy to see how an organisation might spend a huge amount of money developing a complex system which had only minor additional benefits over a simpler system.

Cost models

Prior to looking at costing systems in more detail, we need to consider the types of cost models that could be utilised. A cost model is basically a picture of where the costs of the organisation are incurred and the relationships and cost flows between the different activities and units incurring those costs. The costing system will be built around a particular cost model, and typical generic cost model for public services is shown in Figure 7.4.

A number of points of clarification can be made about this cost model:

- Buildings and equipment costs are initially shared over all the other departments and units (medium grey lines).
- The costs of administrative departments (including their share of buildings and equipment costs) are then shared over all departments (light grey lines).
- The costs of support departments (including their share of buildings/-equipment, and administrative costs) are then shared over all front line service units (dark grey lines).
- The costs of front line service units (including their share of buildings/equipment administrative costs and support costs) are attributed to final cost centres.
- Certain costs are directly assigned to final cost centres.

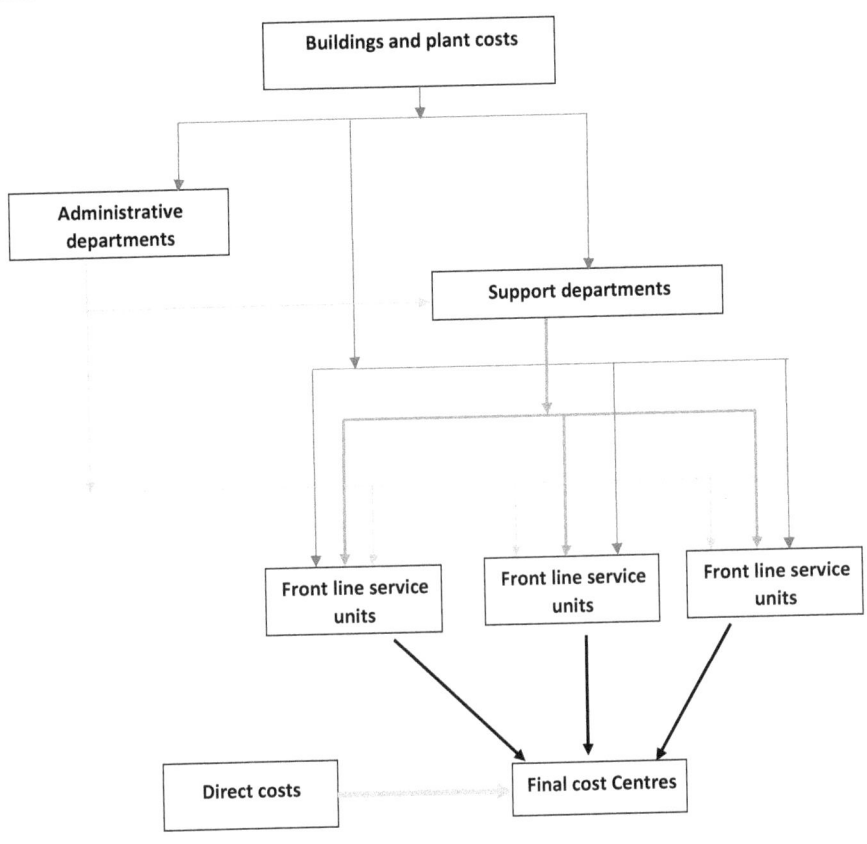

FIGURE 7.4
Generic cost model for public services.

This cost model might be referred to as a cascade model because the costs flow down a hierarchy of cost centres to the final cost centres. Thus, all the costs of the organisation will ultimately be assigned to final cost centres. The way in which this model can be applied to public services is shown in Table 7.4.

Costing systems

In designing a costing system around the cost model, there are four factors which need to be considered:

- *Final cost centres* – these are the cost centres where all of the various costs in the organisation ultimately end up having flowed down the cost hierarchy. In a manufacturing organisation they would probably be referred to as product costs. In public services they would depend on the type of organisation, but examples of such final cost centres are shown in Table 7.4.
- *Cost centre structure and hierarchies* – the costing system will have a series of cost centres where information about income and costs in the

TABLE 7.4

Examples of cost centres in public service organisations

	Hospital	College/University	Police Authority
Fixed assets	• Buildings and plant • Equipment • Vehicles	• Buildings and plant • Equipment • Vehicles	• Buildings and plant • Equipment • Vehicles
Administrative departments	• Finance • HR • Procurement, etc.	• Finance • HR • Procurement • Registry, etc.	• Finance • HR • Procurement, etc.
Support departments	• Catering • Cleaning • Maintenance • IT, etc.	• Library • Student services • Catering • Cleaning/ • Maintenance • IT, etc.	• Catering • Cleaning • Vehicle maintenance • IT • Communications
Front line units	• Wards • Theatres	• Academic departments	• Geographic divisions • Specialist policing functions
Final cost centres	• Medical specialties • Diagnostic groups • Individual patients	• Individual courses • Individual modules • Individual students	• Individual divisions • Community programmes • Individual events or incidents

organisation are collected. What is shown above are just the broad categories of cost centres. In practice, cost centres in public service organisations could number many tens or hundreds. These will need to be identified and organised accordingly. The relationships between each cost centre in terms of cost transfers will need to be clarified.

- **Methods of cost attribution to and between cost centres** – methods need to be established to effect the recording of costs to cost centres. As has already been seen, in some cases, cost may be directly allocated to a particular cost centre but this may not always be possible. In other cases costs are transferred from one cost centre to another by a process of apportionment (or sharing) on some suitable basis. As will be discussed below, in recent years the approach known as activity-based costing (ABC) may have replaced this traditional overhead apportionment approach in some cases.
- **Management reports** – consideration will need to be given to what types of routine reports will need to be produced by the costing system. These could concern the costs incurred by final cost centres and/or cost reports

of individual departments or units in the organisation. These reports will form an input to the budget system of the organisation.

TRADITIONAL OVERHEAD COSTING AND ACTIVITY BASED COSTING (ABC)

As already noted, traditional approaches to costing involved the allocation of direct costs, where possible, while indirect costs were usually apportioned using an appropriate basis involving some measure of production/service volumes. These approaches to costing were seen as acceptable for many decades and applied in most costing systems in public services.

In the USA, in the 1990s, US academic Robert Kaplan (Kaplan and Bruns 1987) noted that over a 40–50-year period, the composition of product costs in manufacturing industry, in developed countries, had altered substantially. The main reasons were the following: -

- Direct materials – the direct materials element of product costs had remained largely unchanged.
- Direct labour – through the introduction of automation and IT the direct labour element of product costs had fallen dramatically.
- Overheads – overhead functions, such as materials handling, quality assurance and marketing, had grown substantially and the element of product cost they represented had grown to match the fall in direct labour costs.

Subsequently, it was recognised that in this situation applying crude approaches to the treatment of overhead costs, which were now such a high proportion of cost, was severely distorting total product costs and cost accounting methods needed to change. ABC was the approach to costing which was subsequently developed as an alternative to traditional costing models.

ABC uses more sophisticated approaches to attributing overhead costs to products or services involving identifying what activities in the organisation actually "drive" the level of particular types of cost rather than a statistical share. It therefore eliminates much of the distortion.

Using material stores costs as an example, the traditional crude approach would be to apportion the total material store costs over products pro-rata to the volume or value of the products involved. However, ABC recognised that material store costs have three different elements and that a different activity drives the level of cost in each case. ABC would analyse the number of batches of materials received, relating to the different products and apportion materials receipt costs pro-rata to the number of batches in each case. Different calculations would be needed for materials storage and materials issue. This is illustrated in Figure 7.5.

Under traditional costing methods, the basis for apportioning indirect costs would be some measure of production/service volume. The difference between traditional costing and ABC is that the latter recognised that many overhead costs are not volume related but are driven by complexity or diversity. By

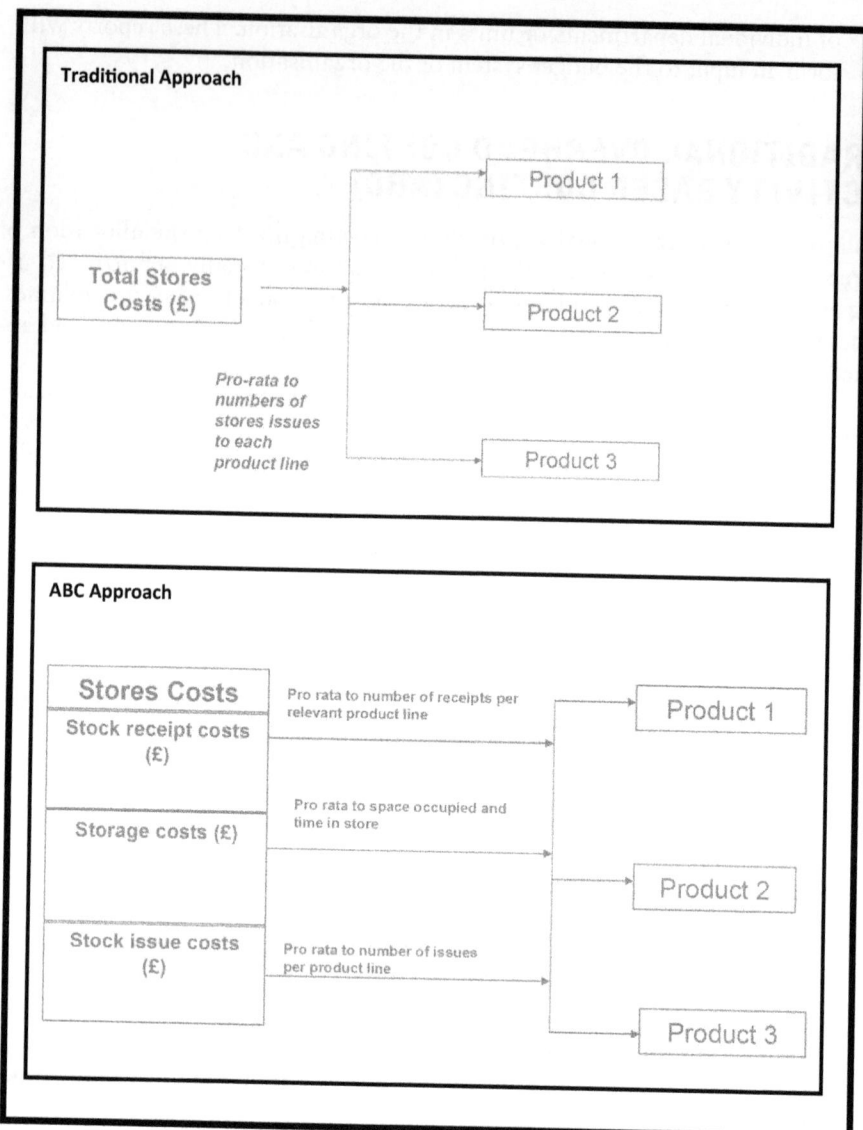

FIGURE 7.5
Activity-based costing.

applying the ABC approach a cost model can be developed for each specific service which identifies the discrete activities involved in each service and the cost drivers of each of those activities.

The differences between ABC and the traditional method are shown in Case study 7.2.

Traditional overhead costing versus ABC: the cost differences

A government agency has a commercial arm which produces a wide range of publications (e.g. guidance, information, etc) for sale to individuals and external organisations The customer services department of the agency undertakes three main functions – order processing, customer enquiries and credit checks. The department employs 20 people, and the total salary bill is £560,000 per annum. The organisation has three main products: A, B and C. The total number of orders of product in the year is 49,000 broken down as follows:

- Product A 18,000 units
- Product B 21,000 units
- Product C 10,000 units

Using a traditional costing approach, the total costs of customer services might have been apportioned over products pro-rata to number of orders. Thus, the cost apportionments would be as follows:

- Product A £205,714
- Product B £240,000
- Product C £114,286

However, the customer service department involves three separate activities: processing customer orders, answering customer queries and making credit checks on customers. Surveys of staff have indicated that their workload and associated cost is distributed as follows:

Function	% of Workload	Staff Cost
Process customer orders	70%	392,000
Handle customer enquiries	10%	56,000
Perform credit checks	20%	112,000
Total	100%	560,000

Using ABC, the calculation of a cost driver rate for each of the three activities is shown. Costs of these activities are then attributed to products on the basis of volumes and cost driver rates.

(continued)

	Process customer orders	Handle customer enquiries	Credit checks	Total
Assigned cost	£392,000	£56,000	£112,000	£560,000
Total activity levels	49,000 orders	1,400 queries	1,000 checks	
Cost driver rate	£8/order	£40/enquiry	£112/check	
PRODUCT A				
Level of activity	18,000	900	100	
Cost attributed	£144,000	£36,000	£11,200	£191,200
PRODUCT B				
Level of activity	21,000	100	150	
Cost attributed	£168,000	£4,000	£16,800	£188,800
PRODUCT C				
Level of activity	10,000	400	750	
Cost attributed	£80,000	£16,000	£84,000	£180,000

If we compare the results of the traditional methods of costing with ABC, we see the following:

	Traditional overhead costing (£)	ABC (£)	Difference (£)
Product A	205,714	191,200	−14,514
Product B	240,000	188,800	−51,200
Product C	114,286	180,000	+65,714
Total	566,000	566,000	0

Clearly, the ABC approach shows big differences in cost distribution largely as a consequence of much higher credit checks (which is an expensive activity) for Product C customers. However, it must be recognised that the ABC approach is more accurate, in that it recognises the operational reality of what is happening in the department.

Time-driven ABC

Many organisations have moved from conventional ABC approaches (often called driver-based ABC or DBABC) to a different ABC approach termed time-based ABC (or TBABC). It is often argued that TBABC provides a method which is both simpler and better. Although both forms of ABC have the same starting point, namely to improve on traditional overhead costing approaches, there are key distinctions which are summarised below:

- *Driver-based ABC* – the example used in Case study 7.2 utilises DBABC. It will be noted that employees in a department are first asked to estimate how much time (and hence cost) they spend on each of the activities in department. Using this cost data and estimates of the volume of activities, a cost driver rate is calculated for each activity. This rate is used to assign costs of each activity to individual products.
- *Time-driven ABC* – TDABC starts from a different point. Staff are not asked to estimate how their overall time is utilised over the various activities in the department. Instead, they are asked to estimate (in minutes) how much time they are likely to spend in completing a single activity (e.g. one order). At the same time, the department will calculate its overall "practical" capacity (in minutes) of all the staff in the department. Practical capacity is calculated by starting with total capacity (number of staff x working time available) but then deducting a reasonable percentage (maybe 15–20%) to deal with inevitable downtime. Using this practical capacity, the department can calculate the cost per minute of employee time. A cost driver rate can then be calculated for each activity by multiplying the cost per minute by the time estimates of staff for completing a single activity. Clearly, there will be a learning curve since staff estimates of time to complete an activity may be very inaccurate in the first instance but will improve over time. Many will argue that this is a simpler approach with particular application to labour-intensive services such as public services. More information about TDABC can be found in Kaplan and Anderson (2004).

ABC in public services

The principles of identifying activities and establishing the cost drivers also apply in public services. Using domiciliary social care as an example, a simple ABC model which identifies the activities and associated cost drivers of service delivery might be as shown in Table 7.5.

This aligns with the discussion in Chapter 2 about the need to review service delivery processes to seek improvements. Undertaking an ABC approach on this model means the impact on costs of changing the way in which services are delivered can be assessed. Thus, ABC may assist in getting a better understanding of how public service costs behave. However, two common problems can arise:

- The lack of suitable data on activities to establish bases for cost attribution
- The relatively high costs associated with setting up an ABC system

Case study 7.3 looks at an application of TDABC in a hospital setting.

> **TABLE 7.5**

Activity-based costing in domiciliary social care

Activity	Cost Drivers
Initial client assessment	• Number of clients • Complexity of client needs • Complexity of assessment process • Distance between clients
Direct services delivery	• Number of clients • Number of visits per client per day • Volume and type of services needed to be delivered (determined by need, independent living skills, etc.) • Skill level of staff used to deliver services
Record keeping	• Number of clients • Complexity of record keeping • Technological sophistication
Supervision (including client satisfaction)	• Number of clients • Distance between clients • Number of staff to be supervised

> **CASE STUDY 7.3**

The use of ABC in the hospital sector to improve resource use

Four hospitals have shared concerns about the way in which their imaging departments function and the costs incurred. The imaging department is that part of the hospital responsible for the capture, processing and reporting on images of the body obtained using radiological techniques including:

- MRI scans
- CT scans
- Ultrasound scans
- X-rays

Within each of the above categories, there are subcategories representing different parts of the body (e.g. cranial MRI, limb MRI, etc.). The conduct of an imaging procedure comprises a series of largely sequential steps starting with referral and ending with reporting results. Although the steps were broadly similar, there were important differences between Trusts in terms of the number of stages and which staff were involved at each stage. These differences were likely to influence overall costs.

The hospitals had little information about clinical outcomes or costs of the various imaging procedures.

Each hospital initiated an approach to TDABC. However, the same approach to costing was applied in each of the four hospitals to facilitate comparability. This involved the following steps:

- The first stage was to map out the processes involved in undertaking different types of imaging and to identify the types of resources involved.
- Each stage of the process was then analysed to identify the resources and costs at each stage.
- Staff were asked to estimate the time required (in minutes) to undertake each separate stage in the imaging process. This was done for each type of imaging procedure.
- In line with TDABC approach the practical capacity (in minutes) of different classes of staff in the imaging department was calculated. Practical capacity is the mathematically maximum capacity less an amount for inevitable down time.
- Dividing practical capacity into staffing costs a cost driver rate (cost per minute) is calculated for each stage in the process.
- The above stages are also repeated for other types of resource. Non-staff would be calculated in a similar manner to pay costs by asking for estimates of the resources being used at each stage in the process and estimating the costs involved.

The results of the costing exercise are as shown below:

	Hospital A £p	Hospital B £p	Hospital C £p	Hospital D £p	Weighted Mean £p
MRI Cost per procedure	213.05	209.46	197.82	102.4	177.81
CT Cost per procedure	54.33	79.81	101.2	76.71	78.43
Ultrasound Cost per procedure	21.45	23.65	49.71	42.06	29.12
Plain X-rays Cost per procedure	34.82	30.04	26.79	31.95	30.77

Clearly, there are significant differences in cost between the hospitals which may or may not be justified. The hospitals agreed to work together to investigate whether the differences in costs can be justified in terms of better or worse outcomes and/or patient experiences.

IDENTIFYING AND ESTIMATING COSTS IN PUBLIC SERVICES

We have discussed the potential and actual uses of cost information in public services, the various ways of classifying costs and the nature of costing systems. An important question to consider is the different ways in which this cost information might be generated within the organisation. If a public service has a need for a particular type of cost information, then there are two main ways in which this information might be produced:

- Formal costing systems of the organisation
- Special costing exercises

Formal costing systems

All organisations will have main financial systems to record transactions and manage the finances of the organisation. While the details of such systems will vary from place to place it will suffice to say here that such financial systems will record the individual financial transactions (e.g. invoice payments, employee payments, etc.) of the organisation, and this will form the basis for completion of the financial accounts of the organisation and provide a range of financial information for management. However, the capabilities of such financial systems to produce detailed costing information will vary from place to place, and no generalisations can be made. However, it is probably true to say that in most organisations the minimum capabilities of the main financial systems to produce cost information could probably be summarised as follows:

- The direct running costs (pay and non-pay) of departments are identified to those individual departments with a further sub-analysis to units within those departments.
- The costs of support service costs departments are identified to individual support departments, and such costs may subsequently be attributed to individual front line departments using a broad-based method of apportionment.
- Within departments only limited information would usually be available on the costs of discrete activities and services delivered by the department. For example, colleges would not have routine cost information about course costs, and hospitals may not normally have routine cost information about disease treatment costs.
- Information on the costs of depreciation of buildings, equipment, etc., would be limited, and such costs would not usually be attributed to individual departments or activities. In the past this may not have been seen as a problem but, as noted later, the growth in the use of IT in public service provision might provoke a rethink.

The above is very much a generalisation, and clearly, there will be organisations who have much more sophisticated costing systems. However, the above comments imply that the range and quality of cost information that can be generated by existing costing systems in is often somewhat limited.

In situations where the existing costing system is deemed inadequate and the conduct of special exercises will not give the routine cost information required by management then the only remaining alternative is to consider acquiring some form of new costing system. Two approaches may be involved:

- To procure a completely new suite of financial systems which incorporate the costing modules appropriate to the information needs of the organisation. This will be an expensive proposition and not one likely to be considered if the existing suite of financial systems is not seen as being ready for replacement. If the public service organisation aims to go down this route, then normal systems design and procurement arrangements for IS/IT need to be applied.
- To procure a system which would be an "add on" to the existing financial systems and which would provide the costing analysis needed to produce the cost information required. It is quite common in large organisations to see individual departments use such systems to take financial information from the financial ledger and undertake secondary cost analysis for the departments own purposes. Sometimes such systems may be a suitably designed spreadsheet, but special proprietary systems can be purchased.

Special costing exercises

If the existing costing systems cannot produce the information needed or cannot be "tweaked" to produce that information, then recourse may involve undertaking some form of once-off special exercises. Such exercises would involve finding ways of obtaining and collecting relevant data on activity and costs in order to undertake a costing exercise designed to produce the information needed.

The data for such exercise might be collected in a number of ways including the following:

- Obtaining activity and/or cost data from other information systems in the organisation
- Undertaking surveys of staff to obtain estimates of
  - time spent on activities
  - consumables used in relation to particular activities
- Undertaking observations of activities to identify the resources (and hence costs) used
- Asking operational staff to give best estimates of how their time might be split over several types of activity

The data obtained may then be suitably analysed to produce estimates of costs. These could be the costs of undertaking a new activity or changing the level of existing activities. In estimating the costs of an activity, the purely variable costs and the purely fixed costs are easy to estimate but the difficulty comes in relation to semi-fixed costs where the relationship between activity and costs may be unclear. There are a number of different approaches to estimating costs that can be used:

- **Managerial judgement** – This approach basically involves managers using their judgement to classify costs as exhibiting certain behaviours. From these subjective profiles of behaviour, the magnitude of semi-fixed costs can be estimated.

- **The engineering approach** – this approach to estimating costs involves studying the processes that result in the incurrence of a cost and focusing on the relationships that should exist between inputs and outputs. It may also involve the use of time and motion studies (or task analysis) where employees are observed as they undertake work tasks and activity-based approaches extend task analysis to the study of indirect activities and costs.

- **Quantitative methods** – there are also a number of approaches to estimating costs using quantitative methods. A scatter diagram can be plotted enabling one to visualise the relationship between cost and the level of activity and make estimates accordingly. Alternatively, the high-low method involves taking the two observations with the highest and lowest level of activity to calculate the cost function as somewhere in between. However, both these methods lack quantitative rigour, and so recourse might require the use of multiple regression analysis (Drury 2004). This is a statistical technique which aims to identify a quantitative relationship between a dependent variable (i.e. costs) and one or a number of independent variables which are believed to influence that level of cost. Multiple regression equations will take the following forms:

$$c = m1f1 + m2f2 + m3f3 + m4f4 + \ldots\ldots + z$$

Where:
- c = cost
- f = factors which drive costs
- m = coefficient of each factor
- z = residual factor which reflects random cost variations not captured by the main independent variables

By collecting enough data points for each magnitude of cost (and the associated magnitude of the factors) a regression equation can be developed where the various coefficients and the residual factor can be established. This equation is then, effectively, a financial model, and the estimated costs of changes in activity can be estimated by plugging suitable numbers into the regression equation and calculating the costs involved.

In public services an example of the use of such a multiple regression approach might concern making estimates of changes in hospital ward costs consequent on changes to the type and level of activity undertaken by the ward. A multiple regression equation might be identified which provides a good predictor of ward costs taking account of the following factors:
- Patient numbers on ward
- Average length of patient stay
- Average age of patients on ward
- Diagnostic mix of patients
- Severity level of patients on ward

Quite often it might be the case that much of the variation in costs can be explained by just two or three factors with the remaining factors having only limited impact. Also, it is important to look at the regression equation and the independent variables being used to see if they make sense. Quite often, it is easy for regression equations to suggest relationships which are spurious in nature.

However, a word of warning is necessary here. There are a number of reasons why these regression equations may not prove stable over time. Some examples of these include the following:

- *Learning effects* – over a period of time staff become more proficient at performing tasks with the result that the time taken, and the costs involved, reduce over time.
- *Practice changes* – changes in professional practices are introduced which will impact on the time taken and the costs involved.
- *Staff changes* – new staff will impact (in either direction) on time taken and the costs involved and also the use of other resources.

Clearly, such special exercises may be time-consuming and expensive to undertake and hence should be treated with caution. They may be appropriate where a once-off view of costs is appropriate but if such cost information is needed on an ongoing basis then it would be more appropriate to implement a new costing system.

Some examples of costing developments in public services are shown in Case studies 7.4 and 7.5.

CASE STUDY 7.4

Patient-level costing in health

Health service costing, in the UK, has evolved and become more sophisticated over a period of decades. Up until the 1970s, the only cost information produced was an analysis of expenditure by resource type. In the 1980s, the idea of specialty costing (the costs of individual medical specialties) became commonplace and expanded the range of cost information available. Other subsequent costing initiatives have involved DRG costing, HRG costing and service line reporting introduced by Monitor (Prowle and Harradine 2012). However, the ultimate goal has always seemed to be the introduction of patient-level costing approaches. Early approaches to this (Prowle 1981) outlined the potential application of such costing but at that time, NHS information systems were incapable of supporting the concept on an ongoing basis.

In recent years, costing in the NHS has undergone a major change with the development of costing systems which identify the costs of the actual care individual patients receive. Patient-Level Information and Costing Systems (PLICS) brings

(continued)

together healthcare activity information with financial information and provides detailed information about how various resources are being utilised at the patient level. PLICS, combined with other data sources, provides hospitals with a rich source of information to help understand their patients and their services.

An NHS hospital conducted an "in-depth" review process to agree the income and expenditure methods in the patient-level costing system in order to identify areas of improvement and to check that the data were as expected. This was a rolling process which, over time, included all specialties across the hospital. A breast surgery review, led by the costing team, required input from one of the breast surgeons, the directorate management team and the finance manager for the service, with additional support from clinical coding when required. Through this patient-level costing review, the team found weaknesses in existing costing methods which meant that certain procedures were being wrongly classified. Correction of these errors resulted in the hospital gaining an extra £160,000 per annum in income.

While this example involved NHS hospitals using costing data to maximise income, the UK NHS also now has a strong focus on value-based health care (VBHC) and linking patient-level costs with health outcomes allows the NHS to try and improve value for patient.

CASE STUDY 7.5

Course and programme costing in higher and further education

In many countries, institutions delivering higher education (universities) and further education (colleges) receives funding based on the number of students they recruit and an amount per student payable by the student and/or the government, which may vary according to the type of course studied.

Such institutions usually have fairly well-developed costing systems which identify and analyse costs to individual support departments (i.e. library, human resources) and to individual academic departments (e.g. business, history, computing). However, usually, little routine information is available below the academic department level.

Now for planning, control and decision making, it would be useful to know the costs of delivering various academic course or programmes for comparison against the income likely to be received for students participating in these courses/programmes. Unfortunately, this is not usually available.

However, many institutions have made progress in this area and have developed costing systems to enable them to identify course and programme costs.

In an effort to develop an accountability framework for Manitoba's post-secondary education system, the Manitoba Council on Post-Secondary Education (COPSE) developed a common programme costing methodology in conjunction with its colleges and universities. The COPSE programme costing methodology states that common definitions (such as definitions of programs, full load equivalent students and departments) should be used for all institutions. Furthermore, all costs are to be as closely associated as possible with their sources, and the programme costing methodology seeks to deal with every facet of institutional operations. At its simplest level, the COPSE programme costing methodology can be summed up as follows:

Total program costs = direct costs + indirect costs + overhead

Obviously, however, common definitions of each category of costs are necessary as are the methods of attributing the various costs to individual programmes.

(Hanover Research 2010)

DIFFICULTIES AND COMPLEXITIES OF COSTING IN MODERN PUBLIC SERVICES

There are a number of specific difficulties and complexities in operating costing systems in public services which need to be highlighted. To a large extent, these are applicable to all service organisations be they public or private. These are as follows:

- "Product" costing in public service organisations
- The problem of joint costs
- Multi-agency working

"Product" costing in service organisations

When the pioneers of cost accounting developed formal product costing systems, the economy was dominated by manufacturing businesses, for which these systems were intended. Today's economy (particularly in economically developed countries) is dominated by service organisations, and the application of conventional product costing methods can be problematic in such organisations (Prowle and Lucas 2016). The potential difficulties relate to the nature of the cost structure of some service businesses and also to possible problems of defining "the product". The same comments can be applied to public services.

Conventional wisdom and empirical evidence suggest that in manufacturing businesses, product costs are used for various purposes, including (1) stock valuation, (2) product pricing and mix decisions and (3) management planning and control. In the service sector the validity of these three specific uses is questionable for the following reasons:

- Stock valuation is not a major issue in service organisations, as the inherent perishability of services meant that they cannot be stored.
- Not all service organisations use total product costs for pricing, and in public services, pricing is often not a major issue.
- It is often the case that the organisations costs were planned and controlled via responsibility centres linked to functional activities rather than via their products/services, which did not seem to be a useful unit of analysis.

However, "product" costing is seen as an important issue in many public service organisations for a number of reasons:

- For certain organisations such as hospitals, knowing the total costs is important in order to compare with the national financial tariffs paid by government for services provided. Similarly, education establishments might need to know the costs of their activities in order to set a price for courses.
- As discussed in a later chapter on performance improvement, having total product cost data available in public services would provide for meaningful comparisons between providers and provide a basis for cost improvement.
- Public service funds are limited, and having total cost data on their "products" assists in understanding where the funds are being used.

There are a number of features of public services which have implications for costing practices.

- **Product definition** – in manufacturing industry, the product is tangible and is easily defined for product costing purposes. In the service sector, and public services, the definition of the "product" to be costed is not so clear. For example, in hospitals is the product an individual patient, a disease, a treatment, etc? In the earlier discussion on costing models, it was noted that a number of definitions of final cost centres (products) were possible in public services. To clarify this matter, it is important to consider how such service (product) costing might be used and where the focus of management control should lie.
- **Labour-intensive nature** – due to their inherent nature, the activities of public services are generally labour intensive. The direct material cost is either small or non-existent. The labour cost (i.e. salary and wages) constitutes a significant portion of the total operating costs of a service sector entity. The problem is that to obtain reasonable accurate estimates for labour costs it is necessary to obtain data on how labour is being used. Professional staff in public services are often resistant to recording such data.
- **Overhead costs are large** – the overhead cost component of a public service "product" cost is often quite significant and has changed and increased over the years. The approaches to apportioning overhead costs to products, while defensible, are often lacking in sophistication and do not fully

reflect the overhead burden of the different products. The ABC approach discussed above might, if applied, improve the accuracy of attributing overhead costs to products.

The problem of joint costs

These are costs which can only be assigned to individual products in an arbitrary way, so the resultant product cost has little if any economic meaning. This raises the question as to the logic of assigning such costs to products at all. Examples of resources that manifest *"jointness"* between cost objects are information technology, corporate marketing and PR, and most intellectual property assets. Information technology, like a database, once available can be used by lots of other activities in the organisation with little or no marginal cost of usage. Most information provision within the organisation will possess elements of jointness. The increasing importance of joint costs in public services creates another area where conventional "product" costing (i.e. ascertainment of unit product cost) may be inapplicable.

Multi-agency working

This has been mentioned elsewhere in this book and involves several public agencies working collaboratively, rather than independently, to deliver a service to an individual. It is a policy which has been promoted by governments for many years as it is seen to have potential benefits in terms of the quality of service provided (e.g. better integration) and improved resource use (e.g. the avoidance of duplication). It is further discussed in Chapter 13 under the heading of inter-organisational cost management where the aim is to reduce overall costs by better multi-agency working along the lines of improved supply chains in the commercial sector. The costing problem is twofold. First, the individual agencies may have very different costing policies and practices such that the two sets of agency costs are not comparable to begin with. Second, there may be difficulties in tracking cost savings actually made through better joint working because of the inadequacies of existing costing systems.

DEVELOPING COSTING SYSTEMS IN PUBLIC SERVICES

Finance is a key resource of a public service organisation, and hence, good quality information on the costs and revenues of the organisation is a pre-requisite for effective decision making. In considering the development of costing systems in public services, it is important not to just consider the need for cost information in current circumstances but to think ahead about future needs as well. Looking ahead, there are a number of areas where an improved range of financial information may be required. These include the following:

- *Financial Strategy* – the ongoing pace of change and the degree of uncertainty will necessitate the development of robust corporate strategies in public services which will be supported by a number of resource strands including, of course, financial strands or strategies. To do this, there will probably be a need for an increased range of financial information about the various activities of the organisation.

- *Internal Resource Allocation* – public service organisations require robust approaches to allocating resources internally in order to achieve equity between different services, different geographic areas and different client groups and to facilitate the best use of public funding. As resources become tighter, the pressures to do this are likely to increase. A key aspect of internal resource allocation is knowing what things currently cost to provide, and such information is not always easily available in the organisation. Again, this suggests a need for more sophisticated costing approaches.
- *Departmental Activity Analysis* – as already noted, while, the costs of individual departments in a public service organisation are always identified it is less common for more detailed cost information to be available about the costs of undertaking specific activities and delivering specific services from the department. However, the resource pressures likely to impact on public services in the next few years suggest that a greater analysis of costs within departments will be required in the future.
- *Value for Money* – linked to the above, public services are certain to be under ongoing pressure to improve the VFM of public services, and to do this, it will probably be necessary to have more sophisticated analysis of costs than has been the case in the past.
- *Pricing Decisions* – some public service organisations may find it necessary to introduce further charges for services and so prices will need to be set. Cost information which is a key element of pricing will therefore need to improve.

In the light of the above, it is pertinent to ask whether the current approach and current generation of costing systems in the public sector will be adequate and appropriate. The answer to such a question is probably "no", and therefore, consideration needs to be given to the design of future costing systems.

There are a number of key stages, which should be followed in the development of effective approaches to costing in public service organisations, as follows:

Costing strategies and policies

Before launching into any systems development, public service organisations need to give substantial consideration to the development of longer-term strategies and policies for costing including the following:

- Identifying longer-term needs for cost information
- Identifying future costing systems architecture and cost flow structures
- Reviewing strengths and weaknesses of existing information systems (financial and non-financial) – existing systems may be adequate with some "tweaking"
- Establishing likely resource availability – the amount available for costing systems development is inherently limited

At this point great emphasis must be made about the "cost of costing".

Costing systems development

There will be a need to produce a costing systems development plan, which should include the following:

- Identification of detailed information needs
- Development of detailed costing approaches and methods
- Enhancement of existing systems
- Selection of new systems or selection of a new provider

Implementation and training

It is important to have a realistic plan for the implementation of a new costing system taking account of the potential problems of switching from one system to another. Clearly, if the cost information produced through new systems is not fully utilised by managers and service professionals then the investment in such systems may have been wasteful. Hence, it is vital to provide adequate training to all relevant staff about interpreting the cost information and how it can be used to improve decision making.

Management accounting and operational/tactical decision making in public services

INTRODUCTION

In Chapter 2, we discussed the operational management aspects of service design and delivery in public services. It can be seen from that discussion that operational management issues in public services are very varied and often very complex in nature.

Consequently, decision making in relation to operational/tactical issues in public services can also be complex and multi-faceted and will (or should) consequently require financial inputs.

In this chapter on operational decision making we consider the following:

- Operational/tactical and strategic decision making: the distinction
- Operational/tactical decision making in public services
- Management accounting methods

OPERATIONAL/TACTICAL AND STRATEGIC DECISION MAKING: THE DISTINCTION

At the outset, there is a need to distinguish between operational/tactical decision making and strategic decision making which is the subject of a later chapter. The distinction between the two types of decisions is, in no way, clear-cut and there are often overlaps. However, it is suggested that the distinction between them can be delineated by reference to the following features:

- **Timescale** – Operational/tactical decisions involve decisions with relatively short- to medium-term timescales and thus are made generally on an annually, monthly or even weekly basis. Hence, they focus mainly on the details of operations scheduling, day-to-day resource allocation, etc., to ensure the efficiency of operations and an optimised flow of services.

- **Scope** – Strategic decisions tend to be very broad and cover a wide range of factors both internal and external to the organisation. On the other hand, operational/tactical decisions will generally be narrower (but not necessarily narrow) in scope compared with strategic decisions and will take account of fewer factors.
- **Goals** – Operational/tactical decisions are made (or should be made) to execute the short-/medium-term plans and processes with the aim of achieving the longer-term goals set by the strategy.
- **Volumes** – Operational/tactical decisions tend to be ones that are imposed in high volumes in the organisation. These types of decisions are essential to every organisation, no matter what size, because of how often they are made. It is in the nature of many operational/tactical decisions to be easily repeatable, because one of their primary characteristics is being consistent at following defined rules or guidelines. On the other hand, strategic decisions tend to be made far less frequently.

OPERATIONAL/TACTICAL DECISION MAKING IN PUBLIC SERVICES

In this section we consider a number of fairly common types of operational/tactical decisions that often need to be made in public services. Later in the chapter, we will see how management accounting can assist with decision making on operational/tactical issues by providing robust financial information and analysis about the options being considered.

It must also be repeated that although we are talking here about short–medium-term operational/tactical decisions, it is almost inevitable that these decisions will also have a strategic dimension which also needs to be considered, alongside operational aspects, when making the necessary decisions. In simple terms, Figure 8.1 shows the aspects of operational/tactical decision making.

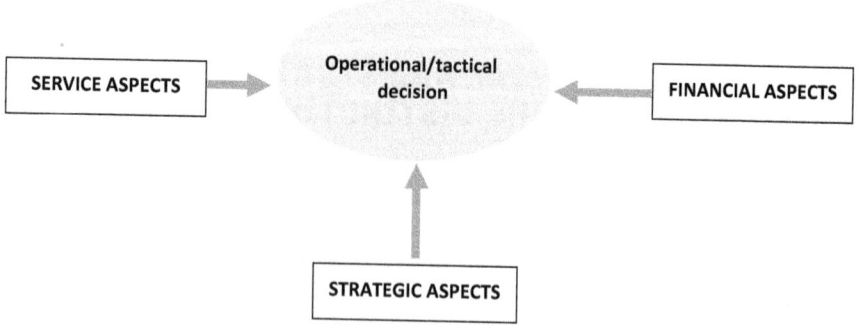

FIGURE 8.1
Aspects of operational/tactical decisions.

Thus we can see that operational/tactical decisions in public services will have both financial aspects and service aspects to be considered, but it (or should) also be considered in the context of the strategic aspects concerning the decision issue in question. This point will be exemplified further below.

Production decisions

In manufacturing industry, there is a constant need to make decisions about the volume and mix of products that the company is going to produce over the next day, week, month etc. These decisions have financial implications which need to be considered. In public services, the situation will vary. With some public services (e.g. benefit payments), the workload pattern will be determined by service demand that being who turns up on the day. If demand exceeds capacity, then the service recipient will have to queue. In other situations, the number of service recipients may be largely known in advance and the services to be provided can also be known in advance (e.g. pupil numbers in schools). However, for some public services there will be a need for decisions akin to production decisions in manufacturing industry. For example, elective surgery in hospitals or buildings' maintenance jobs in many public services are situations where the volumes and types of services will need to be considered, estimated, planned and resourced accordingly.

Capacity decisions

Again, in manufacturing industry, there are decisions which frequently need to be made about the capacity (physical, human, financial) that is needed to produce the planned mix and level of product. Similar decisions also have to be made in some public services. For example, an area police commander has to make decisions about the number of police officers that will be required for particular periods such as public holidays, sports events, etc. where the demand for policing might be higher than normal. Similarly, a nurse manager in a hospital will have to make decisions about the nursing cover that will be needed for a particular period based on likely patient needs. Many other examples can be quoted. As financial resources for public services are largely finite, operational managers will have to balance the needs of the service with the costs involved and management accounting has a key role here.

Make or buy decisions

This is a classic decision that needs to be made in many types of organisations, both public and private. While there are certain activities which have to be undertaken by the organisation itself using its own staff and other resources (core activities), there are other activities which might be undertaken by an external organisation using a contractual arrangement. A typical example of this in the commercial sector concerns a company which needs a component to use in the manufacture of its main product. It could decide to purchase that component from another company or, alternatively, it could decide to manufacture the component itself. This is where the term "make or buy" comes from. Such decisions are often complex and have many strands associated with them concerning strategy, finance and security of operations in the company.

Public service organisations often have to make similar types of decisions which vary considerably in nature. Just a few examples are as follows:

- A decision whether to contract out the maintenance of specialist equipment to a private company or develop an in-house capacity and capability to undertake the work.
- A decision whether to continue providing support services in-house or contract them to a private company. Examples here could be cleaning or catering.
- A decision by a public hospital whether to contract out some elective surgical operations to a private hospital in return for payment as an alternative to increasing in-house capacity.

Clearly, the financial aspects of these decisions will not necessarily be the only issue or even the most important issue in the decision, but the financial aspects of the options cannot be ignored.

Capital expenditure decisions

Capital expenditure is defined as money spent by an organisation on acquiring or maintaining fixed assets, such as land, buildings and equipment. Now in public services, capital expenditure can often be concerned with very large projects involving multi-millions (or even billions) of pounds of expenditure. These can be referred to as strategic capital expenditure and will be discussed further in Chapter 9.

However, capital expenditure can also be incurred in public services at a smaller (but not necessarily small) and more mundane level. However, this still involves significant amounts of money and is vitally important for the delivery of public services in the short/medium term. Some examples here might include investment on energy conservation, new equipment or vehicle acquisition. These can be regarded as operational/tactical decisions concerning capital expenditure, and management accounting has a key role to play in providing the financial input into such decisions.

Pricing decisions

As discussed in Chapter 1, the vast bulk of public services are financed through the proceeds of taxation and therefore are free to users at the time of receipt. Consequently, charges for public services represent a small proportion of public service funding and so pricing decisions are limited.

However, there are situations where public service organisations do levy charges on service users and these require pricing decisions to be made. In making pricing decisions, there are a number of (financial and service) factors to be taken into account associated with the activity or service being priced. In addition, individual pricing decisions need to be taken in the context of the overall pricing strategy established by the organisation and this is discussed in Chapter 9.

Regarding the financial aspects of pricing, there are basically three broad approaches to costing which should be considered in relation to individual pricing decisions.

Total cost pricing

A general rule when making pricing decisions is that price should be set by reference to the total costs of the service being considered and this can be regarded as being the sum of:

- direct costs (e.g. staff, travel, materials)
- an appropriate share of indirect costs (e.g. administration, maintenance)

This does not mean that the price must equate to the total cost and indeed the price may be above or below the total cost depending on circumstances. Before making a pricing decision it is essential for the public service organisation to ensure that all relevant costs are taken into account. It is often the case that the direct material costs of services are quite small but direct labour and direct overhead costs are quite large. Hence there needs to be reasonably sophisticated arrangements for identifying those costs. Also, there is often an issue about the extent to which indirect costs should include a charge for the use of fixed assets in the organisation. Although these are sunk costs, they will suffer wear and tear and will eventually have to be replaced.

Contribution-based pricing

The concept of contribution and break-even analysis is important in making pricing decisions in the commercial world. It recognises that pricing decisions are dynamic and must consider the relationship between demand for a product and its price. This approach then involves optimising the price–volume relationship in order to obtain maximum revenues and profits for the company. This is illustrated in Table 8.1.

TABLE 8.1

Contribution-based pricing

1	Level of production (units)	50	75	100	140	200
2	Variable cost per unit of production	£2	£2	£2	£2	£2
3	Total variable costs (1 × 2)	£100	£150	£200	£280	£400
4	Sale price per unit	£3	£2.90	£2.80	£2.20	£1.80
5	Volume of sales (=production)	50	75	100	140	200
6	Total sales revenues (4 × 5)	£150	£218	£280	£308	£360
7	Contribution to fixed costs (6–3)	£50	£68	£80	£28	−£40
8	Fixed costs	£30	£30	£30	£30	£30
9	Surplus/deficit (7–8)	£20	£38	£50	−£2	−£10

It can be seen that the optimal position is a level of production/sales of 100 items which maximises the financial returns.

For the reasons discussed earlier, it seems unlikely that public service organisations will use this approach very often but there may be cases where it is relevant.

Marginal cost pricing

The marginal costs of a service are the additional costs that a public service organisation would actually incur if they undertook some additional activity. Thus, for small increases in service activity, the labour and overhead costs might remain unchanged but consumables costs would increase. In certain specific circumstances it may be appropriate and acceptable to base pricing decisions on the marginal costs of the service provided rather than the total cost. Hence the price may be set at a level which exceeds the marginal cost but is below the total cost.

MANAGEMENT ACCOUNTING METHODS

There are a number of management accounting methods which are relevant to operational and tactical decision making and these are discussed below.

Relevant costing

This was discussed in Chapter 7 and we saw that the basic principle here is that decisions should be based only on those costs which are relevant to that particular decision. The principle is that decisions should be based only on those costs that change as a result of the particular course of action chosen. The more complex a decision is, the more difficult it may be to establish which costs are relevant and which are not but an attempt must be made. The distinction between relevant and non-relevant costs is summarised in Table 8.2.

Thus, relevant costing is of great importance in a variety of operational decision making, in particular to make or buy decisions. However, the process of judging what costs are or are not relevant is not always clear-cut, and judgement is needed. This is illustrated in Case study 8.1.

TABLE 8.2

Relevant costs for decision making

Relevant Costs	Non-Relevant Costs
• Variable/marginal costs	• Sunk costs
• Incremental fixed costs	• Committed costs
• Opportunity costs	• Notional costs

Operational decisions and relevant costing

The buildings maintenance department of a local authority has a section that manufactures a variety of PVC doors and windows for use in maintaining its own housing stock. It has been approached by a private customer regarding the urgent manufacture of an agreed volume of two items.

The department wishes to put forward a price for this contract and needs to establish the *relevant* costs associated with each item.

Basic information

The following information is available about each item.

Material resource requirements

	Doors	Windows	Both
Direct material W (units)	1,000	200	1,200
Direct material X (units)	1,000	–	1,000
Direct material Y (units)	500	600	1,100
Direct material Z (units)	–	200	200

Labour resource requirements

	Doors	Windows	Both
Direct labour type A (hours)	100	50	150
Direct labour B type (hours)	20	–	20

Direct labour costs

Labour costs per hour	£
Direct labour A	25
Direct labour B	30

Direct materials availability and costs

Material	Units already in stock	Book value of units in stock (£/unit)	Realisable value (£/unit)	Replacement cost (£/unit)
W	0	–	–	16.00
X	600	12.00	11.00	15.00
Y	1,200	13.00	10.00	14.00
Z	0	–	–	13.00

(continued)

Overhead costs

	Doors	Windows
Variable overhead (£)	2,000	1,500
Fixed overhead (£)	5,000	4,000
Total overhead (£)	7,000	5,500

The following information should also be noted:

- Material W would need to be purchased as there are no existing stocks.
- Material X is used regularly by the department and if units of X are required for this job, they would need to be replaced to meet other demands.
- Sufficient material Y is in stock due to previous over-buying. No other use could be found for material Y and if not used on this job it would have to be sold off as scrap.
- There is no material Z in stock and the lead time for its supply is so long that it could not be obtained in time for the completion of this contract. However, the department does have another material J which could be used as a substitute but is currently needed for a different item and would have to be replaced. Supplies of material J can be obtained quickly at a cost of £19/unit.
- The employees in labour pool B are currently short of work and could easily absorb this contract into their existing workload.
- Manufacture of item Beta would require the purchase of a new machine at a cost of £5,000. The machine would have no use at the end of the contract and would be scrapped.
- Manufacture of item Alpha would require the use of an existing machine which is currently lying idle. The machine costs £20,000 to purchase and is being depreciated over a ten-year period.

Relevant costs

The relevant costs for each item are as follows:

Doors

	Amount	Relevant unit cost (£)	Total cost (£)	Explanation
Direct labour A	100	25	2,500	Must be acquired at going rate
Direct labour B	20	Nil	Nil	Slack capacity so no cost
Direct material W	1,000	16	16,000	No stocks – must be purchased

	Amount	Relevant unit cost (£)	Total cost (£)	Explanation
Direct material X	1,000	15	15,000	Stocks must be replenished by new purchases
Direct material Y	500	10	5,000	Only alternative use is for scrap – therefore scrap value
Direct material Z	–	19	Nil	None needed
Machine costs			Nil	Depreciation is a non-cash and sunk cost
Overhead costs			2,000	Variable only
Relevant costs			40,500	

Windows

	Amount	Relevant unit cost (£)	Total cost (£)	Explanation
Direct labour A	50	25	1,250	Must be acquired at going rate
Direct labour B	Nil	Nil	Nil	Not needed
Direct material W	200	16	3,200	No stocks – must be purchased
Direct material X	–	15	–	Not needed
Direct material Y	600	10	6,000	Only alternative use is for scrap – therefore scrap value
Direct material Z	200	19	3,800	Substitute material J at a replacement cost
Machine costs			5,000	New machine
Overhead costs			1,500	Variable only
Relevant costs			20,750	

The relevant costs have been established as being £40,500 (doors) and £20,750 (windows). Thus, the department needs to price the prospective contract above those figures.

Capital investment appraisal

In this section some techniques are outlined which can be used to appraise and evaluate public sector capital projects. First, the basis of the technique will be described and then its applicability in the public sector will be considered. The techniques discussed can be classified twofold:

- Financial appraisal – discounted cash flow (DCF)
- Economic appraisal – cost–benefit analysis (CBA)

The techniques of economic appraisal are probably more suited to strategic capital investments and will be discussed in Chapter 9. In this chapter, we will discuss financial techniques. There are various approaches to capital investment appraisal which are outlined below:

Payback

The payback period is both conceptually simple and easy to calculate and is commonly used in commercial organisations. The payback period is the time taken to recover the initial investment. So, a £1 million investment that will make a surplus of £200,000 a year has a payback period of five years. Investments with a shorter payback period are preferred to those with a long period. In theoretical terms, the payback approach has a number of weaknesses:

- It attaches no value to cash flows after the end of the payback period.
- It makes no adjustments for risk.
- It is not directly related to wealth maximisation as is net present value (NPV; see below).
- It ignores the time value of money (see below).
- The "cut-off" period may be arbitrary.

Accounting rate of return (ARR)

The accounting rate of return is a very simple rate of return on an investment project, calculated as:

$$\text{ARR} = \frac{\text{Average return (over a period of years)}}{\text{Project investment}} \times 100$$

Average means arithmetic mean, and the profit number used is operating profit from the particular project.

ARR is most often used internally when selecting projects. While ARR overcomes some of the weaknesses of payback, it still has the following problems:

- ARR does not take into account the time value of money – the value of cash flows does not diminish with time as is the case with NPV and Internal rate of return (IRR).
- It does not adjust for the greater risk to longer-term forecasts.
- It tends to favour higher-risk decisions because future profits are insufficiently discounted for risk, as well as for time value, whereas use of the payback period leads to overly conservative decisions.

Discounted cash flow (DCF)

The main weakness of the above approaches is that the only issue considered here is the size of the various cash flows associated with a project and they ignore what is termed the "time value of money" since the timing of the cash flows is not considered. Thus, they assume that £100 received or paid in year 1 is equivalent to £100 received in year 2 and so on. However, economics teaches that money has a time value as well as a magnitude and argues that £100 received in year 1 has a greater value than £100 in year 2 (which has greater value than £100 in year 3, etc.). Similarly, £100 spent in year 1 has a higher cost than £100 spent in year 2. This is for two main reasons:

- the future is uncertain and £100 receivable today is preferable to £100 in a year's time when one may no longer be able to enjoy the benefit of that £100.
- £100 today can be invested to produce a return which will be in excess of £100 in a year's time.

This basic principle of time value of money leads to the discounted cash flow (DCF) approach which takes account of both the magnitude and the timing of the cash flows involved when evaluating capital projects. In public service organisations it is this DCF approach which should be used for the financial appraisal of projects. It is not possible here to give a full explanation of the DCF approach and the interested reader is referred to the many excellent books on the subject, but an attempt is made here to give a brief explanation of the rationale of the method.

With DCF, cash flows, whether they are inflows or outflows, in whatever time period they occur are converted to a common point of reference, namely a present value. Present value is essentially the converse of compound interest. Assuming an interest rate of 10%, then if £100 is invested, it has a potential future value of £110 in a year's time. The converse is that £110 receivable in a year's time has a present value of £100. Similarly, £121 receivable in two years' time has a present value of £100. Thus, all cash flows can be converted to a present value. When inflows and outflows are combined, the present value becomes an NPV.

Let us look at a simple practical example. An organisation is considering two possible projects involving investment in new equipment both of which have a capital cost of £100,000. The organisation can borrow money at 10% to purchase the equipment. Both types of equipment have a four-year life and will be used to manufacture different products. There will be production costs associated with the manufacture of the products and revenues from the sales of the products. The financial implications are shown in Table 8.3.

Three points should be noted about these results:

- In terms of total cash flows, project Y has a larger positive net cash flow than project X;
- Both projects have a positive NPV;
- Project X has a larger NPV of cash flows than project Y. This is because the larger positive cash flows in project X occur earlier in the lifespan of the project and thus generate higher present values than cash flows occurring later in the project.

TABLE 8.3

Use of discounted cash flow

Project Data

| Year | Project X | | | Project Y | | |
	Production Costs	Sales Revenues	Net Cash Flow	Production Costs	Sales Revenues	Net Cash Flow
	£	£	£	£	£	£
1	−20,000	60,000	40,000	−25,000	38,000	13,000
2	−30,000	65,000	35,000	−35,000	65,000	30,000
3	−30,000	65,000	35,000	−20,000	65,000	45,000
4	−20,000	36,000	16,000	−20,000	62,000	42,000
	−100,000	226,000	126,000	−100,000	230,000	130,000

Project Analysis

| Year | Project X | | | Project Y | | |
	Net Cash Flow	Discount Factor	Net Present Value	Net Cash Flow	Discount Factor	Net Present Value
1	40,000	1.00	40,000	13,000	1.00	13,000
2	35,000	0.91	31,850	30,000	0.91	27,300
3	35,000	0.83	29,050	45,000	0.83	37,350
4	16,000	0.75	12,000	42,000	0.75	31,500
Total	126,000		112,900	130,000		109,150

DCF techniques provide two decision rules for the financial appraisal of potential capital projects:

- In purely financial terms, projects which show a positive NPV should be undertaken, while those which have negative NPVs should not be undertaken. In this case, project X should be undertaken but project Y should not.
- Where several competing projects have positive NPVs but only one can be undertaken (e.g. because of limited investment funds available), the project with the highest positive NPV should be chosen.

The results of a DCF analysis will be significantly affected by the discount rate used in the analysis. In the above example, for simplicity, a discount rate of 10% was used. In commercial companies, the investment discount rate is derived from the interest rates the company might have to pay to fund the investment from different sources. Thus, a company would calculate its weighted average cost of capital

(WACC) as its discount rate. For public services it is different. Public service organisations in the United Kingdom are expected to use the discount rate set down by HM Treasury which is referred to as the test discount rate (TDR). The TDR is a rate which aims to value what is termed the social time preference of society. This is a measure of a society's willingness to postpone private consumption now in order to consume it later and is calculated by HM Treasury. Currently, the TDR is set at 3.5% for most projects but other rates might be employed in specific services (Green Book). Similar financial regimes will exist in other countries.

When we look at the applicability of DCF in public service organisations, we see several different applications:

- Some public service organisations such as service providers may find it necessary to appraise potential capital investments in a manner similar to the above. They would need to set the capital costs of a new project and the associated running costs against the income likely to be generated from the project. An example might be a new piece of medical equipment which would attract additional patients and hence additional funds.

- In another public service organisation, the generation of additional revenues may not be the main reason for capital investment. However, DCF may still be relevant in the situation where a public service organisation decides to invest large sums in computerised energy management systems. DCF can show the present value of energy savings made against the capital costs involved.

- In many public service organisations, the costs of a capital investment will need to be set against the service benefits that the investment will bring. This will be discussed further in the section on cost–benefit analysis, but it will suffice to say that DCF can be of relevance by being a technique which reduces all of the cash flows associated with projects to a single figure (an NPV) which simplifies the decision-making process.

Technical aspects of DCF

Within the public sector, guidance is usually available on the appraisal of capital investments in public services. Typically, such guidance might discuss the following points:

- **Timescales of appraisals** – the cash flows from projects usually will have a fairly limited life and thus any financial appraisal would probably not cover a period greater than 25 years. However, the economic benefits will flow for a much greater period and thus the economic appraisal may cover a much longer time period – possibly up to a hundred years.

- **Discount rate** – as already noted, in public services the discounting calculation should be undertaken using the discount rate set out under finance ministry guidance for public sector investments.

- **Inflation** – the valuation of costs or benefits should be expressed in "real terms" or "constant prices" (i.e. at "today's" general price level), as opposed to "nominal terms" or "current prices". If thought necessary and material, the effect of expected future inflation in the general price level should be removed by deflating future cash flows using the relevant deflator. Leaving aside general inflation perhaps of more relevance is specific price inflation where particular prices are expected to increase at significantly higher or lower rate than general inflation. In these cases, this relative price change should be calculated. Some examples where relative price changes may be material to an appraisal include high-technology products, prices which may be expected to fall in real terms and fuel prices, where the resource supply is scarce.

- **Risk and uncertainty** – issues of risk and uncertainty in public services management are discussed in detail in Chapter 12. However, the basic distinction between the terms is that risk exists where there is a probability, based on past experience, that can be attached to an event. Uncertainty is where there is no such probability available. In investment appraisals, there is always likely to be some difference between what is expected, and what eventually happens because of biases, risks and uncertainties. Two issues need to be looked at critically:

  - **Inherent bias** – there is a demonstrated, systematic, tendency for project appraisers to be overly optimistic. This is a worldwide phenomenon that affects both the private and public sectors. Adjusting for such optimism should provide a better estimate, earlier on, of key project parameters. Such adjustments for optimism may be reduced as more reliable estimates of relevant costs are built up, and project-specific risk work is undertaken.

  - **Rigour** – in assessing uncertainty, an expected value is a useful starting point for understanding the impact of risk and uncertainty between different options. But however well these are identified and analysed, the future is inherently uncertain. So, it is also essential to consider how future risks and uncertainties can affect the choice between options. Sensitivity analysis is fundamental to appraisal. It is used to test the vulnerability of options to unavoidable future risks and uncertainties. Therefore, the need for sensitivity analysis should always be considered and, in practice, dispensed with only in exceptional cases. Scenarios should be chosen to draw attention to the major technical, economic and political risks and uncertainties upon which the success of a proposal depends.

As a consequence of the above phenomena, risk management strategies should be adopted for the appraisal process. Appraisers should calculate an expected value of all risks for each option, and consider how exposed each option is to future uncertainty. Before and during implementation, steps should be taken to prevent and mitigate both risks and uncertainties. It is vitally important to be transparent about the potential impact of risks and bias on proposals. Relating back to the behavioural aspects of management accounting in Chapter 6, this is an area where risks and uncertainties can be underestimated in an attempt to get a project approved.

Marginal costing

The nature of marginal costing was discussed in Chapter 7. Marginal costing is a useful tool in relation to public services, especially with regard to:

- Assessing the cost implications of operational changes in service activity and mix levels.

- Operational pricing decisions are made on a marginal cost basis. The example in Table 8.4 illustrates this.

Having identified the total costs and marginal costs, the organisation can fix a price anything in excess of £2,200 and in doing this, it will need to take account of a variety of factors such as how much do they want the work, risk, cost uncertainties, etc.

However, caution is needed in the use of marginal costing. If all service activities were priced on a marginal cost basis, there would be a risk of generating

---

▶ TABLE 8.4

Marginal cost pricing in a university

A university undertakes a variety of short courses in various aspects of business management. It has been asked to quote for a once-off job to provide a series of courses for a local private company.
Using total costing principles, it calculates the costs associated with this work as follows:

- Materials: £1,200
- Staffing: £10,500
- Variable overheads: £1,000
- Fixed overheads: £2,000
- Total costs: £14,700

However, an examination of each of the cost elements suggests the following:

Cost type	Comments
Materials	Materials are available at costs shown above.
Staffing	The work associated with these courses can probably be absorbed by the existing lecturing staff.
Variable overheads	There is some uncertainty about these costs.
Fixed overheads	These are definitely fixed.

The costing results are shown below:

Cost type	Comments	Amount (£)
Direct materials	Assume directly variable	1,200
Direct labour	Assume it can be absorbed by existing staff	Nil
Variable overheads	Assume directly variable	1,000
Fixed overheads	Definitely fixed	Nil
Total marginal costs		2,200

The university is keen to win this work because it could be the prelude to a longer-term relationship with the company. However, it does not want to set a precedent by offering a very low price which is unsustainable. They are also aware that the company will also be asking other universities and private providers in the city to quote.
Hence it submits a quotation of £12,000, which is well above the marginal cost but slightly below the total cost.

insufficient revenues to finance the overhead costs of the service. Thus, it should only be undertaken in the following circumstances:

- The proposed activity is for a once-off event of fairly short term in nature. Thus, it is not applicable to ongoing activities.
- Pricing the activity at marginal cost will not affect the price charged for the mainstream provision of the same activity. For example, a client given a once-off price based on marginal costs cannot ask for this to be repeated.
- The proposed activity level is a fairly small proportion of the existing workload of the service department and thus most costs would remain unchanged.

Management accounting and public service strategy

INTRODUCTION

In Chapter 3, the issue of public service strategy was discussed in some depth. In this chapter, we consider, in more detail, the ways in which specific management accounting methods can contribute to strategic decision making in public services.

Initially, it is probably worth recapping on a few key points in relation to the concept of strategy:

- The term strategy or strategic management comprises three aspects – strategic planning, implementing strategy and strategic control.
- Strategy is concerned with identifying the longer-term objectives of the public service organisation and what it needs to do to achieve those objectives.
- Strategies that are developed need to be assessed for their strategic feasibility (can they deliver the organisations' objectives?) and resource feasibility, especially financial feasibility.
- Implementing strategies will usually involve a significant element of organisational change. This will need to be properly planned and resourced.
- Management accounting has a large contribution to make with regard to a number of strategic issues. This contribution is not always optimised.

In this chapter, we describe and discuss a number of management accounting approaches which can be used to facilitate the strategy process in public service organisations. These are

- Cost and income benchmarking
- Strategic capital investment appraisal
- Strategic cost improvement
- Programme/client group analysis and budgeting

- Strategic options evaluation
- Strategic financial forecasting
- Decision support models (DSM)
- Pricing strategies
- Strategic financial leadership

COST AND INCOME BENCHMARKING

Most public services are not delivered in any form of competitive market environment. Classical economics would, therefore, argue that, in this situation, they will receive no market signals about the prices they charge and the cost levels they incur. Thus, in attempting to assess the reasonableness of their cost base they have to fall back on making comparisons with others or have a culture of looking for continuous improvements.

Benchmarking is a technique which can help assess the performance of public service activities and which can form a basis for preparing future strategies. A public service organisation might attempt to compare its costs and income levels against benchmarks derived from the costs and income levels of other organisations in the same sector and/or other comparable organisations. Inferences could then be made about those activities which might inform future strategies. For example, why should there be *significant* differences (which there often are) between, for example:

- The cost of collecting a refuse bin in local authority areas
- The conduct of an MRI investigation in hospitals
- The cost of teaching a student on a health and social care course in colleges
- The cost of making a social benefit payment in various towns and cities etc.
- The income collected per service recipient for social care

There may be legitimate reasons for such reasons but, in some cases, there may not be good reasons.

Types of benchmarks

A number of different types of benchmarks can be identified.

Internal benchmarks

For activities which are generic to departments within *the same* public service organisation, a series of internal benchmarks could be developed including, for example, the following:

- Average vehicle utilisation for a local authority transport fleet
- Average class contact hours per member of academic staff in a college
- Average drug prescribing costs per general medical practitioner

Another approach would be to use temporal benchmarks whereby an organisation might consider trends in its own internal costs over a period of years after adjusting for the effects of inflation. If unit costs (in real terms) have changed over time, then the reasons for this might be considered.

External sector–specific benchmarks

Another approach might be to benchmark activities in one public service organisation against those in other public service organisations *in the same sector.* This could be done in two distinct ways:

- Using benchmarks derived from all relevant public service organisations in the sector (e.g. all local authorities)
- Using benchmarks derived from a sample cohort of comparable public service organisations (e.g. urban local authorities)

The necessary information could also be obtained in two ways:

- **Using publicly available information** – performance could be compared against other public service organisations by using information which is in the public domain such as: government statistics, annual accounts, professional associations, etc. Although some interesting comparisons can be made using this information, two key factors limit its usefulness. These are
    - The information is usually at too high a level of aggregation to make meaningful comparisons at an individual functional level. So, greater granularity is required.
    - Considerable concern exists about the degree of consistency, between public service organisations, in the methods they use to record and calculate the publicly available information. This undermines the confidence in any such comparisons that may be made.
- **Special exercise** – the alternative to using publicly available information is to undertake a special exercise to collect information from other public service organisations. The advantage of this approach is that one can define, specifically, the type of information one wishes to collect. The major disadvantage is that, as experience has shown, it is often very difficult to get cooperation from other public service organisations in terms of sharing information. The term *"commercially confidential"* is often used as a reason for not sharing information, but it is often an excuse for avoiding such comparisons being made. However, the following approaches might help to increase the level of cooperation:
    - An offer could be made to the other public service organisations to share the findings of the study on a non-attributable basis.
    - An attempt could be made to undertake the exercise collaboratively with each institution sharing the costs of the exercise and sharing the results. The information might be collected by a third party who keeps the results of individual public service organisation confidential. This is often done by having a contract with a commercial company which collects information from many organisations and provides information about the performance of a public sector organisation compared with an anonymous and comparable set of other organisations. Many public service organisations subscribe to such commercial benchmarking services.

Although this approach to benchmarking using external benchmarks is obviously attractive, the difficulties of getting comparable information should not be underestimated.

External generic benchmarks

The current performance of a public service organisation might be compared against that for a range of other organisations of various types. This is particularly relevant for those functions which are generic and not sector specific such as payroll, payments, human resource management, administration etc. Comparisons might be made against any of the following:

- Public service organisations in other sectors
- Comparable public service organisations in other countries
- Private sector organisations operating in similar business areas (e.g. private training organisations or private health organisations)

A wide range of information is publicly available through trade associations, professional bodies etc. However, most of the organisations involved will be considerably different from public service organisations in terms of organisation, business profile, cultural background, level of technology etc., so the comparisons should be used with caution.

Benchmarking in context

Although the thrust of the benchmarking exercise would relate to the benchmarking of costs and income, for the process to be useful a wide range of other information might also need to be collected to assist with the interpretation of the cost and income data. This would include

- Cost information
- Income information
- Information about volume of activity/workload to establish unit costs
- Organisational arrangements
- Process descriptions etc.

The results of the benchmarking exercise are unlikely to be definitive and will need consideration and interpretation. After this has happened, any significant differences in unit costs and income between organisations may, after investigation, be found to be justified but this should not be assumed at the outset. Higher unit costs may be a consequence of higher wage rates, economies of scale, greater levels of social deprivation, population age structures, geographic location etc. and these matters should be investigated. It is also important that one should not assume and assert, as often happens, that higher unit cost means higher standards. This should also be investigated and not just assumed. The overall aim of the benchmarking exercise would be to try and identify areas where the public service organisation might be able to improve its financial performance and for this to be incorporated into its strategy.

STRATEGIC CAPITAL INVESTMENT APPRAISAL

Public service organisations undertake many different types of capital investment on things like buildings, plant, equipment, IT etc. Many such investments are *relatively* small in expenditure terms and involve operational considerations which were considered in Chapter 8. An example of this would be an investment in buildings insulation to improve energy efficiency. In this section, we consider the appraisal of what we term strategic capital investments.

One of the major features of strategic change in public services is the prevalence of major strategic capital investment. Major projects like this tend to have the following features:

- They involve large amounts of expenditure which can be multi-million or even multi-billion-pound projects.
- The projects are effectively irreversible once implemented.
- The projects will have implications for public service delivery for many decades to come.
- They are complex and multi-faceted in nature.
- The have implications for the revenue cost base of the public service involved.
- They are often politically contentious.

Hence it is absolutely vital to try and get the decision making around these projects as optimal as possible which is not always easy given their multi-faceted nature. Now, nobody would suggest that decision making on such large projects should be based purely on financial criteria, but the financial criteria are important. Contrary to much popular opinion, strategic investments in the commercial sector are not based purely on financial criteria as other strategic considerations are also important. However, good management accounting practices can guide decision-makers to understand the financial complexities of different projects in a manner which can simplify their decisions.

Too often, capital investment appraisal is seen as just a collection of techniques and it is important to focus on the distinction between

- Financial and economic techniques
- Management decision framework
- Decision guidelines

Financial and economic techniques

These techniques fall into two groups – financial and economic. The financial techniques were already discussed in Chapter 8 and are just listed below:

- **Payback** – The length of time it will take for returns from a capital investment to repay the initial capital cost.
- **Accounting rate of return (ARR)** – The returns over the whole life of a project assessed by providing a comparison of the overall profit generated by the investment, over its lifespan, with the cost of the investment. This is then expressed as a percentage return.
- **Net present value (NPV)** – This approach is the recognition that cash flows have a time value as well as a magnitude and, thus, earlier cash inflows have greater value than later inflows and earlier cash outflows have greater cost than later outflows. The NPV approach converts all cash flows to a single point of reference in time (the present time) through a process called

discounting. The discounted cash flows can be added together to give an NPV. While NPV is the theoretically correct approach for financially appraising possible investments, it is not always used. The discounting approach is not always well understood and there are doubts about the veracity and reliability of the discount rate used. Many managers prefer methods like payback and ARR because they can easily understand them.

Other techniques for appraising strategic investment projects are termed economic techniques. Two such techniques are outlined below.

Cost–benefit analysis (CBA)

The above techniques are concerned only with the income and costs associated with an investment project. However, public services are usually concerned with the benefits to be derived from public service provision as well as financial costs. CBA is a tool of economic appraisal which involves, as its name suggests, identifying both the costs and benefits associated with a project. In addition, the identification of costs should incorporate social costs as well as financial costs. As a consequence, CBA is, largely, a tool which is used in the public sector rather than the private sector.

A full CBA for a large infrastructure project like a new motorway or a new urban tram line would utilise a variety of techniques to quantify and monetarise the benefits. This is a complex and expensive process which can take many months (or even years) to complete. Thus, it is usually reserved for large-scale infrastructure projects. For smaller (but not small) projects, a simpler approach can be applied which is as follows:

1. Identify and quantify the financial costs associated with the project and any cost savings that can also be identified.
2. In collaboration with key stakeholders, identify what are seen as the key benefits and social costs that might be associated with the project.
3. Identify and utilise any quantitative data that are already available concerning the benefits and social costs associated with the project.
4. Where such data are lacking, undertake a survey of stakeholders asking them to give their opinion of the level of benefits that have accrued to the project on the basis of a number of agreed criteria and utilising a five-point ranking scale.
5. Present all of the results obtained in an appropriate manner to indicate the cost–benefit aspects of the project.

CBA evaluations may also need to address two other important issues:

- **Attribution effect** – benefits can be attributed to a number of causal factors. Thus, it is important that we consider what level of benefits can realistically be attributed to the investment project as opposed to other causal events that may take place at the same time. It may be difficult to obtain sufficient numeric data to have any degree of precision about this issue but it might be possible to get a qualitative "feel" about what can be achieved. Also, a scenario analysis may be undertaken using a range of different attribution factors to estimate extent of effect to estimate the extent of impact.

- **Distributional effect** – CBA is essentially a utilitarian tool which looks at the overall benefits and overall costs associated with a particular investment project. However, with any project there will, inevitably, be gainers and losers. Some individuals/groups may realise benefits, while others do not. In the same way, some individuals/groups may incur costs (financial or social), while others do not. Hence, whatever the overall results of the CBA, it is also important to pay some cognisance to the distribution of benefits and costs associated with the change. Again, in the absence of numeric data, having a qualitative "feel" is important as well as undertaking a scenario analysis similar to the above.

Cost–utility analysis (CUA)

CUA is a method which is most often used when benefits cannot be expressed in monetary or metric values. It is commonly used in the healthcare sector. As its name suggests, it involves a comparison of options in terms of their costs and the utilities they generate. These utilities are often expressed in terms of what are termed quality-adjusted life years (QUALYs). QUALYs indicate the average number of years of quality life which a person with a defined health status will be able to live if a certain health intervention is carried out. The intervention could be a new drug, a surgical technique, an implant etc. CUA, therefore, shows the cost of intervention with regard to a specific outcome – quality of life. It is commonly used in the healthcare sector particularly in relation of pharmaceuticals but could be applied to some capital investment options.

Capital investment appraisal – conflicting perspectives

As already noted, financial appraisal and economic appraisal of potential capital investments have different perspectives. Financial appraisal is concerned with the financial impact on the service delivery organisation of undertaking the investment, while economic appraisal is concerned with the broader impact on society of undertaking the investment. These perspectives can sometimes conflict as illustrated by the example of an urban tram system in Case study 9.1

In Chapter 3, there was a discussion of situations in public services where there is a separation of the service commissioner from the service provider and, consequently, different perspectives about service provision. In these situations, to some extent, these different perspectives are reflected in the respective standpoints of the service commissioner and the service provider. Basically, since service-provider organisations are quasi-commercial in nature and have business-type objectives, to achieve the objectives they are more likely to find the financial appraisal technique of discounted cash flow as being of greatest relevance to them. For example, a service-provider organisation needs to assess whether investment in a new piece of equipment will generate savings and/or additional income streams that will outweigh the costs of investment and, therefore, improve its financial performance. On the other hand, commissioners are more concerned with need for service and whether a piece of equipment will improve the quantity, quality etc. of service provision. Hence, they are likely to find the economic techniques of CBA of greatest relevance. In this case, there are likely to be situations where such conflicts arise where projects which are economically desirable do not provide the delivery organisation with a financially sound case for proceeding.

CASE STUDY 9.1

Financial versus economic evaluation

In a large European city, an old bus line has been replaced by a modern tramway. Simultaneously, the road-space has been narrowed by about a third. A survey of users of the tramway indicated that the tramway hardly generated any shift from private cars towards public transit mode but it did generate shifts from bus and subway towards the tramway, and from existing roads towards the ring road for cars. The various benefits and costs of these changes were evaluated.

The welfare gains made by public transport users are more than compensated by the time losses to the motorists, and in particular, by the additional cost of road congestion on the ring road. The same conclusion applies with regard to CO_2 emissions. The reductions caused by the replacement of buses and the elimination of a few car trips are less important than the increased pollution caused by the lengthening of the automobile trips and increased congestion on the ring road.

The results of the economic evaluation are summarised below:

	Initial (millions of euros)	Annual (millions of euros)
Initial investment	−444.34	
Transport company operating surplus		1.00
Benefits to public transport users		
Time savings	2.69	
Comfort gains		2.69
Subway decongestion		5.71 to 9.43
Car user benefits		
Welfare losses		−6.73
Time losses	−1.83	
Externalities		
Time losses on ring road		−30.00
Additional CO_2 emissions	−0.10	
Total	−443.58	−27.33 to −23.61

Even if one ignores the initial investment of 350 M€, the social impact of the project, as measured by its NPV, is negative. The NPV of the project, calculated at the official discount rate over 30 years varies from −868 M€ (with the lower estimate of the subway decongestion benefits) to −806 M€ (with the higher estimate). This is especially true for suburbanites. The inhabitants of the city reap the main part of the benefits while supporting a fraction of the costs. Not only did it require a major investment but its yearly costs are greater than its yearly benefits.

However, we should also note that on, purely, financial grounds, the project is generating a one million Euro surplus per annum. This is clearly a function of the operating costs of the tram system and the revenues earned through the charges levied on users. A key question would be that of what would be the impact if significantly lower fares were levied for using the trams than is currently the case? Two impacts might be anticipated:

- The tram system might have lower fare revenues and would make a smaller operating surplus and may even have a large operating deficit. This could only be sustained through some form of public subsidy to the tram system. However, the lower fare might generate additional traffic that would compensate for the lower fare and so increase the surplus. There would then be concerns about the ability of the system to cope with the extra traffic.
- The economic aspects might change. Lower fares might encourage more car users to leave their cars at home and use the tram instead. They have a personal calculation to make here about the relative costs of car versus tram transport. However, such a shift in transport patterns may significantly alter the overall economic benefits (and hence the NPV) of the tram project.

Hence, we have a situation here where use of public funds to provide a subsidy might reap large-scale economic benefits. However, caution is needed here. Clearly some of the above estimates are more uncertain than others. Three in particular must be considered fragile: the comfort gains generated by the tramway, the subway decongestion benefits and the time lost by vehicles entering or leaving the city. The authors of the study recognised that "*In these cases, available data does not make it possible to produce very solid figures*".

Thus, the key question must be whether the use of public funds (for a subsidy) can be justified on the basis of a very "soft" economic analysis.

Management decision framework

In the previous section, we have summarised the main financial and economic techniques that can be used to undertake an appraisal of proposed capital investments. While such financial analysis is extremely important, perhaps, it is vital not to over-emphasise its importance vis-à-vis other factors which are discussed below. Indeed, it seems somewhat strange that many books with a general management accounting focus almost entirely on financial techniques to the exclusion of the other aspects of capital investment appraisal which are at least as important (and sometimes more important) than the financial aspects.

Also, in many areas of management, it is often the case that there is an over-focus on the use of techniques and a failure to consider how techniques should be used and integrated into what might be defined as a management decision framework. Such a framework would consider matters such as what projects are to be appraised, how many alternative options have been identified, how the appraisal should be conducted, who will be involved, who will make the decisions and how the results are to be used.

In relation to capital investment appraisal, the key elements of the framework can be summarised below:

- **Involvement** – who is to be involved in the appraisal exercise? Clearly, there will need to be technical experts used to working with the various financial techniques but there are others. For example, functional managers at various levels need to be involved and it may be thought appropriate to involve service users.
- **Approach** – the approach to the appraisal exercise needs to be clearly defined and the various tasks identified. The type of appraisal method to be used needs to be established and the process of interpreting and acting on the results needs to be clarified.
- **Responsibilities** – the process can be quite a complex exercise with various stages concerning options, decision criteria, information gathering, assessment etc. It is important to have a proper project plan and be clear about who is doing what. The importance of this cannot be over-emphasised.
- **Consultation** – in addition to establishing a core project team for the exercise, it is important to consult a wider audience to gain knowledge about the area of activity being considered. Thus, consultation arrangements need to be clarified.
- **Reporting** – it needs to be clear how the results of the appraisal exercise are to be presented and to whom they should be reported.
- **Decision forum** – how will the final decision on which projects to undertake be considered and agreed.

Decision guidelines

The decision framework for capital investment decisions should incorporate a number of key guidelines including:

- **Strategic investment objectives** – there should be clear investment objectives which are derived from the strategy of the public service organisation.
- **Investment options** – a common weakness of investment appraisal is that insufficient investment options have been identified and considered. Thus, the decision framework must be organised in such a way as to encourage the formulation of options. This should be a serious exercise and not just a case of putting forward the preferred option alongside a number of weaker options that have not been fully explored and therefore look weak.

- **Decision criteria** – these should be decided and the methods of evaluating them agreed *at the outset*. In this way, criteria cannot be formulated or adjusted during the course of the process to favour a particular project. A range of criteria could be applied to each investment project including:
  - Strategic relevance
  - Service outcomes
  - Financial impacts
  - Impacts on other resources (e.g. staff)
  - Availability of resources
  - Risks and uncertainties
  - Social and political issues
- **Implementability** – How easy would it be to implement a particular capital investment choice and what would be the barriers to smooth implementation (e.g. inability to recruit skilled labour). Where there are a multiplicity of projects which are all seen as having positive benefits, then the order of implementation might be influenced by these factors.

STRATEGIC COST IMPROVEMENT

Overview

The term cost improvement (or similar titles such as cost savings, efficiency improvements etc.) has been common parlance in public services for many years, and the onset of austerity provided an increased emphasis on this topic. Traditionally, much of cost improvement in public services was seen as an annual tactical issue which involved examining individual services, activities, units etc. with the aim of identifying and implementing a variety of cost improvements. Sometimes, public service organisations just apply an across the board target for cost improvement from all departments and services. The individual cost improvements identified may not have been that great but added together they constitute a significant sum which meet the organisational requirements.

This tactical approach to cost improvement is simply not effective today. Such solutions, despite consuming considerable resources in their development, have failed in many organisations to deliver the planned reductions to the cost base and have not contributed to financial sustainability in longer term. In some cases, the cost savings required just cannot be identified. In other cases, the cost savings achieved in the short term have leaked away and the cost base has returned to previous high levels but with the result of considerable damage to the organisation.

In its place, public service organisations need to look at cost improvement as a strategic issue. It is important, today, to have a structured and systematic approach to strategic cost improvement and one such approach is summarised below:

1. **Confirm** the organisation's strategy and strategic imperatives and adjust as necessary given forward-looking perspectives on sector evolution.
2. **Assess** the major cost elements across the organisation which are of strategic importance in order to understand the cost drivers, the levers for change and strategic choices. The Pareto's rule often applies in that 80% of the costs are accounted for by 20% of cost elements.

3. **Plan** a change programme that achieves significant strategic cost reductions while building a sustainable strategic cost management capability.
4. **Implement** strategic cost reductions, with focused programme management and clear accountability for results. Linked to this is a need to develop and monitor assessment criteria to review the achievement of savings identified in the initial strategic cost improvement.
5. **Sustain** the results by deploying appropriate tools and decision mechanisms to instil a cost management culture and build lasting organisational capability.

Now it is easy to say and write the above but difficult to put into practice, so further consideration is needed.

The value chain

The concept of value chain and value chain analysis (VCA) came from business management and was first described and mostly popularised by Michael Porter (Porter 1985). VCA is a process where an organisation identifies its primary and support activities that add value to its final product and then analyses each of those activities with the aim of reducing costs or increasing differentiation. All activities are divided into two value streams:

- **Primary activities** – Those related directly to the physical creation, sale, maintenance and support of a product or service.
- **Support activities** – Those supporting the primary functions and including procurement, human resource management etc.

VCA can be applied in public services but needs some amendment, and the value chain needs to be amended to fit the context of public service organisations. Heintzman and Marson (2003) suggest that the public sector value chain might look something like that shown in Figure 9.1.

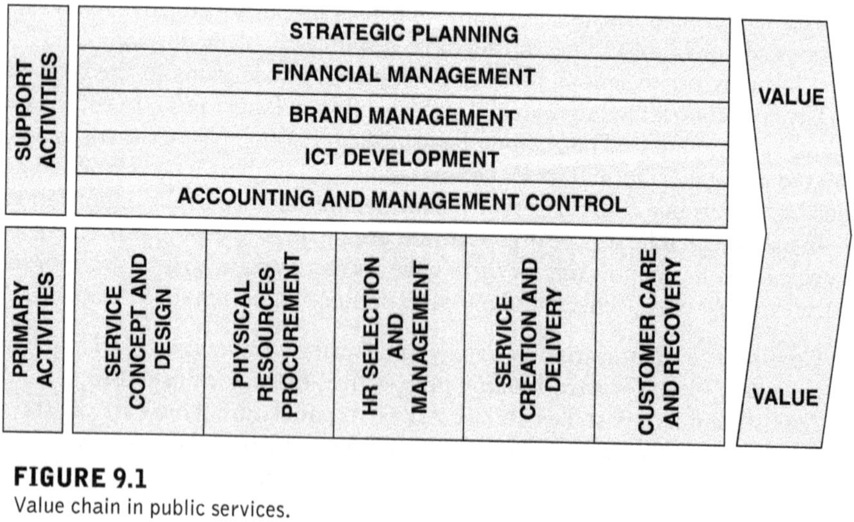

FIGURE 9.1
Value chain in public services.

Now it is not necessary to accept this value chain model for one's own organisation, but it is important to have some form of value chain model to understand the flow of value and cost in the organisation and to undertake strategic cost analysis (SCA). Hence individual public service organisations may wish to experiment with the above model and adapt for their own circumstances.

Strategic cost analysis

Strategic cost analysis (SCA) is often considered alongside the concept of VCA. SCA is basically a framework for *systematically* analysing each element of the value stream of the organisation (as shown above) as a means to focus on the following three key issues:

- What does a particular public service activity do that will *add value* for a client and what are its costs?
- Can the costs of that activity be reduced without impinging on the value received by the client?
- Can the value to the client be enhanced without impinging costs of the activity?

In relation to cost structures, SCA draws a distinction between two types of cost drivers which can be identified in the value stream. These are

- **Strategic cost drivers** – These relate to *strategic* choices the organisation has undertaken in relation to a series of factors including organisational structures, client mix, operational processes, physical layouts and locations, human resource configurations etc. Basically, greater complexity is likely to lead to a higher level of costs.
- **Executional cost drivers** – These relate to way in which the strategic choices have been implemented or executed and how well it has been done.

In the light of the above, SCA involves undertaking the following tasks:

1. Identify the appropriate value chain and assign costs and assets to it.
2. Diagnose the cost drivers of each value activity and how they interact.
3. Compare value chains and costs with that of other comparable organisations and the sources of any cost differences (see section on cost and income benchmarking above).
4. Develop a strategy to lower cost position through controlling cost drivers or reconfiguring the value chain.
5. Test the strategic cost reduction strategy for sustainability.

Making strategic cost improvements

Strategic cost improvement implies building on the findings of SCA to improve the cost base of the organisation. The emphasis here is on strategic improvements which suggest that the changes involved are likely:

- To be of significant size in terms of potential cost improvements
- To involve complex changes to many parts of the organisation
- Not to impinge on the value received by the client

The changes needed to deliver significant strategic cost improvements are likely to be complex and difficult to implement and thus require good implementation planning and change management. Furthermore, while they are likely to have significant financial implications, these sorts of changes are likely to have associated risk and need to be carefully analysed together with an adequate risk analysis. Also, these sorts of changes may have significant non-financial implications such as political implications, human resource implications, risk profiles etc. Once again, these need to be adequately assessed and considered alongside the financial implications for the simple reason that changes of this magnitude can have huge implications for the organisation.

For public service organisations some of the major strategic choices which will have implications for its cost base include the following:

- **Physical assets** – numbers, types, conditions, layouts etc. of buildings and associated equipment.
- **Service delivery arrangements** – this could include the modes of service delivery, processes, locations be they be centralised, distributed, domiciliary online etc. Also, the range of accessibility of the services in terms of days, times etc.
- **Workforce** – it has already been mentioned that public services are labour intensive and labour costs are a large component of the public sector cost base and of strategic importance. Issues here concern numbers, mix, working arrangements, terms and conditions, recruitment and retention etc.
- **Extent of outsourcing** – a possible means of achieving economies of scale and utilisation efficiency is the outsourcing of functions that can be performed by another entity more cost-effectively due to the outsourcer's scale economies and utilisation efficiencies.
- **Consumables and services** – a variety of changes can be made to the supply chain of the public service organisations in order to generate strategic cost improvements and other benefits. Some examples of these include rationalisation of the number of supply lines, strategic purchasing partnerships etc.

In Chapter 1, we discussed the idea of organisational inertia which is often prevalent in many public service organisations. Such inertia often favours the continuation of well-established and what are seen as tried and tested methods of working. On the other hand, SCA and improvement is doing the opposite of looking at new ways of doing things, at lower cost, and there is often resistance to doing this. Once again, the management accountant needs to be aware of this phenomenon and the ways of overcoming it through change management approaches.

PROGRAMME/CLIENT GROUP ANALYSIS AND BUDGETING

If we think about a public service, the organisation involved in delivering the service comprises a number of departments and units which hold financial budgets for the services they are responsible for and the objectives they seek

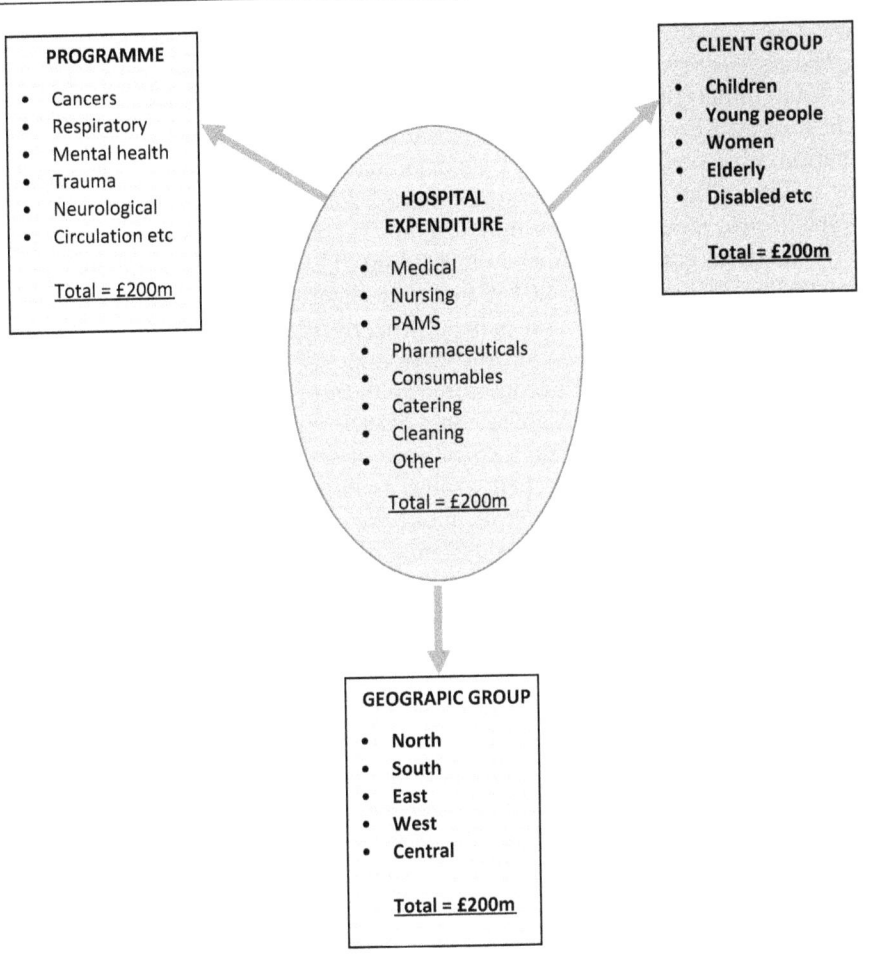

FIGURE 9.2
Programme/client group analysis.

to achieve. However, the other dimension of these departments and budgets concerns the expenditure programmes and client groups in society who use the services.

An example of this is illustrated in Figure 9.2 using a hospital as an example.

Programme analysis would involve disaggregating the expenditure of the organisational departments and units over the various health programmes shown and also assigning that expenditure to one or more of the identified client/geographic groups. In this way the total expenditure of the hospital would be re-classified by programme and client group. Alongside the costs associated with each programme or client group, there would also be:

- The needs of the community being served and the role of the programme
- The goals and objectives of the programme
- The nature of the client groups
- The outputs of the programme

Now a word of caution is needed here. Conceptually this programme and client analysis is easy to define but much more difficult to do in practice. The data needed to undertake the analysis may not be available or difficult to access in the right format. Resort will have to be made to a variety of methods involving estimation, statistical analysis and even data analytics as described in Chapter 13. The results of the analysis need to be treated with caution and in some cases a complete programme analysis may just not be possible. However, the results of the analysis can make interesting reading. The Welsh Government (2019) analysed health spending in 2017/2018 over client groups and found the three largest areas of expenditure on patients with mental health problems (11.4%), circulation problems (7.4%) and cancers/tumours (7.1%).

As well as undertaking a programme analysis of expenditure for one organisation (a hospital) such an exercise could also be undertaken on a multi-agency basis as shown. In this case the expenditure of several agencies and services is disaggregated over a series of client groups as shown in Figure 9.3.

However, in spite of the caveats about the robustness of the analysis, programme and client group analysis can provide a useful strategic tool. Patterns of programme and client group expenditure could be compared over time periods, and/or with other organisations or multi-agency partnerships, to see what significant differences might exist and whether they are justifiable. This can provide a basis for developing future strategies.

Whereas programme analysis is a "relatively" easy (albeit time-consuming) task of analysis, programme budgeting has far more intractable problems. Whereas programme analysis is limited to the production of information about programmes and client groups, there is no change in the budgeting process and the authority to incur expenditure. Under a true programme budgeting system,

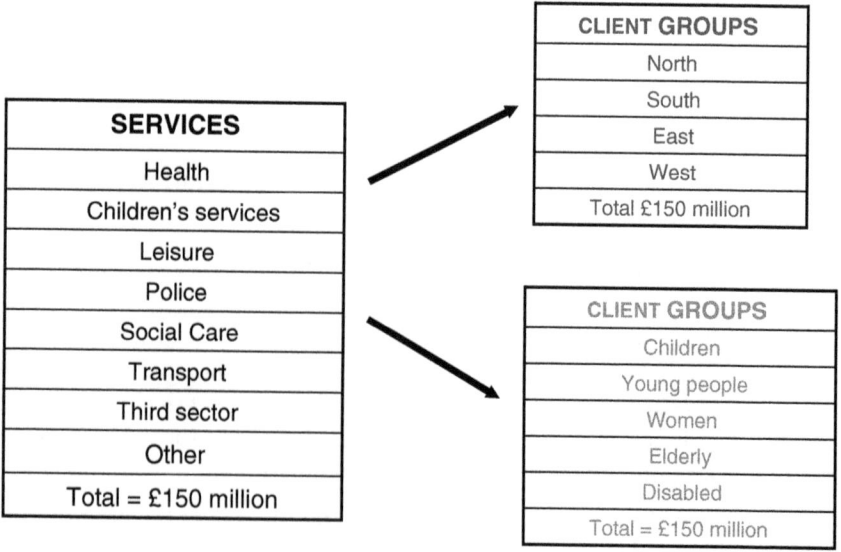

FIGURE 9.3
Client group analysis in multi-agency working.

the responsibility for incurring expenditure (and the subsequent accountability) would shift from the service or departmental managers to a series of programme and client group managers who would hold the overall budget for services to the programme or client group. They would then commission (and pay for) services from departments based on the overall needs of the programme and client group users. Similarly in the multi-agency example, the budgetary power would shift from the individual agencies in the partnership to a series of client group managers who would commission (and pay for) services from the various agencies in the partnership again based on the overall needs of the client group.

Programme budgeting is not a new idea. It had great popularity in the 1960s and 1970s in the US Federal Government and in a number of public and local authorities in the United Kingdom (Kluvers 2001). In spite of its great attractiveness as a rational means of allocating resources according to the needs of client groups, it must largely be judged as a failure and by the mid-1970s most of the euphoria about programme budgeting had disappeared, at least in the United Kingdom. Clearly many of the earlier problems associated with programme budgeting concerned the complexity of the associated administrative and data handling procedures and the IT revolution and the existence of high-speed and accessible computing power have simplified the approach. However, the main obstacles are largely political (small p) and cultural. Traditional service managers in public services are often very powerful and jealously protect the power that comes with responsibility for resources from (what they would see as) interference of a group of programme and client group managers with different ideas about how funds should be spent. Furthermore, the spending power of these programme and client group managers would be spread across a number of different service units and it would probably be difficult for one programme manager working in isolation to affect the sorts of changes in service delivery that would be required by their client group. The past experience of programme budgeting suggests that it is difficult to break into the "silo" mentality that often pervades service departments.

In recent years the emphasis on public sector partnerships, service commissioning and joined up government has led to renewed interest in programme/client group analysis and budgeting. These approaches would seem to lend themselves to the philosophy underlying partnerships working with the emphasis on multi-agency delivery of services to identified client groups. However, as already noted, although modern IT can simplify much of the earlier complications of programme analysis and budgeting (e.g. programme costing), the political and cultural problems still exist. It is quite probable that considerable efforts will be put into the programme analysis of partnership activities, but it remains to be seen whether sustainable and effective forms of programme budgeting can realistically be achieved. Only time will tell.

STRATEGIC OPTIONS EVALUATION

One of the criticisms often levelled against public service strategies are that too few options are considered and developed during the preparation of the strategy. Thus, in preparing strategic plans, public service organisations should develop a number of different strategic options or pathways.

The next stage is to evaluate those options and this process must concern both strategic feasibility and resource feasibility, particularly financial feasibility. Hence the organisation should undertake an evaluation of the financial implications of the various strategic options which have been identified over a period of years. Just some examples of the sorts of options which might be developed and evaluated include

- **Commissioners** – Options concerning different commissioning strategies in perhaps involving a stronger role for new service providers.
- **Providers** – Options concerning:
  - Reconfiguration of the range and/or volume of service provision
  - Rationalisation or amendment of methods and/or locations of delivering services
  - Rationalisation and reconfiguration of physical estates facilities etc.
  - Combinations of the above and others
- **Partnerships**
  - New partners
  - Change in focus of service mix
  - Changed distribution of service responsibilities

None of these changes can be achieved in one year and thus there must be a multi-year strategy.

One issue often discussed is the time period for preparing such plans – should it be three years, five years, ten years etc. Too often, organisations slavishly follow the requirements or guidelines of their own funding body without considering their specific circumstances. While organisations will need to meet, as a minimum, the requirements of their funding bodies, there is nothing to stop them preparing forecasts for longer periods should they deem this necessary. Again, in all of these situations it would be beneficial if organisations could develop a financial planning model (or models) to assist with this.

STRATEGIC FINANCIAL FORECASTING

Financial forecasting is an important tool for appraising public sector strategies and an effective financial forecast allows for improved strategic decision making. However, the forecast should not stand alone. The future is uncertain and so future financial forecasts will also be uncertain. The underlying assumptions and methodology behind the forecasts should be clearly stated and made available to stakeholders so that they can judge what the forecasts are actually saying. Also, the forecast should be regularly monitored and periodically updated in the light of changing circumstances.

Forecasting is not just about spreadsheets and statistical methods. A forecasting project requires a framework which is illustrated in Figure 9.4.

Forecasting process

In undertaking financial forecasting in public services, there are a wide range of different techniques which can be utilised. But these techniques should not

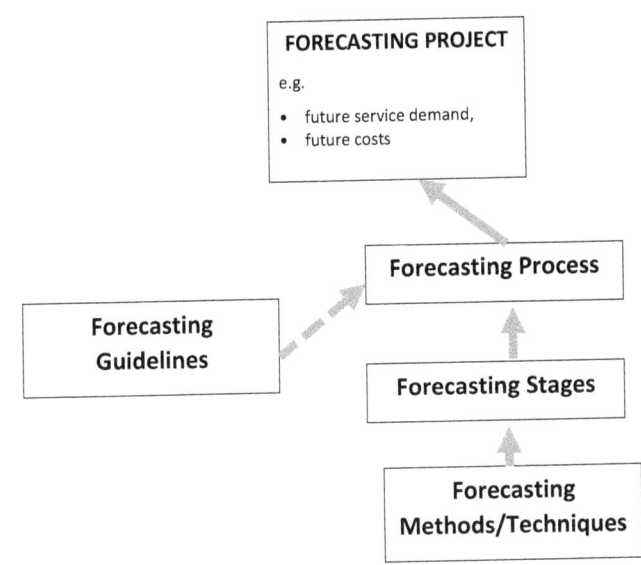

FIGURE 9.4
Structure of a forecasting project.

be considered in isolation but must be integrated into a formal management process which considers matters such as what forecasts are to be made, how they are to be made, who will be involved and how the results are to be used. In relation to forecasting, the key elements of a forecasting process can be summarised below:

- **Involvement** – who is to be involved in the forecasting exercise? Clearly there will need to be technical experts used to working with the various forecasting techniques but there are others.
- **Approach** – the approach to the forecasting exercise needs to be clearly defined and the various tasks identified. The type of forecasting methods to be used need to be established and the process of interpreting and acting on the results needs to be clarified.
- **Responsibilities** – the forecasting process can be quite a complex exercise with various stages concerning design, data collection, interpretation etc. It is important to have a proper project plan and be clear about who is doing what. The importance of this cannot be over-emphasised.
- **Consultation** – as well as establishing a core project team for the exercise, it is important to consult a wider audience to gain knowledge about the area of activity being considered. Thus, consultation arrangements need to be clarified.
- **Reporting** – it needs to be clear how the results of the forecasting exercise are to be presented and to whom they should be reported. Also, the structure of the report on the exercise should be considered.

Forecasting guidelines

There are nine overarching principles (Armstrong et al. 2010) that can help to improve forecasting accuracy and the relevance of the forecasts to the tasks in hand.

1. **Match the forecasting method to the situation** – conditions for forecasting vary. No single best method works for all situations. Consider the methods available and select the most appropriate based on evidence available. Interestingly, generalisations based on empirical evidence sometimes conflict with common beliefs about which forecasting method is best.

2. **Use existing domain knowledge** – managers and analysts typically have useful knowledge about situations. While this domain knowledge can be important for forecasting, it is often ignored. Managers' expectations are particularly important when their knowledge about the direction of the trend in a time series conflicts with historical trends in the data. If one ignores existing domain knowledge about contrary series, large errors are likely.

3. **Structure the problem** – one of the basic strategies in management research is to break a problem into manageable pieces, solve each piece, then put them back together. This decomposition strategy is effective for forecasting, especially when there is more knowledge about the pieces than about the whole. Decomposition is particularly useful when the forecasting task involves extreme (very large or very small) numbers. When the components of the series can be forecasted more accurately than the global series, using causal forces to decompose the problem increases forecasting accuracy.

4. **Model the experts' forecasts** – expert systems represent forecasts made by experts and can reduce the costs of repetitive forecasts while improving accuracy. However, expert systems are expensive to develop. An inexpensive alternative to expert systems is termed judgmental bootstrapping. It translates an experts' rules into a quantitative model by regressing the experts' forecasts against the information that was used. Bootstrapping models apply an experts' rules consistently, and studies have shown that decisions and predictions from bootstrapping models are similar to those from the experts.

5. **Represent the problem realistically** – this has been discussed earlier. It is common practice to start with an existing model and attempt to generalise to the situation. Instead, one should start with the situation and develop a realistic representation in the model. Realistic representations are especially important when forecasts based on unaided judgment fail.

6. **Use causal models when you have good information** – an important advantage of causal models is that they reveal the effects of alternative decisions on the outcome. However, this means that the forecaster must understand the factors that have an influence on the variable to forecast and possesses enough data to estimate a regression model. To satisfy the first condition, the analyst can obtain knowledge about the situation from domain knowledge and from prior research.

7. **Use simple quantitative methods** – there is a danger of automatically preferring complexity over simplicity. Complex models are often misled by noise in the data, especially in uncertain situations. Thus, using simple methods is important when there is much uncertainty about the situation.

8. **Be conservative when uncertain** – one should make conservative forecasts for uncertain situations. If historical trends are subject to variations, discontinuities and reversals, one should be cautious with extrapolating the historical trend. Only when historical time series show a long steady trend with little variation, should one extrapolate the trend into the future.

9. **Combine forecasts** – combining is especially effective when different forecasting methods are available. One could use as many as five different methods, and combine their forecasts using a predetermined mechanical rule. Lacking strong evidence that some methods are more accurate than others, one could use a simple average of forecasts.

Stages in forecasting

Forecasting can also be considered as a number of fairly discrete and sequential stages as shown below:

1. **Determine the purpose** – this is fundamental to the exercise and involves deciding what the purpose of the forecasting exercise is and what we are trying to find out.

2. **Establish time line** – the amount of time available to undertake the forecasting exercise will be limited, but it is likely that a longer time horizon will provide for more detailed and sophisticated forecasting to be undertaken. Thus, at the outset of the exercise it is important to establish a time line.

3. **Identify items to forecast** – a forecasting exercise can involve forecasting a wide range of items (e.g. income, costs, client numbers, demand etc.). Consequently, it is vital to identify the precise items which need to be forecasted, over what period, to what level of disaggregation etc.

4. **Select relevant forecasting methods** – at this stage it will be necessary to select the relevant forecasting methods to be used whether they be qualitative and/or quantitative methods. This is discussed in more detail below.

5. **Gather data** – the forecasting exercise should be based on the purpose identified and not the data that are easily available. Thus, once the purpose has been clarified and the relevant forecasting method agreed, it is necessary to undertake data collection exercises. Some data may be already available or easily accessed, while other data might require a specific data collection exercise. If some data are impossible to obtain within the required timescales, then an estimate should be made but the results of the forecasting exercise will now subject to some form of sensitivity analysis around these estimated variables.

6. **Make forecasts** – in this stage the forecasting methods and the data will be combined to make the required forecasts. It will usually be appropriate to also undertake some form of sensitivity analysis to consider the likely impact of uncertainty around certain input variables.

7. **Validate forecasts** – once the forecasts have been prepared, it is important to try and understand how much reliance can be placed on their accuracy. To achieve this, forecasters try to validate their forecasts.

8. **Decision making regarding results** – it is therefore important that the results of the forecasting exercise are reviewed and some decisions taken even if that decision is to do nothing in the short or longer term.

Forecasting approaches and techniques

Forecasting techniques can be of two broad types:

- **Quantitative forecasting methods** – these are statistical techniques designed to make predictions about the future, which use numerical measures and prior effects to predict future events. These techniques are based on models of mathematics and in nature are mostly objective. They are highly dependent on mathematical calculations. There are two types of quantitative forecasting methods which are listed below:
    - **Time-series models** – these models examine the past data patterns and forecast the future on the basis of underlying patterns that are obtained from those data. There are many types of time-series models like simple and weighted moving average, seasonal indexes, trend projections, simple mean and exponential smoothing.
    - **Associative models** – these are also known as casual models. The model assumes that the variable that is being forecast is associated with other variables. The predictions are made based on these associations. Linear regression is one of the simplest forms of an associative model of forecasting. This regression line forecasts the dependent variable based on the selected value of the independent variable.

    Quantitative forecasting methods are used to make predictions very easily based on the underlying information. The data can be used to forecast automatically without many complications. Any person can easily forecast on the basis of available data. One of the main disadvantages of this method is its dependence on the data. The entire forecasting depends on the data of the underlying model. An error in the available data can lead to wrong forecasting. These methods can also be used only if the proper data are available. This method cannot evaluate the effect of changes in the other variables involved.

- **Qualitative forecasting methods** – these are techniques used to make predictions about the future which rely on the subjective opinion and judgment of consumers, experts etc. when past data are not available or are insufficient. Examples of qualitative techniques include
    - Structured interviews
    - Executive surveys
    - Scenario building
    - Delphi exercises
    - Guided discussions

    Sometimes qualitative approaches are ignored in forecasting because they are seen as being subjective in nature. However, commonly held subjective opinions, about a particular issue, from several different persons suggest a degree of objectivity. Also, when using quantitative data, one must also be cautious about elements of subjectivity that have crept into the data collection process.

Both quantitative and qualitative approaches have a role to play.

Further detailed information about forecasting in public services can be found in the CIPFA publication "A Guide to Forecasting Methods in Public Services".

DECISION SUPPORT MODELS AND STRATEGIC FINANCIAL FORECASTING

Decision support models (DSM) can be of great use when undertaking forecasting for a number of reasons. First, speed – they can undertake the necessary calculations to make a forecast very quickly, when to do it manually might take a long period of time. Also, they can undertake mathematical tasks which might prove impossible for all practical purposes. Thus, the use of such models can enable the public service organisation to look at a much wider range of scenarios, in a lot more detail, than they might otherwise have been able to do.

There are many different types of DSM and they can be classified in several ways. A possible classification of some types of model is as shown below.

* Dynamic simulation models
* Systems dynamics models
* Optimisation models
* Heuristic models
* Multiple regression analysis models
* Financial models
* Strategic resource planning models

Also, it should be noted that the issues of data analytics, artificial intelligence and machine learning are discussed in Chapter 13.

Strategic resource planning models

Of particular note in this chapter is the potential use of strategic resource planning models. Such models can be developed to forecast the impact on the organisation's resource inputs (e.g. staffing, space, consumables, finance etc.) of changes in service levels, service mix and other base level assumptions which have been derived from a variety of different strategic scenarios. Such models can be fairly simple or more complex dependent on the time and cost being devoted to such a development. For example, a university could develop and use such a model designed to assess the impact on buildings space, staffing and finance, of changes in the numbers and mix of students attending the university as well as the different modes of teaching. In this way, the university can see, quickly, the impacts of different development scenarios being considered. Similarly, in healthcare services, a model could be designed and used to evaluate the impact on beds, staffing and finance of strategic options concerned with the transfer of patients from institutional to community care or some other form of major service re configuration.

Stages in DSM development

Decision support modelling should not be regarded as just the task of acquiring some form of IT hardware, software or consultancy. In reality, DSM has no more to do with IT than (say) word processing in that both use software packages as tools. If one is to make maximum use of DSM in forecasting, one must have a clearly thought-out plan involving a series of sequential stages. Decision support modelling can be considered as involving the following main stages.

- **Problem formulation and clarification** – the key issue at the outset is to formulate and clarify what is the problem or issue to be addressed through DSM. In relation to forecasting this can mean such things as: what variables are to be forecast, over what time periods, with what degree of disaggregation, with what degree of accuracy etc. It is important that these matters are agreed before any model development takes place.
- **Modelling design and capacity** – once the issue has been formulated and clarified and it is agreed that some form of modelling may assist with the tasks, then consideration may be given to what sort of modelling is appropriate and how the organisation is going to obtain the necessary modelling capacity to do the job.
- **Data collection** – relevant data must be obtained in order to populate the model. Some data may already be easily available or obtainable with a small amount of effort. However, to undertake a modelling exercise some form of data collection exercise may also need to be initiated to obtain critical data. This could, for example, be some sort of survey. However, the important point to note is that the task of data collection follows the task of problem formulation and clarification. The data are collected to deal with the issue identified and not the easily available data are used as far as possible. Too often modelling is initiated on the basis of what data are currently available and not what issue needs to be addressed.
- **Review and audit** – given that critically important decisions about public services may be made on the basis of forecasting data produced, it is important that the modelling undertaken is robust. Thus, before the model is used "live", it is important that a technical audit of the construction of the model in terms of formulas, links etc. is undertaken by a suitably skilled person and appropriate checks are undertaken. It is not uncommon in public services to see decisions made using spreadsheet models which have not been accurately developed by suitably skilled persons. Also, it is quite possible that the statutory auditors of a public sector organisation may wish to examine the DSM on which managerial decisions have been made.
- **Model calibration and validation** – if possible, some attempt should be made to validate the predictive accuracy of the model by comparing actual changes with those predicted by the model.

Key features of a DSM

In summary, whatever modelling approach is used for forecasting, there are some key features which should be borne in mind at all times:

- The model must be "fit for purpose" in that it delivers the output required. This may fail to happen if the model is data-driven rather than problem-driven.
- The model must provide a realistic representation of the "real world" and must reflect the "business" of the organisation. This does mean that the model should not be over-simplistic, although clearly one does not wish to introduce complexity for its own sake. To achieve this, the modeller will need a good understanding of the "business" of the organisation.
- The model must be technically robust in terms of instructions, calculations etc. This is not always the case.
- The model must be developed on the most appropriate application package.
- Model construction must be in accordance with certain set of procedures designed to facilitate good practice.
- The model must be capable of being audited and validated by a third party.
- The model must be reasonably user-friendly.
- Good model documentation must be available.

PRICING STRATEGIES IN PUBLIC SERVICES

As discussed in Chapter 1, the vast bulk of public services are financed through the proceeds of taxation and therefore are free to users at the time of receipt. Consequently, charges for public services represent a small proportion of public service funding. However, in saying this, two points need to be noted:

- The pattern of charges will vary greatly between countries, and sectors.
- Some charges for public services are designed to cover the full cost of the service provided, but the majority of charges are only intended to cover part of the costs.

The reality is that for many public services, the public body involved has no discretion over the charge since the charge is already set nationally by the relevant government department. In these cases, there is no real decision to be made and no pricing strategy is needed.

Beyond that, where there is local discretion on pricing, there are four main factors to consider when developing a pricing strategy. These are discussed next.

Conflicting objectives

In the commercial world, a company may set prices for its products or services on the basis of what price will maximise revenues and/or market share taking account of the interplay between price and demand. It is not the same in public services. Where public authorities have discretion about charging, they have to recognise that the charge levied will impact on two factors:

- The revenues raised from the charge levied,
- The level of demand for the public services provided on which the charge is being levied.

There is usually a trade-off to be made here. A higher price might raise more revenues but may also curtail the demand for public services which may be socially undesirable. Take, for example charges levied for the prescription of medications to patients. The levying of a charge will raise more revenue but may also deter some people from obtaining medication prescribed for them by a doctor with possible health consequence and future health costs. Equally, charges for public sports centres will raise revenues but, if set too high, may deter people from taking exercise or practising sports with consequent impacts on health status or levels of youth crime. Hence, for most public services, public authorities will be concerned to ensure that the level of charges does not markedly reduce service demand with damaging consequences for the individual and society.

However, charges for public services can also be used with the primary purpose of reducing demand for public services. Examples here concern possible charges for refuse collection and charges for the use of roads. In these cases, the primary aims are to reduce refuse collection volumes (by encouraging greater recycling) in the light of climate change or reducing road use and congestion (by people making greater use of public transport). In these situations, the revenue generation is portrayed as being a secondary objective although some evidence suggests that charge payers just do not believe this and see the charge as a means of getting more money.

Competition

For many public services where charges are levied there is no alternative supplier and the public body involved is essentially a monopolist or monopsonist. Take for example, fees for social care, local college fees or fees to access the National Archives where there is no alternative provider.

However, for other public services the public body may face competition from other public bodies and/or from the private sector. Take for example, public leisure services which may be competing against several private leisure companies in the same area. Alternatively, school lunches where students may be able to get lunch from external providers or take a packed lunch. It goes without saying that in these situations, the public body has to take cognisance of the fees being charged by alternative providers.

Administration

With any system of charging for public services, there has to be some level of administration concerning recording of the service received, billing, income collection follow-up etc. Clearly the costs of administration detract from the levels of revenue to be raised from the charge. In broad terms, it is probably true to say that the level (and cost) of administration will be influenced by a number of factors including the complexity of the charging system and the means of collecting the income. Thus, while some complex charging systems might be good at ensuring that vulnerable people are not adversely affected, the systems can have high levels of administrative cost associated with them.

Cost

In developing a pricing strategy for a public service, the costs associated with that service will be a relevant input. In particular, there is an issue about whether the charge should cover the total cost of the service or only part of it. If the charge only covers part of the cost then, by definition, the service is being financed or subsidised from some other source. Hence, there is an opportunity cost involved. Clearly the charge to be set will need to be considered alongside the other three issues already mentioned, since there are clear trade-offs between them. The ways in which costs might be identified, for pricing purposes, are discussed in a later section.

At this point it is important to distinguish between pricing strategies and pricing tactics. When one goes into a supermarket to buy something, the price of the product is indicated. There is no negotiation about this price and the only choice is to buy or not buy the product from this shop. On the other hand, if one is purchasing a car or having building work done on the house, there is considerable scope for negotiation of the price with the supplier of the goods or services in question. From the point of view of the supplier of services, these sorts of negotiations concern tactical pricing issues concerned with a specific pricing decision. That tactical decision may be influenced by short-term pressures like current workloads, state of the market etc.

Pricing strategies are concerned with longer-term aspects of pricing taking account of the four factors discussed above. It should be the case that tactical pricing decisions will recognise the pricing strategy in which they are contained, but the danger is that too often specific factors are allowed to distract from the strategy to the extent that strategic considerations no longer apply. The classic example of this is the argument that a particular bid should be submitted on a loss-leader basis, since it might then generate future work and income streams. In this case the old adage "loss-leaders lead to losses" should be borne in mind. Thus, it is important, when making pricing decisions, to strike a reasonable and realistic balance between strategic considerations and specific factors.

For the vast majority of public services where charges are levied, there is likely to be little or no price negotiation. The service user must pay the stated amount or not receive the service. This price might be set by statute or by local decisions made by the public service organisation. However, there will be situations where tactical issues are important in public services. A common example is argument, referred to above, that a particular bid should be submitted on a loss-leader basis, since it might then generate future work and income streams. Such claims should be treated with caution.

Cost inputs into pricing decisions

The costs of delivering public services are clearly an important input into pricing decisions, but the key issue is "which costs". There are basically three broad approaches to costing which should be considered in relation to pricing decisions. These were discussed in Chapter 8 on operational aspects of pricing but are summarised, briefly, here.

- **Total cost pricing** – a general rule when making pricing decisions is that price should be set by reference to the total costs of the service being considered which can be regarded as being the sum of direct costs and indirect costs. The price might be set at above, equal to or below the total cost.
- **Contribution-based pricing** – this approach then involves optimising the price–volume relationship in order to obtain maximum revenues and profits for the company. For the reasons discussed earlier it seems unlikely that public service organisations will use this approach very often but there may be cases where it is relevant.
- **Marginal cost pricing** – this involves setting a price by reference to the marginal costs of the activity of service being undertaken and priced.

Special factors related to pricing in public service organisations

Beyond the factors described above, there are likely to be a number of other sector-specific factors which may impinge on pricing strategy decisions in public service organisations. Some examples of these are discussed below:

- **Avoidance of unfair competition** – public service organisations particularly need to avoid any charges of unfair competition either, through accusations of forming cartels with one another in breach of the anti-competition legislation or by making unfair pricing decisions. These issues might result in the public service organisation being accused, by commercial organisations, of unfair competition through the use of their public subsidy to charge lower prices.
- **Accountability for the use of public funds** – chief executives of public service organisations are accountable for the financial health of their organisation and for their use of public funds. In making pricing decisions, public service organisations need to ensure that they are not planning to use public funds to subsidise the delivery of private services and also that there is minimum risk to public funds should some problem arise in relation to the activities involved. Before embarking on a particular venture, public service organisations need to conduct a thorough risk analysis and identify both means of minimising any related risks and of dealing with unforeseen events should they occur.
- **Equity of access** – the pricing of particular services may affect the degree of access available for different individuals or organisations. A price which is too high may inhibit access for certain individuals and organisations, for example, particular groups of individuals such as the unwaged or particular types of organisations such as charities may be inhibited from accessing the services due to the price. These considerations may be of little relevance to a commercial organisation but to a public service organisation these are relevant as it receives large amounts of public funds and has a high degree of public and political accountability. Any concerns in this area may lead to substantial public disquiet and bad publicity for the public service organisation involved.

CASE STUDY 9.2

Pricing and unfair competition in public services

A public hospital occupies a large city centre site and manages a major laundry facility located on this site. As well as providing laundry services for itself, the hospital also provides services to other local public hospitals. In spite of this, the laundry found itself with slack operational capacity probably because of a major shift to disposable items. Hence, it decided to offer laundry services to local private sector organisations at a very competitive price.

This move had serious implications for local laundry service companies who immediately complained to their national trade organisation. This organisation took up the matter with a health minister who ordered an enquiry into whether the hospital laundry was providing unfair competition to local private laundry providers.

An independent review of its pricing arrangements established that the prices charged by the hospital laundry covered the marginal costs of providing additional laundry services as well as making a reasonable contribution to its fixed overheads. Thus, the charge of unfair pricing was not deemed to be substantiated.

STRATEGIC FINANCIAL LEADERSHIP

Management accountants need to display strategic financial leadership in public services. Putting it another way, this means taking the lead regarding the financial aspects of public service strategies. If management accountants do not take on this role, it is not clear who will.

Research done a few years ago (Prowle et al. 2013) suggested that although the basic operational functions of finance were being provided satisfactorily, in many public service organisations, the strategic role for finance was limited and was in danger of being further reduced because of the need for sort-term efficiency savings. In some cases, removing a layer of management as part of a cost-saving programme meant that the most senior financial post was now an operational and not a strategic role, with a consequent gap in representation at the most senior level of management. Furthermore, strategic working at the multi-agency level is also generally seen as an important issue for service provision and public value. In practice, however, it is often seen as "too difficult" and senior managers, including finance managers, are often unable to devote sufficient time to it because of other pressures.

There are four distinct ways that management accountants in public services can orient themselves:

- **Responder** – in this role, the management accountant can support the organisation's strategy development by helping decision-makers to quantitatively analyse the financial implications of different strategy choices. To be an effective responder, the management accountant should ensure there is a central financial planning and analysis capability that delivers the relevant analyses and data to the organisation whose leaders have primary responsibility for generating strategy alternatives.

- **Challenger** – as a challenger, the management accountant should examine the strategy process and the strategic options by critically examining the outcomes and risks associated with each strategic alternative. Where there are concerns, the management accountant should be prepared to challenge what is being proposed and work to look for solutions. This goes beyond narrow financial issues and the management accountant should be prepared to challenge any aspects of the proposed strategy where there are concerns about its outcome which may well have financial implications.
- **Creator** – in this orientation, the management accountant works jointly with others to work in shaping strategic choices and applying financial strategies to complement and maximise the value of particular strategies. This goes beyond the challenger orientation to enable the financing of innovative initiatives through varied finance strategies and finance arrangements with suppliers, customers or delivery channels. To effectively deliver the creator orientation, the management accountant needs to establish mutual trust and working relationships with others at the outset of setting the strategy process.
- **Transformer** – as a transformer, the management accountant becomes involved in shaping and executing future strategy. Management accountants as transformers proactively engage in addressing core questions in a strategy process, and then develop and execute options through finance in a way that allows the organisation to shift its strategy effectively.

Now some reading the above may find these roles daunting and falling outside the traditional roles of the management accountant. However, the finance function in public authorities is itself financed from public funds and is therefore subject to the same austerity pressures as all other public services – hence it, too, must demonstrate what value it is adding to the provision of public services. Hence it is important the management accountants in public services display strategic financial leadership. This is especially important given the growing use of accounting technologies (see Chapter 13) which will take over some of the traditional functions of the management accountant.

Management accounting and management control in public services

INTRODUCTION

This chapter discusses the topic of management control in public service organisations from both a strategic and an operational standpoint. It then considers the roles of management accounting in this area. The chapter is structured as follows:

- Key management tasks
- Nature and purpose of management control
- Operational/tactical management control
- Cash and working capital control and management
- Budgeting systems and budgetary control in public service management
- Strategic management control

KEY MANAGEMENT TASKS

Recapping from an earlier chapter, management in any public service organisation involves achieving a complex set of objectives both strategic and tactical/operational. As such they will have a wide variety of objectives to achieve but it is possible to distil this multiplicity of objectives down to three main groups which are illustrated in Figure 10.1.

1. **Services** – the organisation must deliver public services of the right quantity and right quality which can be defined as the right standards at the right times and in the right places. In cases where there is a commissioner–provider split, the objectives will be largely determined by the contract. In other cases, they will be influenced strongly by regulatory bodies, professional standards, client views etc.

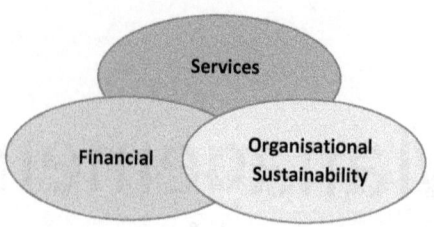

FIGURE 10.1
Key management tasks.

2. **Financial** – all public service organisations will have some sort of financial objectives, either internally generated or externally imposed. These objectives may be complex or simple but will usually involve keeping expenditure within income and possibly generating a financial rate of return. This is a complex area since decisions about financial objectives may clash with service objectives and may also have implications for sustainability which are discussed below.

3. **Organisational sustainability** – the reality is that many, if not most, public service organisations are not sustainable, in the longer term, in their current form (e.g. social care, healthcare). Thus, there must be a process of strategic change taking place in the organisation to achieve long-term sustainability.

Tasks 1 and 2 basically concern tactical/operational objectives to be achieved. These might be seen as "relatively" straightforward to achieve, although there are many examples of public service organisations which have succeeded at one objective but failed on the other and vice versa. There are examples of organisations who have succeeded with objective 1 but failed on objective 2. They have taken remedial action only to find the situation completely reversed the following year. However, objective 3 is a major strategic issue which will have to be addressed over a period of years. Thus, the management task involves progressing the strategic change over several years while at the same time successfully delivering services and achieving financial objectives each year as far as possible. This is a challenging agenda which requires effective management control.

NATURE AND PURPOSE OF MANAGEMENT CONTROL

A control system can be defined as a device which manages, commands, directs or regulates the behaviour of other devices or systems. In the most common form, the feedback control system, it exists to control a process such that its output follows a control standard, which may be a fixed or changing value. The control system compares the output of the process to the control standard, and applies the difference as an error signal and initiates action to bring the output closer to the control standard.

There are a variety of different types of control systems but one that often comes to mind is the linear feedback system which incorporates a control loop, comprising sensors, control algorithms and actuators, arranged in such a fashion as to try to regulate a variable at a set point or reference value. An example of this in the physical world is a thermostat designed to control the room temperature. When the temperature, measured by a thermometer within the system, drops below the set temperature, the thermostat triggers the heating system to raise the temperature back to the standard set, at which point it switches off the heating system. Equally, if the temperature rises above the set limit, then the heating system is turned off or the air conditioning might be switched on.

Management control systems are basically an application of control systems theory to the management of an organisation. A management control system is a system which gathers and uses information to evaluate the performance of different organisational resources and activities. Basically, it involves a structured and systematic approach comprising:

- The setting of standards for the organisation consistent with planning objectives;
- The design of appropriate information feedback systems which report what actually happened compared with planned, in order to determine whether there are deviations of any significance from planned performance;
- The taking of any actions required to ensure that all resources are being used in the most effective and efficient way possible, in achieving corporate objectives.

Some commentators also emphasise a behavioural element which, in defining management control, refers to the way in which an organisation influences its sub-units and members to behave in ways that lead to the attainment of organisational objectives. However, some public service organisations are described as "complex adaptive systems". These are defined as organisational systems in which a perfect understanding of the individual parts does not automatically convey a perfect understanding of the whole system's behaviour. Thus, it is only possible to influence situations and not necessarily control them mainly due to people and unpredictability of their behaviour. Therefore, the importance of adaptable leadership, a well-communicated inspirational vision and alignment of individual, team, sub-unit and organisational objectives is increased. These are difficult to capture in control algorithms but need to be important considerations.

It was noted earlier that the origins of management accounting lie in the emergence of improved costing methods in the early 20th century. Shortly after this, in the 1930s another central plank of traditional management accounting emerged and began to be widely adopted, namely budgetary planning and control. Thus, management accounting has always had an important control function role in most organisations of any size. However, management control also has a strategic dimension as well as an operational dimension. These issues will be discussed in turn.

OPERATIONAL/TACTICAL MANAGEMENT CONTROL

The reality is that private and public sector organisations will have a wide range of operational/tactical control systems covering different activities including

- Service production controls
- Quality controls
- Human resource controls
- Fixed asset controls
- Information and IT controls
- Financial controls etc.

In this section we will consider two financial aspects of control in a little more detail, namely cash and working capital control and budgetary control.

CASH AND WORKING CAPITAL CONTROL AND MANAGEMENT

In the commercial sector, cash is the lifeblood of a business and it is vital that a business generates enough cash to meet its liabilities as they fall due. The worst thing that can happen to a business is that it runs out of cash due to failure to plan and control cash flows adequately. Such an event will have a much greater and quicker impact than failing to make a profit in a particular year, although, clearly, a continuation of such losses will itself ultimately impact on the company's cash flow and its sustainability. Also, such an event reflects badly on the financial competence of management and a bank manager would be unlikely to be sympathetic in providing overdraft facilities to such a business.

In order to manage its cash flow, a business must also control the other elements of working capital which determine the timing and amount of cash received and paid out. Working capital is defined as current assets (principally inventory, debtors and cash) minus current liabilities (principally creditors and any short-term loans).

In the public sector, the management of cash and working capital is perhaps not as important because:

- public services have relatively low volumes of stocks of goods and, as service organisations, nil volumes of work in progress and finished goods since such items are not relevant;
- public services, in general, obtain the vast bulk of their funding from the national or sub-national government and so have a fairly definitive idea of when they will receive funding during the year. This contrasts with the private sector where there is always some uncertainty about sales income. This certainty about income makes the management of cash flows and working capital easier in public services. However, there are some public service organisations which are not so government reliant and rely on the generation and receipt of income in return for services. In this situation, the management of cash flows and working capital is very important. This

could be the case, for example, in universities where reliance on government might be lower and thus there are a variety of cash flows such as student fees.

At the outset it is important to consider the relevance of the cash cycle. The cash cycle is equal to the number of days it takes to sell your inventory (DIO), minus the days it takes you to pay your vendors (DPO), plus the days you need to collect on your invoices (DSO). Thus, it is

$$CC = DIO - DPO + DSO$$

- Days inventory outstanding (DIO) – the number of days on average that your company turns your inventory into sales. The smaller this number, the better.
- Days payable outstanding (DPO) – the number of days it takes you to pay your accounts payable. The higher this number, the longer you can hold onto cash, so a longer DPO is better.
- Days sales outstanding (DSO) – the number of days you will need to collect on the sales of that inventory after the sale has been made. The lower the number, the better.

Let us look at a hypothetical example. The following information is known:

- The organisation purchases from its suppliers and takes an average of 35 days to pay them.
- On average, the purchased goods remain in stock for 25 days.
- It takes an average of 50 days for customers to pay.

The "cash cycle" is the time elapsed from paying suppliers to receiving cash from customers, which is:

$$Cash\,cycle = DIO - DPO + DSO = 25 - 35 + 50 = 40\,days.$$

This means that the organisation must have enough cash to bridge this gap. The length of the cash cycle (and hence the amount of cash required) will depend on how soon suppliers are paid, how much stock is held and how quickly the business collects money from customers and these timings must be monitored and controlled. Management accountants will need to prepare ongoing cash and working capital budgets to see where problems might occur and be planned for. These budgets will have to build in other aspects of cash such as salary payments, payments to suppliers for services etc. Such budgets might be prepared monthly, weekly or even daily where deemed necessary.

Management accountants in public services may also, where appropriate, make use of the following working capital measurements as a guide to the situation:

1. **Stock turnover ratio** $= \dfrac{\text{Stock held}}{\text{Annual sales (at cost)}} \times 365$

2. **Debtor collection period** $= \dfrac{\text{Amount owed by trade debtors}}{\text{Annual income}} \times 365$

3. **Creditor payment period** $= \dfrac{\text{Amount owed to trade creditors}}{\text{Annual credit purchases}} \times 365$

Finally, it must be emphasised that the relevance of the above methods to public services depends on the nature of the public service organisation itself and this must be considered.

BUDGETING SYSTEMS AND BUDGETARY CONTROL IN PUBLIC SERVICE MANAGEMENT

Budgeting systems are a very important part of management control in public service organisations. However, budgeting systems also have other important roles to play as well. These will be discussed below.

Purpose of budgeting systems

Traditionally budgeting systems in public service organisations would probably be seen to have had three main purposes:

1. **Plan** – a (one-year) financial plan for the organisation indicating the purposes on which public funds were to be spent.
2. **Resource allocation** – a method of internal resource allocation for distributing resources to different parts of the organisation.
3. **Control** – a system of management control to control income and expenditure within budgets and to clarify authority and responsibility within the organisation for performance in this area.

While these purposes are still very relevant, the budget system may also have other more modern but important roles:

- **Delegation** – once organisations reach a certain size, they become too large and complex for one individual to manage and make all the decisions. This would probably be the case in all public service organisations and many third sector organisations. Delegating certain decisions to lower levels of management is one way of resolving this problem. However, delegating the power to make decisions without also delegating the power to use resources and to spend money would not be a very effective way of working. Hence the process of delegation can be aided by utilising a system of budgets. Giving a subordinate manager a budget delegates the authority to incur expenditure up to the budget level, and in line with the strategy without the requirement to refer the expenditure decision to higher authority. Such an approach should lead to quicker decisions and possibly better decisions because the person closer to the action is better informed than someone higher up the chain. However, delegation of budgets must be treated with care. It would be counter-productive to delegate budgets to managers or service professionals who were unwilling to manage budgets effectively, did not see it as their job or did not have the requisite skills needed to manage such budgets. Such a situation could herald a severe loss of management control. Whereas in the private sector budgetary management skills would usually be seen as a prerequisite for being an effective manager, in the public sector this is not always, and perhaps not usually, the case. Sometimes, service professionals such as doctors, nurses, teachers, social workers etc. do not see budget management as part of their job but regard it as an administrative chore which they are required to undertake. If such a culture is prevalent in a public service organisation, it is easy to see how the budgetary system can become ineffective and lead to financial control problems. Sometimes it is necessity that drives the non-finance professionals to become effective budget managers (e.g. where financial pressures exist, it affects every-day operational decision making) and, therefore, the "frontline" professionals make it their business to understand their budgets and help prioritise their own objectives. Equally, it must also be said that in some public service organisations, senior finance managers are often risk averse and have a strong reluctance to decentralise budgets further down the organisation. This may be because of a perceived loss of financial control, a lack of trust or a concern that an increasing number of budget holders will require increased support from finance staff.

- **Prioritisation** – the onset of financial austerity has created major challenges for all public service organisations. Many organisations have had to cope with lower growth in resources than has traditionally been the case, while others have suffered large real term reductions in funding. Funding changes of this magnitude mean that it is often difficult, if not impossible, to deal with them by shaving relatively small amounts off the whole resource base of the activity or unit. Instead it might be necessary to consider the degree of importance and priority attaching to each activity or unit and, possibly, discontinuing the lower-priority activities or units or transforming that activity to deliver it in a more efficient way, for example using technology, different methods of delivery etc. This will be discussed further under zero-based budgeting (ZBB)/priority-based budgeting (PBB) later.

- **Performance** – as will be discussed later, a key component of the budget process is the setting of budgets whether that be an annual process or longer term. Either way, this process provides an opportunity for the public service organisation to review the way it does things and the way it uses resources. If improvements can be identified, then these can be incorporated into the future budget as a means of promoting its implementation.

- **Strategy** – as discussed earlier, public service organisations have faced, and will continue to face, a situation of continuous and ongoing change. Such changes may be organisational, procedural, cultural, political etc. Consequently, they will need to prepare strategic plans and associated financial strategies to deal and assist with the changes deemed necessary. It is one thing to prepare a strategic plan and another to implement that plan, and situations have arisen where public service organisations have failed to implement the strategy they have prepared for a variety of reasons. The budget system of a public service organisation can be one key mechanism by means of which expenditure priorities for future years are decided upon. Thus, the budget process should be a means for facilitating the implementation of a strategic plan by ensuring that future expenditure priorities take cognisance of and reflect the content of the multi-year strategic plan. This is not always achieved and as we shall discuss later, there is often a discontinuity between strategic planning and budgeting in public service organisations. This discontinuity is because the usefulness of budgeting goes beyond just operational/tactical purposes into strategic issues.

- **Motivation** – perhaps the most commonly neglected aspect of budgeting is that of employee and managerial motivation. Much evidence exists to show that budgeting systems are not behaviourally neutral (Hopwood 1972). The way in which budgets are set and budgetary control operated can have a considerable impact on the managerial performance of an individual manager. Thus, in setting budgets in public service organisations, it is important to keep in mind the impact that the budget setting process may have (in a positive or negative sense) on departmental and managerial performance and morale. Thus, the operation of an effective budget system requires consideration of:
  - aspiration levels and their impact on motivation,
  - degree of participation in setting budget targets and its impact on motivation/commitment to budget targets,
  - communication of budgets, objectives and priorities,
  - management style and its impact on behaviour.

Hopwood (1972) identified three different approaches to the way senior management used budget information in the evaluation of manager performance in the commercial sector:

1. **Budget-constrained style** – in which the manager's performance is evaluated rigidly on the basis of his/her ability to achieve (short-term) budget targets.
2. **Profit-conscious style** – in which the manager's performance is evaluated on the basis of his/her ability to improve the general effectiveness of his/her centre's operations (e.g. profitability, productivity), with budgetary information used in a more flexible manner in conjunction with consideration of other factors/information.
3. **Non-accounting style** – in which budgetary information plays a relatively unimportant role in the evaluation of a manager's performance.

Thus, a thought must be given to how budget information is to be used in order not to provide the wrong motivation to managers.

Components of a budgeting system

Any budgeting system can be thought of as comprising three main component parts as shown in Figure 10.2.

This will apply as much in a public service organisation as in any other type of organisation and each of these components are discussed in some detail below.

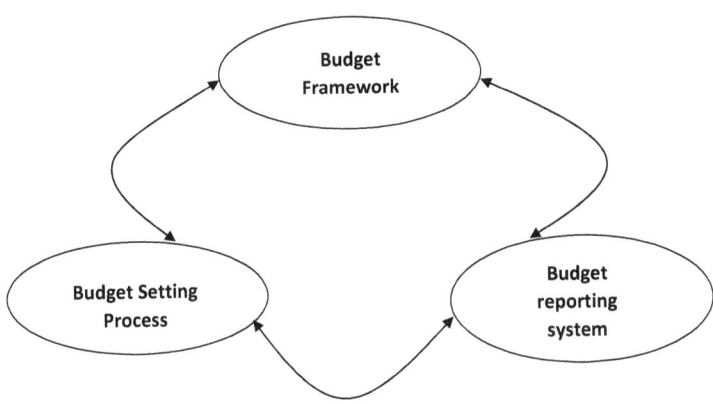

FIGURE 10.2
Components of a budgeting system.

Budget framework

The role of the budget system as a means of delegation and empowerment within an organisation has already been discussed and therefore a budget system must reflect the framework of responsibility and accountability in the organisation. This means answering the following questions:

- Who are to be the budget holders in the organisation?
- What specific activities are they responsible for?
- What items of expenditure are to be included in their budgets?
- What items of income are to be included in their budget?
- What workload and performance standards are required from them?
- What powers of authority do they have in relation to their budgets? For example, are they able to switch funds between different budget categories or do they require higher approval to do this?

Answers to these questions are never clear-cut and will vary. No two organisations will have the same organisational and managerial arrangements and consequently neither will they have the same budgeting framework. Furthermore, it must be recognised that many organisations, including some public service organisations, do not have a rational and tidy budget framework along the lines described above. Quite often, one sees examples of individuals having responsibility for activities but having no control over resources and expenditure items with no nominated person responsible for controlling them. Such situations can lead to major failures of financial control. Thus, the framework described above must be seen as something to be aimed for and not something which already exists.

Budget setting process

Whatever budget framework is adopted, there will be some process or mechanism for setting expenditure (and income) budgets for individual departments or units. Budgets will usually be set for a 12-month period but, as noted earlier, in some public service organisations budgets may be prepared for several year's

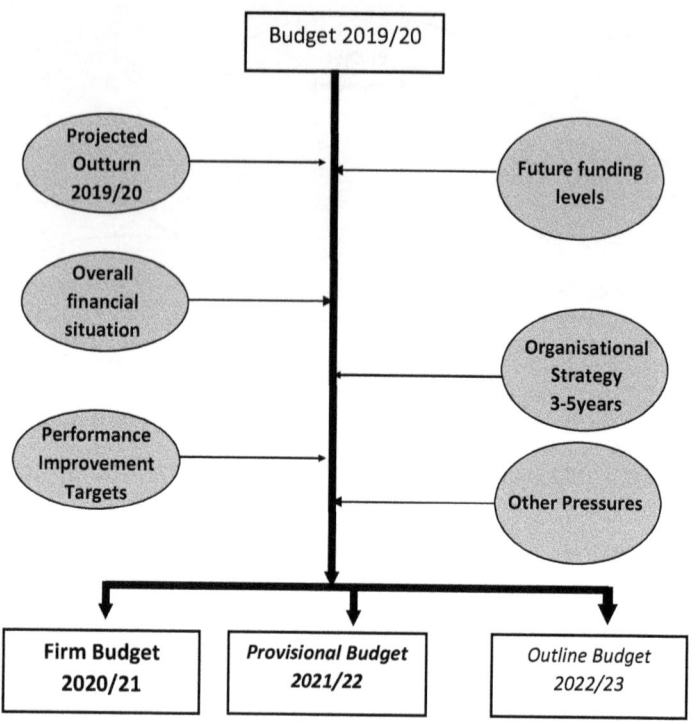

FIGURE 10.3
Budget setting factors.

duration with the first year being firmer than the later years. This would operate as a rolling process with the outline budget for year 2 being converted into a firm budget the following year and so on.

The factors which may influence budget setting in a public service organisation are shown in Figure 10.3.

Starting with the budget for 2019/2020, the budget setting process moves towards the construction of budgets for future years. In constructing such budgets there will be a number of influencing factors of which the following are suggested as being of greatest importance:

- **Projected outturn for 2019/2020** – the projected outturn expenditure for a department for the current year (compared with budget) will be relevant, since it will be important to know whether the departmental budget will be over or under spent and whether such under/over spendings are a once-off event (non-recurrent) or have taken place over a number of years (recurrent).
- **Future funding levels** – public service organisations usually have some indications of likely funding levels for future years and the likely levels of growth (or contraction) of resources they are likely to get. Within those overall figures it is possible that there may also be an indication of the likely levels of resources which will be available to fund specific services in years to come. These projections will inform the budget setting process.

- **Overall financial situation** – this means the overall financial situation of the public service organisation itself and, for example, whether it is in a financial surplus or financial deficit position, what sort of financial reserves it has, working capital position etc.
- **Performance improvement targets** – many public service organisations operate in a regime where it is necessary for them to demonstrate improved performance from one year to the next. This requirement will need to be factored into the budget setting process.
- **Strategy** – the budget is one of the key means of implementing the overall strategy of the public service organisation. Thus, aspects of the strategy which require shifts in resources will need to be taken account of in setting budgets. For example, the aim may be to reduce one service and expand another or change the location where a service is delivered. These changes will have clear budgetary implications and should form part of the budget setting process.
- **Other pressures** – a whole range of other factors may impinge on the budget setting process including political pressures, current service shortfalls, contingency reserves etc.

Within this overall budget setting process a number of different models of budget setting may be applied. Three of these models are briefly outlined later, but it must be recognised that in practice the budget setting approach will probably be based, to some degree, on a combination of these broad models.

Incremental budgeting

With this model, the main determinant of the expenditure budget of a department will be the previous year's expenditure budget. Thus, this year's budget will be largely determined by the previous year's budget. Adjustments will be made for the effects of inflation, new developments, changes at the margin or the need to generate across-the-board efficiency improvements. However, the budget of the department is not linked to its projected workload, planned strategic change or efficiency level and no attempt made to justify the historic level of the budget. Such an approach to budget setting is not necessarily desirable but, traditionally, is quite common in the public sector. The main weakness of this approach is that the base budget is not queried for appropriateness and relevance and no link exists with the overall workload, only with marginal changes in workload. Such budgets are effectively fixed budgets, as they will not usually be changed in-year in response to changing workload demands placed on the department. Furthermore, there is a layering effect of year-on-year changes, through this method in moving the organisation further away from rapidly changing priorities.

Workload-based budgets

With some types of budgets, or parts of budget, the budgeted level of expenditure can be linked to the planned level of workload in the department. Take for example a catering budget in a public service organisation. The expenditure of the department will, clearly, be influenced by the number of meals served. Hence the budget also needs to be based on the number of meals actually served and can be flexed as the meal numbers change up or down. Budgets such as these are termed flexible budgets, as the overall budget level will be flexed in accordance with the level of activity undertaken. However, for setting workload-based budgets there are a number of prerequisites:

- **Measures of workload** – there is a need for credible measures of workload available on which those budgets can be based? The catering example above has a clear measure of workload. However, in many public service areas such workload measures are not easy to come by and so workload-based budgets cannot easily be developed. For example, consider the difficulty of identifying suitable workload measures (which could be used for budget setting) for policing services in different areas. Should budgets be based on number of crimes, number of arrests, social deprivation in the area etc?
- **Workload data** – there would need to be reasonably accurate data on the workload levels of the function or department being undertaken. This requires the existence of suitable measures of workload and information systems to capture these data.
- **Unit costs** – to set budgets there needs to be agreement as to the unit cost to be applied to workload units and this requires good costing systems and data.

Zero-based budgeting (ZBB)/Priority-based budgeting (PBB)

These related approaches were developed to overcome the main weaknesses of the incremental approach of failing to look at the base budget of a department and of the workload-based approach which only looks at volumetric variations in workload and not the efficiency of operation. ZBB/PBB approaches are particularly applicable to central support departments in a public service organisation rather than to service departments. PBB is essentially a simpler and more pragmatic version of ZBB, but the thrust is the same in both cases.

Under ZBB/PBB, no budget is automatically rolled forward as is the case in the incremental approach. Rolling forward budgets can have the undesirable effect of rewarding under-performers and penalising over-performers. For example, the cost base for a poorly performing unit is often higher than the cost base for a high-performing unit, and therefore poor performers have greater £ per unit to spend. Organisations therefore must have some mediation/challenge/benchmarking process to balance this dilemma and the decision packages approach described below is often the vehicle for such challenge.

Thus, expenditure budgets must be fully scrutinised and managers of departments (or decision units) must indicate

- the decision packages they currently undertake or might wish to undertake in future,
- the costs attaching to each of those decision packages,
- the benefits and priority of undertaking each of those decision packages.

Senior management can then scrutinise all decision units in the public service organisation and compare the costs with the benefits and priorities attaching to each package or activity. They can decide to fund decision packages, in priority order, up to the limit of resources available.

The terms "decision unit" and "decision package" need a little explaining:

- **Decision units** – this is the term used to define the operational or support units in the public service organisation around which budget setting process will operate. Decision units could be individual departments, units within a department, sub-units or geographic areas. The aim is to base budget setting on the most appropriate level in the organisation for decision making about priorities. A larger number of decision units might provide a more meaningful analysis than a small number of decision units but would also be more complex. Thus using a university as an example, a decision unit could be the whole university, a faculty, a department, a subject area or an individual course. Overall, a decision unit should have the following characteristics:
  - A single manager should be clearly identifiable as being responsible for its activities.
  - It must have clear and measurable objectives.
  - It must have clear and measurable outputs.
- **Decision packages** – for the purpose of a ZBB/PBB setting process these activities must be classified into what are termed "decision packages". This involves categorising the various activities of a decision unit as a set of decision packages which describe how the unit achieves its objectives. Thus, decision packages are concerned with identifying different ways of performing the functions of the unit and meeting its objectives. Such decision packages can be of two main types:
  - **Mutually exclusive packages** – these are packages where the only alternative to undertaking and funding the package is not to undertake and fund it. There is no middle way. In public services it may be difficult to think of many such services since most services are either statutory in nature or can be provided at different levels.
  - **Incremental** – these are packages where the decision package can be undertaken at different levels such as: minimum level, current level, enhanced level etc. Thus, health checks on patients could be provided at different levels of sophistication and thoroughness.

Whatever the merits of ZBB/PBB in principle, there are some clear practical problems:

- Whatever the ranking process produces, the reality is that some activities or decision packages must be undertaken by statute and thus there is limited discretion over this.
- The procedures are cumbersome and time-consuming. Consequently, in some organisations the ZBB/PBB process might be applied to individual decision units every three years rather than every year.

- It will probably be difficult to switch resources between areas of activity without retraining staff and/or making redundancies.
- There will inevitably be strong organisation resistance to implementing the outcomes of the process.
- The process is open to "game-playing" whereby managers rank their weakest packages most highly thus giving the best chance of getting across the resource threshold.

Some public service organisations use an approach similar to ZBB/PBB not for budget setting as such but for the purposes of identifying where reductions in expenditure might be achieved as a consequence of resource pressures. Once again, decision units are required to identify and rank those decision packages which could constitute cuts in expenditure. The packages for all decision units are submitted to senior management who rank the proposals in order and identify the cuts to be made based on the overall priorities of the organisation.

Overall, it is probably the case that most public service organisations have difficulty with the concept of ZBB/PBB. There are often difficulties in identifying clear decision packages and in identifying the objectives and impact of those packages. Consequently, there are difficulties in ranking packages in priority order. Furthermore, some public service organisations feel uncomfortable about the idea of cuts in expenditure resulting in the cessation of lower-priority activities in some departments. Also, some managers often feel happier with a situation where every department and activity bear an equal percentage cut because they see it as "fairer". However, it is suggested that in an environment of limited growth in public funding such a process of prioritisation will be of increasing importance. In fact, the author would argue that this process of identifying the priority order of existing activities in terms of value added is one of the most important aspects of public service management today.

> **CASE STUDY 10.1**
>
> # Budget prioritisation in social care
>
> In many countries, the combination of ageing populations and financial austerity is putting social care budgets under extreme pressure. The social care department of the Flatborough City Council was faced with a severe budget deficit amounting to almost £8 million. It has recognised that it cannot resolve this financial problem by a combination of top-slicing everyone's budget and discontinuing politically uncontentious (but potentially valuable) activities, which it has done in the past.
>
> It recognises that, in future, in making budgetary decisions, it needs to consider the relative value and cost of the various activities it undertakes by using a targeted budget approach. This means that savings of the required amount should be obtained by identifying those activities which are a combination of lowest priority and greatest ease of discontinuation.

Under this approach, departmental managers were required to put forward plans which would indicate how each manager would make savings at the following levels: 3%, 5% and 7%. In putting forward their plans, each manager also had to score each proposal (on a scale of 1–3, with 1 = low and 3 = high) against the following criteria:

- Ease of deliverability
- Policy/strategy compliance (will it cause more problems in the medium term?)
- Standards/vulnerability (adverse impact on discharge of statutory responsibility/professional standards as they effect vulnerable people)
- Public/user risk (general impact on users and upon public perception – political test?)
- Organisational risk (impact/implication for functionality of organisation)
- Performance risk (adverse impact on performance measures)
- Reputational risk

These criteria were not weighted (but could have been) and an overall score was calculated.

Senior managers in the department evaluated the proposals put forward and considered the balance between the magnitude of cost savings and the various criteria. Departmental managers were also questioned about their proposals to assess the robustness of their risk evaluations and cost estimates.

The outcome of this process was that senior management in the department identified which activities should be eliminated to achieve the savings target and an action plan was prepared.

The implementation of this savings plan was closely monitored using a traffic lights system, and half way through the financial year, the situation was as shown under:

- Savings achieved (green) £4.6 million
- Progress being made (amber) £1.6 million
- Difficulties being encountered (red) £1.8 million

The overall view in the department was that although this process was laborious and time-consuming, the final outcome was fairer and much more satisfactory in minimising the impact on services.

Also, they concluded that they had underestimated the degree of resistance to the process of prioritisation such that the implementation plan was showing a shortfall on the level of savings anticipated. More effort needs to be put into the management of the implementation process.

Mixed approaches to budget setting

The above three approaches to expenditure budget setting are not mutually exclusive and all three can often be found in a single organisation to some extent. For example, the provisions element of a catering budget might be a flexible or workload-based budget, whereas the catering staffing budget might be a fixed budget established by the incremental or PBB method.

Budget reporting system

The provision of budgeting information must be a clear part of the information and IT strategy of the organisation. Although the precise configuration of information systems will vary considerably between organisations, a number of common themes can be identified which are applicable to all budgeting information systems:

- **Relevance** – budget managers need relevant information. This relates to issues of responsibility and control as managers require information on those items of expenditure over which they have responsibility and can exert control. This point may be obvious but is not always seen in practice.

- **Frequency and timeliness** – historically, in many organisations budget managers used to receive monthly budget reports on paper within a few days of the end of the month. However, with modern information systems managers can often obtain such information, online, at any time via computer terminals within their department. However, even where such budget information systems exist, the timeliness of the information contained will be conditioned by how frequently the ledger and budget system has been updated by the main financial feeder systems such as payroll, payments and income.

- **Format** – the precise format of a budget report varies, but usually shows the following information:
  - Total budget for the year
  - Budget for the month, which may be a simple twelfth of the annual budget or is adjusted to reflect seasonal variations in some type of expenditure such as heating costs
  - Expenditure for the month
  - Variance for the month
  - Cumulative budget for the year to date
  - Cumulative expenditure for the year to date
  - Year-end estimated expenditure
  - Variance for the year to date

- **Accuracy and content** – the accuracy of information is important. An organisation needs to avoid situations where inaccurate data are used to monitor performance which can often lead to demotivation of budget managers and, in some cases, the cause of disaffected managers that push against the organisational objectives and values.

  The information on actual expenditure included in budget reports can be of three main types:
  - Cash payments actually made.
  - Accruals of creditors, this being expenditure on goods and services received but not yet paid for.
  - Commitments, being goods and services ordered for which an expenditure commitment exists but which have not yet been received.

  Budget reports usually include accruals of creditors but they may not include commitments, although this is becoming more common. Budget managers obviously need to be aware of any additional expenditure commitments not included on their budget reports.

- **Support** – support and advice on the content of budget reports are needed by the budget managers. In some cases, departments or directorates might have their own decentralised finance officer, while in other cases support will be given by a central finance department. Provision of such support is a key role of the finance function.

Enhancements to budget reporting mechanisms

A number of enhancements to basic budget models can be identified and may be applied in public service organisations.

Profiling of budgets

In simpler budget systems the monthly expenditure for individual budget headings is compared with one-twelfth of the annual budget and variances are reported. Clearly in some instances, this approach is bound to produce misleading information. Consider the following:

- **Heating costs** – comparing actual expenditure with twelfths of the budget will result in budget overspends in winter months and under spends in summer months.
- **Grass-cutting costs** – comparing actual expenditure with twelfths of the budget will result in budgeting overspends in summer months and underspends in winter months.

These are extreme examples of seasonal variations in expenditure, but there are many examples where expenditure is not incurred evenly throughout the year. Hence more advanced budget systems try to profile budgets to reflect expected expenditure for the months in question. Variations from budget can then be regarded as real and not seasonal variations.

Budget variance analysis

As noted above, a typical budgeting control report might show the variation between actual expenditure and planned budget both for the month and the cumulative position for the year. In practice, variations from budget may occur for a large number of reasons such as workload pressures, price increases or poor expenditure management. A simple budget variance does not indicate the reasons why expenditure has deviated from budget. The technique of budget variance analysis was developed in industry many years ago as a means of explaining the reasons why expenditure has deviated from budget. It has practical application in a public service organisation using a transport unit as an example. A standard budgetary control report would merely show that the transport unit had exceeded its budgets by £4,000, but even a cursory analysis would show that there are three factors at work here, namely:

- The price of fuel
- The mileage covered
- The fuel efficiency

Variance analysis uses this information to disaggregate the causes of an expenditure variance. In saying this, it is important to recognise that variances can be of three types: the controllable, the influenceable and the non-controllable, and the action taken will depend on the type. Furthermore, variance analysis can also identify the department or individual person who should be regarded as responsible and accountable for that particular variance. However, budget managers sometimes try to deflect or hide the real underlying reasons for a variance to avoid it impacting on their perceived performance. It is important that the true underlying source and driver of the expenditure is evidenced and understood.

The earlier example concerns a support function of a public service organisation, but with a little imagination it is easy to see how the variance analysis approach can be used to identify key variances and responsibilities for frontline services. Consider the imaging function as an NHS hospital. In the imaging department, the difference between planned expenditure and actual expenditure for a particular class of imaging could be analysed to produce a number of different variances:

- **Volume variance** – resulting from the actual volume of procedures being more or less than planned.
- **Mix variance** – resulting from the actual mix procedures being more or less than planned.
- **Price variance** – resulting from differences in pay and non-pay costs being different from that planned.
- **Efficiency variance** – resulting from lesser or greater efficiency in the conduct of imaging procedures compared with that anticipated at the planning stage.

Activity-based budgeting

We have seen previously how Activity-Based Costing (ABC) can be used to establish the costs incurred in making products/providing services. However, the principles of ABC can also be applied to the budgeting process. Activity-based budgeting (ABB) focuses on the budgeted cost of the activities required to produce, sell and distribute products and services. In doing this, ABB separates indirect costs into separate activity cost pools. Management can then use the cause-and-effect criterion to identify the cost drivers for each of these indirect-cost pools.

In practical terms, ABB can be looked at in four steps:

- The budgeted costs of performing each unit of activity, in each activity area, must be calculated.
- The demand for each individual activity must be estimated.
- The actual costs of performing each activity must be calculated.
- Provide a description of the budget as the costs of performing various activities rather than budgeted costs of functional or conventional spending categories.

Beyond budgeting

In the late 1990s, there arose the Beyond Budgeting Movement, championed by Hope and Fraser (1993). These writers argued that the traditional budgetary control approach is not appropriate in today's fast moving, uncertain, "information age". Budgets are, it was argued, a relic of the hierarchical command and control organisation characteristic of the industrial age. In the "information age", with flatter, leaner organisations a more informal flexible approach to control, whereby the organisation adapts itself to its rapidly changing environment, is required. In a competitive environment (it was argued), the budget is a barrier to the rapid adaptive behaviour required; it is "out of date before the ink is dry", yet effectively forces managers to strive for targets that are no longer relevant or appropriate. Budgets also encourage dysfunctional behaviour whereby managers strive to achieve budget in ways that are damaging to the organisation as a whole.

Hope and Fraser advocated the abolition of budgets for control purposes and their replacement by a system based on mutual trust among managers. The planning function of budgets would be served by the use of rolling forecasts, regularly updated (say, monthly or quarterly) in response to the rapidly changing competitive environment.

The Beyond Budgeting Movement enjoyed some initial success with some high-profile examples of companies such as IKEA and Svenska Handelsbanken famously abandoning budgets. However, research evidence suggests that today conventional budgeting is very much alive and well! In some ways this is surprising because Hope and Fraser originally wrote in the early days of the IT revolution. Subsequent changes have created a business environment more akin to what they described in the 1990s which would make the Beyond Budgeting Movement more credible today than when they originally put forward the idea.

STRATEGIC MANAGEMENT CONTROL

As we saw in Chapter 3, strategy needs to be implemented and monitored and controlled. Strategic management control processes allow managers to evaluate the organisation's strategic progress from a critical long-term perspective. Such a control framework focuses on the dual questions of whether

- the strategy is being implemented as planned,
- the results produced by the strategy are those intended.

Thus, strategic control goes well beyond just financial measures but financial measures are important.

Strategic management control is probably not an area of great strength in many public services. This is either because the organisational strategy itself is unsound in some way and/or there is a failure to recognise that monitoring the progress of the strategy against plan is important.

Effective strategic control can be considered as comprising four elements listed underneath.

Control of premises or assumptions

Every strategy is based on certain planning premises, assumptions or predictions. This form of control is designed to check methodically and constantly whether the premises/assumptions on which a strategy is grounded on are still valid. If it is discovered that an important premise is no longer valid, the strategy may have to be changed. Financial planning aspects will be critical here.

Implementation control

Implementing a strategy takes place as a series of steps, activities, investments and acts that occur over a lengthy period. Implementation control is the type of strategic control that must be carried out as events unfold and such control needs to be properly resourced to be effective. There are two types of implementation controls: strategic thrusts or projects and milestone reviews. Strategic thrusts provide information that helps determine whether the overall strategy is proceeding as planned, whereas milestone reviews monitor the progress of the strategy at various intervals or milestones. The exact emphasis that should be put on implementation control will vary. The greater the fluidity of activity or instability in an organisation, the greater the need for implementation control.

Strategic surveillance

Strategic surveillance is designed to observe a wide range of events within and outside the organisation that are likely to affect the track of the organisation's strategy. It is based on the idea that you can uncover important yet unanticipated information by monitoring multiple information sources. Horizon scanning or future proofing are essential parts of strategic surveillance.

Unforeseen events control

This is the rigorous and rapid reassessment of an organisation's strategy in the light of an immediate, unforeseen event. Such an event will trigger an immediate and intense reassessment of the strategy and any remedial action required.

The above four elements combined represent a fairly sophisticated and integrated approach to strategic management control. It is a debatable point as to how many public service organisations can claim to be approaching this ideal model in a systematic manner.

Management accounting and performance management/ improvement in public services

INTRODUCTION

Performance management, including the measurement of performance, has always been an important subject in any type of organisation. In the absence of performance management, it is difficult to see how any organisation can make progress in the modern world in which it operates.

All organisations will have a range of objectives which may be: short term/ long term, strategic/operational, financial/non-financial etc. In the absence of any system of performance management, an organisation will find it difficult, if not impossible to:

- identify how well it is performing against its pre-arranged objectives and the deviations from those objectives;
- communicate, internally and externally, its performance against these objectives;
- provide a framework for taking action to bring the organisation back in line with its objectives.

In the past, there has often been debate about the relevance of performance management approaches in public services. However, most people would probably now accept that they do have relevance provided the distinctive nature of public services is not forgotten. One researcher in this field has stated that "while public and private organisations do differ in some fundamentals, the similarities they share in terms of organisational behaviour and managerial practices render a strong platform for public organisations to implant private-born performance management into their organisations" (Mazlan 2008). Thus, provided performance management approaches are developed and used in an interactive way between managers, professionals and politicians they can be extremely useful.

Thus, performance management and performance improvement are key managerial functions in all public services, and management accounting has a key but not exclusive role to play.

This chapter addresses the following issues:

- Nature of performance in public services
- Dimensions of performance
- Systems of performance management
- Performance information
- Improving performance in public services
- Management accounting contribution

NATURE OF PERFORMANCE IN PUBLIC SERVICES

Traditional approaches to performance measurement, particularly in the commercial sector, tended to focus on a fairly narrow range of issues most notably those concerned with financial aspects such as profits, returns etc. While these traditional approaches sufficed at the time, they proved to have severe limitations in a world which was changing dramatically. In the commercial world, during the 19th and early 20th centuries, businesses operated in a largely local or national context but the development of increasingly sophisticated economies in Asia and the shift towards globalisation introduced new dynamics and risks into the business environment. In the commercial world, this development of more complex economic environments necessitated greater sophistication in relation to performance measurement.

Looking beyond the operational issues, it is likely to be the case that commercial organisations will also require a number of strategic performance measures covering such matters as: market share, sales growth, return on capital employed, value added etc. Also, companies showed an increasing interest in product quality and customer satisfaction.

In the public services, the increasing sophistication of clients coupled with the increasing pressures on public funds also led to an increasing emphasis on the development of performance management and performance measures (Elcock 1996) against which public services could be judged. Thus, in the public sector it is also the case that while there has been a continuation of the drive to have financial measures of performance (i.e. efficiency measures), there has also been a strong focus on performance measures concerned with customer or client satisfaction and inherent service quality.

DIMENSIONS OF PERFORMANCE

Performance in public services can have different dimensions and it is important, at the outset, to try and clarify what these dimensions might be. An initial classification is to consider performance from a timescale perspective and thus we have the concepts of operational/tactical performance (short to medium term) and strategic performance (longer term).

Operational/tactical performance

In public services, tactical/operational performance measurement could be considered in a number of ways:

- Service quality
- Use of resources
- Value for money (VFM)

Service quality

Service quality is a very complex issue and there a number of sub-dimensions which need to be considered. These are

- **Service access** – how accessible the services are to service users in terms of time and/or distance, location etc.
- **Service outcomes** – these outcomes are related to the strategic objectives of the service provision and will contribute towards those strategic objectives. Some examples would be educational attainment outcomes (e.g. examination passes) for schools, clinical outcomes for hospitals, crime reduction for police services etc.
- **Service user experiences** – these measures concern the attitudes held by service users and others of services based on their experiences. There are several aspects to this, and one model for measuring them is termed SERVQUAL (Parasuraman et al. 1988).

Use of resources

The second main dimension of tactical/operational performance in public services concerns the use of public resources. There are several ways of expressing this such as:

- **Resource utilisation** – this could include such input ratios as length of stay in hospital, staff, pupil:teacher ratios in schools etc.
- **Unit costs** – traditionally unit costs of support activities in public services (e.g. cost per meal) are readily available with some cost information about frontline services. Further development involves the use of unit costs of frontline service provision (e.g. cost per student for a specific course, cost per patient for a specific condition).

Value for money (VFM)

VFM is a very important aspect of public service performance which has been prominent for several decades. In public services, there is an overriding moral and political imperative to ensure that the taxpayer's pound is used in the most appropriate way to achieve good value given that it is extracted involuntarily under the force of law. Furthermore, given that many public services are delivered in a non-market environment and so are subject to ever-increasing levels of demand, unconstrained by the individual citizen/customer's income, VFM becomes an essential way of meeting seemingly insatiable demand within restricted budgets. "Value for money" is a term used to assess whether or not a public service organisation has obtained the maximum benefit or value from the services it both acquires and provides, within the resources available to it. VFM not only measures the cost of goods and services but also takes account of the mix of quality, cost and resource use, fitness for purpose, timeliness and convenience to judge whether, together, they constitute good value.

The delivery of public services involves the following stages:

- **Expenditure** – expenditure is incurred by the public authority in order to deliver services.
- **Resources** – these expenditures enable the public authority to acquire real resources such as staffing, consumables, equipment in order to deliver services.
- **Operational process** – these resources are then utilised in some form of operational process in order to deliver a public service.
- **Service outputs** – these might sometimes be referred to as intermediate outputs and constitute the initial or immediate measure of delivery of public services. Output measures might include
  - number of students taught in schools,
  - number of patients treated in a hospital,
  - number of miles of roads maintained,
  - number of patrols by police vehicles,
  - number of building inspection by fire and rescue officers.
- **Service outcomes** – these might sometimes be referred to as final outcomes and represent the real purpose for the provision of public services. Following the delivery of a range of service outputs, there would be an expectation that public services would achieve longer-term and sustainable service outcomes. This is a complex area but some examples of service outcomes might include
  - higher employment rates for young people,
  - reductions in mortality and sickness,
  - higher levels of fitness among the population,
  - reductions in the number of road accidents,
  - reductions in crime rates,
  - reductions in the number of fire incidents.

VFM is also usually described in terms of the "three Es", namely economy, efficiency and effectiveness. Figure 11.1 shows the relationship between the 3Es in the stages of delivery of a public service.

- **Economy** – this concerns the expenditure incurred in acquiring the real resources needed to deliver public services. Improved economy would be achieved by paying a lower price for a consumable item or piece of equipment. It may also occur where staff labour rates can be reduced without there being any negative impact on service quality and/or ability to recruit staff.

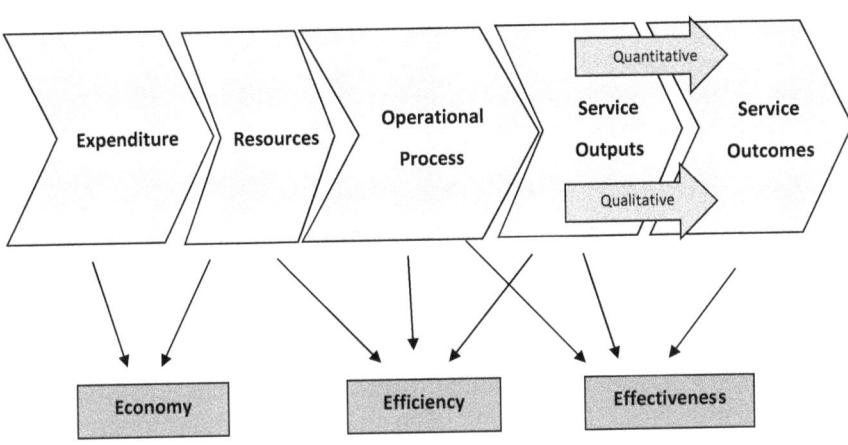

FIGURE 11.1
Value for money and the 3Es.

- **Efficiency** – efficiency is basically the ratio of resource inputs to service outputs. Thus, improved outputs for the same resources or the same outputs for reduced resources will constitute improved efficiency. Such improvements can come about by changing the amount and mix of resources, improving the operational processes etc.
- **Effectiveness** – this is concerned with the extent to which a public service organisation has achieved its preordained service objectives in terms of service outputs and service outcomes. It is basically the extent to which outputs have generated outcomes.

There are certain myths about VFM that need to be dispelled. First, improved VFM is not necessarily obtained by taking the cheapest alternative which is often the view of many service professionals and members of the general public. Although economy is important, efficiency is more important, and the ultimate objective is public service delivery effectiveness. Also, decreasing resource inputs (and hence costs) will not necessarily lead to a diminution of service outputs/outcomes and increasing resource inputs will not necessarily lead to an enhancement of service outputs/outcomes. The link between inputs and outputs is subtle and it is imperative to avoid a mentality of assuming that more always means better and less always means worse. Evidence from within the private and public sectors with regard to approaches, such as lean, show this is definitively not the case in all circumstances.

VFM is a very important concept in public services and a much used term. However, it has a number of interpretations different to the aforementioned which often causes confusion. Also, some elements of VFM may be subjective, difficult to measure, intangible and/or misunderstood. Judgement is therefore required when considering whether VFM has been satisfactorily achieved or not. Thus overall, VFM is possibly best seen as a concept which requires interpretation and judgement rather than just a set of numeric performance measures.

There are many different approaches to identifying potential VFM improvements and these include the following techniques:

- Analysis of available data
- Performance benchmarking
- Analysis of operational process – value chain analysis
- Service user surveys
- Staff surveys
- Strategic evaluations
- Challenge approaches etc.

However, such techniques have limitations and one of the most important issues when trying to improve VFM is to develop an organisational culture which encourages all employees (and other stakeholders) to seek out and identify VFM improvements. This topic was the subject of a 2016 CIPFA publication entitled *"Having a value-focused culture: Continually improving to face the challenges of austerity"*.

CASE STUDY 11.1

VFM and preventative services for children and families

A local authority children's services department delivered a wide variety of preventative services in relation to children and families. These services have the overall aim of improving outcomes of children in disadvantaged circumstances.

The authority needed to undertake a VFM study of three of the services involved. These were

- **Team around the child (TAC)** – This is a nationally used programme with the aim of bringing together different agencies into one meeting where there are concerns about a child or a family (identified within a common assessment framework), but not serious enough for statutory intervention. It also sourced support services and agreed an action plan for implementation.
- **Parenting** – There are many different programmes available concerned with improving parenting skills. The authority was delivering one of the better known and widely used programmes.
- **Haven** – This was a bespoke programme developed within the authority which aimed to provide support to children with disruptive behaviour within the school, rather than placing them in a pupil referral unit which is very expensive to operate and not always best for the child.

The VFM study was undertaken by an external consultant who undertook the following approaches:

- Examination of available data on the programmes
- Interviews with staff
- Interviews with service recipients
- Review of management systems
- Examination of the "track record" of the operational service model being used.

The findings of the VFM review showed quite different findings for the three programmes:

- **TAC** – the programme had clear objectives and good data on both costs and outputs, and was at the early stages of producing outcome measures – a tool had been developed. Staff were very positive about the programme as were service recipients. The TAC approach had been used in many other local authorities with positive results.
- **Parenting** – the model of service delivery being used had been internationally validated as being effective in many organisations around the world. Thus, provided it was implemented correctly, it should prove effective. Staff and service recipients were very positive about the programme. The costs were known as was output data. However, no attempt had yet been made to collect outcome data.
- **Haven** – although staff and service recipients were very positive about the programme, there were no clear objectives. While the costs were known, no data had been collected on outputs, and outcome measures had not really been considered. As the service was a bespoke service, there was no means of assessing whether the approach could be validated as effective from other organisations.
- **Overall** – with two exceptions, the management systems in the department were regarded as being effective and contributed to economy.

Overall, while two of the three programmes can be regarded as having evidence of delivering VFM, the third programme was weak in most areas. This does not mean that it was not delivering VFM but that it could not be demonstrated.

Strategic performance

As well as tactical/operational performance, public service stakeholders will be interested in aspects of longer-term strategic performance of public services. These stakeholders will be considered in a latter section. In reality, it is likely that individual service users will have little interest in such measures, but more sophisticated stakeholders such as government or regulatory bodies will have a strong interest.

One of the best-known models of strategic performance is the balanced scorecard model (Kaplan and Norton 1996). With the balanced scorecard, strategic performance is assessed against four main dimensions of performance (financial, customers, internal business processes, and learning and growth) which are derived from the vision and strategy of the organisation. The original balanced scorecard model was devised, mainly, for commercial organisations but it has been adapted for public services with some modifications to the definition of the performance dimensions used. For public services, these are

- Stakeholders (instead of customers)
- Resource utilisation (instead of finance)
- Management processes (for internal business processes)
- Learning and innovation (for learning and growth)

A further enhancement to the public service balanced scorecard can be seen in the work of Moullin (2017) and is illustrated in Figure 11.2.

This is an integrated (1) strategy mapping, (2) service improvement and (3) performance measurement framework. It extends and adapts the balanced scorecard to fit the culture and values of the public and voluntary sectors. The model focuses on outcomes, service users, strategic and financial matters and the processes that lead to those outcomes, and the capability, behavioural and organisational factors that are needed to support staff and processes. The latter includes trained and motivated people, good partnership working and sufficient resources. Also, a culture of innovation and learning rather than a top-down blame culture is needed – all underpinned by effective and supportive leadership.

Producing a balanced scorecard for a complex public service is a major piece of organisational development work. The main stages in designing and implementing a balanced scorecard are

1. Establishing a sound strategic foundation for the balanced scorecard
2. Producing a multi-dimensional strategic summary
3. Setting objectives for each balanced scorecard perspective
4. Linking objectives via cause and effect
5. Determining measures for each objective
6. Setting targets for each measure in the balanced scorecard
7. Identifying strategic initiatives to deliver targets
8. Full implementation of the balanced scorecard

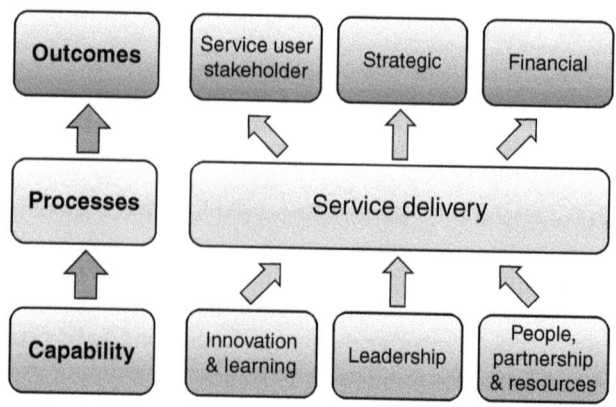

FIGURE 11.2
Public service balanced scorecard.

However, it is also possible to cascade balanced scorecards down to directorate and departmental levels. This means that the scorecard can dominate the monitoring activity of managers. Supporting this scorecard will be a series of initiatives designed to deliver on the targets and objectives so identified.

SYSTEMS OF PERFORMANCE MANAGEMENT

A look at published documents will reveal that there are many systems of performance management which have been developed in public services. However, a consideration of these models suggests many common features and it seems that an effective performance management system in any organisation requires all of the following components:

1. Data on current performance
2. A clear plan for the way ahead
3. Measurable objectives deriving from that plan
4. A measurement device to assess the progress being made
5. A means for communicating the current position throughout the organisation
6. A formal mechanism for reviewing progress
7. A means for promoting management action in areas where performance expectations have not yet been achieved
8. An organisational culture which promotes and rewards improved performance

Quite often it is the case that public service organisations do not have complete performance management systems in that some of these elements are lacking or are inadequate and consequently the task of performance management becomes constrained.

Stakeholder analysis

In designing performance management systems consideration needs to be given to what sorts of people and/or organisations might be interested in the performance of public service organisations. Some possibilities might be:

- Service users
- Prospective service users
- Proxies for service users (e.g. relatives)
- Service professionals
- External experts
- Suppliers
- Media
- Government departments and agencies
- Politicians
- General public etc.

These are termed stakeholders which was a concept introduced by an American management theorist named Edward Freeman (1984). One approach would be

Level of influence

Level of interest		High	Low
	High	A	B
	Low	C	D

FIGURE 11.3
Stakeholder analysis.

to identify what might be (1) the level of interest and (2) the level of influence of these various groups in relation to public service organisational performance. This approach based on the work of researchers (Mitchell et al. 1997) divides stakeholders into four main segments shown in Figure 11.3.

- **Segment A (high interest/high influence)** – key stakeholders: consult, involve and communicate with them. Examples of such key stakeholders in public services could include government departments, MPs, the media, lobby groups etc. This could involve face-to-face meetings and an effective public relations function.
- **Segment B (high interest/low influence)** – keep them in touch with what is happening at minimum cost. Examples here might be neighbouring public service providers. Social media might provide useful tools here.
- **Segment C (low interest/high influence)** – the strategy here is to keep them happy and they would not bother you. An example in this group might be the government tax authorities. Provision of regular written information should suffice.
- **Segment D (low interest/low influence)** – do not spend much time with these. An example of this group might be the suppliers of goods and services to the organisation. Availability of information on the organisations' website might be sufficient.

Some may regard such an approach as overly cynical and not particularly positive in outlook. However, it does represent an approach that keeps the task of performance management manageable in its own right. One problem, however, is that in some public service organisations there may be a large concentration of stakeholders into quadrant A which is a scenario which might not be found in most commercial organisations. However, stakeholder analysis is a useful tool which can be applied to all types of organisations – private, public and third sector.

PERFORMANCE INFORMATION

Information about the performance of public services can be derived from a wide variety of sources. However, it is suggested that performance data and performance measures can be derived from three main sources which are discussed later:

- **Organisational data** – various types of data (volumes, quality, outcomes cost etc.) will be available within the organisation which can indicate performance.

- **Professional judgements** – issues of performance could be derived from peer reviews undertaken by service professionals within the organisation or by specialists from external organisations.
- **Customer/client perceptions** – the views of service users or prospective service users concerning the performance of services available could be obtained by various means.

Using performance information

It is not usually the case that performance information can be used in isolation or in absolute terms. For example, just stating that in a public service organisation the rate of client satisfaction with services is 89% or the cost of an MRI scan in a hospital is £600 tells very little about its performance. Is 89% good or bad for the type of service involved? Is £600 a low cost or a high cost? It is more likely that the information will be used in a comparative manner and a number of different types of comparisons are possible:

1. How good is our own performance in comparison with some predetermined objective.
2. How good is our own performance over time.
3. How good is our own performance compared with others:
   - Other similar units in the organisation
   - Other public sector service providers
   - Other commercial service providers
   - International comparisons

Clearly most public service organisations are unlikely to undertake the whole range of comparisons, but they could probably do more than is currently being done. Indeed, one of the concerns is that public service organisations actually limit quite considerably the extent to which they compare themselves with others:

- Many only compare their performance with other public service organisations in the same sector even though the areas of comparison might have generic applicability to all sectors (e.g. costs of payroll functions).
- Many only compare themselves within a limited geographic area. They might only make comparisons within their own region rather than the country as a whole.

Few will compare themselves internationally because of a possible lack of basic information about other countries and a concern about how relevant such comparisons might be. However, top universities in a country may do so because they regard themselves as working in a global higher education market and they see these as important comparisons to make.

IMPROVING PERFORMANCE IN PUBLIC SERVICES

Over the last 20 years or so the culture of continuous performance improvement in public services has meant that most of the easy improvements have already been achieved (Prowle et al. 2013). Hence public services must now be more sophisticated in the identification of ongoing improvements. The performance of public services (according to the dimensions identified above) can be improved in a myriad of ways but it is useful to consider them in two main groups:

Strategic approaches

Under this heading would be included major changes to the way in which services were provided:

- **Service reconfiguration/transformation** – step changes in the quality and resource efficiency of public services can be achieved by major reconfigurations or transformations of public services in an area. Examples would be the reconfiguration of healthcare services in an area, the rationalisation of schools' provision as a result of falling rolls or changes to refuse collection involving reduced collections and enhanced recycling opportunities.
- **Major investment in technology** – investment in technology can bring significant improvements in the quality and resource efficiency of public services. A good example would be the ability to make returns to government departments using the Internet. Such an approach should reduce costs and also give greater freedom to the individual about submitting their returns.
- **Changes in skill mix** – changes in skill mix often employing less skilled people to do the lower-skill tasks usually undertaken by more highly skilled staff can bring improvements in performance. On the other hand, the less skilled people will be undertaking the same work at lower cost, while the higher skilled people will be concentrating on the more complex tasks thereby improving service quality in those areas. An example here might be the employment of lower skilled support workers who work with qualified health visitors.
- **Fixed asset rationalisation** – there is often scope for public service organisations to rationalise their fixed asset base (particularly property). This would produce benefits in terms of reduced maintenance costs and the generation of capital receipts which can be reinvested elsewhere. This process might be catalysed by changes in the structure and means of service delivery achieved through service transformation/reconfiguration.

Tactical/operational approaches

These are basically changes which could be made to the current operational practices which would generate improved performance.

- **Process improvements** – public services have, for some years, been utilising approaches developed in manufacturing industry in the use of lean production methods to analyse their various operational process and make improvements. This could involve the use of such techniques as value stream mapping, identification of cost Paretos etc. However, also core to the implementation of "lean" are the creation of vision and effective leadership as well as the use of techniques.

- **Improving flow** – many public service activities (e.g. teaching in a class-room) might be regarded as a form of batch production in that the services are delivered to a group of users in one location by a single service deliverer. However, other public service activities involve a flow process akin to assembly line models in manufacturing industry. Frequently it is the case that in flow arrangements, such as this, bottlenecks are experienced in various stages of the flow process and these bottlenecks result in the flow of services being halted or slowed. The consequences of this are delays in the delivery of services (e.g. scans) and possible underutilisation of resources in other stages of the flow process due to the reduction in flow. Thus, one approach to performance improvement would be to identify these bottleneck situations and take remedial action to eliminate them. In this case the flow will be increased and resource utilisation improved.
- **Increased staff productivity** – low productivity is a major concern in the public and private economies of many countries. In the public sector, there are a number of areas where performance improvements can be achieved by means of increasing staff productivity. Key aspects of this might include enhanced remuneration mechanisms, better supervision, outsourcing, improved recruitment and retention, reduced sickness absence levels, better training and more up-to-date technology. Such approaches will require a number of organisational improvements in relation to productivity measurement, leadership, better sharing of good practice and effective change management.
- **Enhanced Procurement** – improved procurement could involve collaborative procurement arrangements, extended use of e-procurement, collaborative IT procurement.

Barriers to performance improvement in public services

As always, there are a wide range of barriers to improving performance in public service organisations. It is suggested that these be classified twofold:

Internal barriers

Some of the barriers to improving public service performance reside within the public service organisation itself, and some examples of such internal barriers include

- **Incomplete performance management system** – at the start of this chapter we discussed what are the key elements in a performance management system in a public service organisation. It is quite often the case that a public service organisation will have an incomplete system thereby inhibiting the improvement of performance.
- **Incomplete and/or inconsistent data** – to identify and implement performance improvements, it is important to have good-quality data. Often public service organisations lack the necessary data (e.g. cost data) or the various datasets available may conflict with one another. However, sources are available such as CIPFA statistics.

- **Lack of managerial skills or capacity** – performance improvement is not an easy task. First good analytical skills are required to identify changes that will make real improvements to performance. Change management skills are often required to ensure the necessary changes are communicated within the organisation and implemented successfully. It is often the case that public service organisation managers are so burdened with the tasks of keeping the organisation going that they just do not have the capacity to deal with these tasks. Alternatively, even if they did have the capacity, they may not possess the skillset needed to deal with the issues involved.
- **Lack of capital resources** – many performance improvements will require substantial capital investment (e.g. improved energy efficiency) and this can be hampered by a lack of access to capital resources.
- **Internal resistance to change** – in Chapter 1, we discussed the issue of organisational inertia. Thus, it is a well-known phenomenon that public service organisations attempting to improve performance suffer from internal resistance from its staff. Such resistance may be reinforced by resistance from labour unions and/or professional bodies. This situation may have worsened in recent years because of austerity and the belief that changes made to improve performance might lead to job losses. Maybe some form of reward mechanism needs to be developed to reward individuals who cooperate with the change process.

External barriers

However, there are also barriers to performance improvement which are external to the public service organisation itself. These barriers are often much more difficult to deal with than internal barriers, and some examples of external barriers include

- **Public opposition** – many changes to public services (whatever their merits) often result in strong public opposition. Such opposition may be genuinely based or may be based on a combination of misunderstanding and/or misinformation. Such opposition may also be fuelled by an often irresponsible and ineffective media.
- **Lack of political support** – politicians have to be responsive to the concerns of their constituents and often such concerns will result in strong political opposition to change. Once again, these concerns may be based on a combination of misunderstanding and/or misinformation.
- **Poor communications** – in both of the previous cases, the opposition generated may be as a consequence of poor communication by the public service organisation which has failed to get its message over.

Some actions which might be undertaken to overcome these barriers to performance improvement include

- **Improved communication** – as a means of overcoming resistance from external parties such as service users and the general public at large good communication is necessary. Effective and proactive (as opposed to reactive) public relations can help here.

- **Effective change management** – performance improvements usually involve some degree of changes in operational and managerial practices, and such changes will create resistance among staff at all levels. Hence, effective programmes of change management need to be applied to overcome such resistance.
- **Adequate information and analysis** – proposed improvements in performance need to have been subject to robust analysis to ensure the case for change is sound. In turn, this requires adequate information on which the analysis is based. This is not always the case and, not surprisingly, half-baked proposals tend to fall apart under the glare of public scrutiny. Hence improvements in information are required.
- **Adequate management resources** – all of the aforementioned factors require an adequate level of managerial resources in order to identify and implement performance improvements.

MANAGEMENT ACCOUNTING CONTRIBUTION

Management accounting has a number of key roles to play in relation to performance management and performance improvement in public service organisations. This applies both to the strategic aspects of performance management as well as operational aspects. The contribution of management accounting to performance management is based on the role it can play in relation to the performance management cycle which is illustrated in Figure 11.4.

The various techniques that are of relevance here have, to a large extent, already been discussed in previous chapters. In this section we look at their applicability to performance improvement and management in public service organisations.

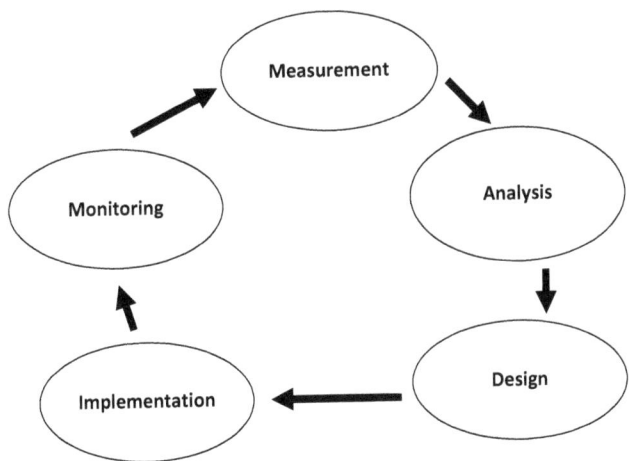

FIGURE 11.4
Performance management cycle.

Measurement

In financial terms, the start point of any performance improvement exercise must be identifying the costs and income associated with the particular entities or activities to be improved. For example, in order to benchmark against others, we must first identify our own costs. More often than not this cost information will not be readily available and some form of costing exercise will need to be undertaken to identify those costs. In such circumstances, it is likely that some form of activity-based costing might be applied. However, there is a balance to be struck here in that the cost information must be of sufficient accuracy to be meaningful while not having taken an inordinate amount of time and effort to compute.

Much of performance improvement will involve changing the relationship between costs and the other dimensions of performance. Thus, in addition, alongside the cost data, there will need to be data about the services themselves such as types, volumes, standards etc.

Analysis

The analysis stage is perhaps the most complex and difficult stage of all. A considerable amount of work will need to be undertaken to analyse the financial and related non-financial data which have been obtained to interpret actual performance. Comparisons with others and over time will be needed. The use of financial benchmarking is well established in public services as a means of analysing and assessing comparative performance and this should be undertaken where possible.

Design

Having undertaken the analysis of existing performance, the next stage is to design improvements that will produce genuine and significant improvements in performance. Such planned improvements may well require changes to a number of aspects of service delivery such as timing, location, method of delivery, type of resource, management etc.

In these situations, it is vitally important that the resource implications of the proposed changes are fully identified and understood before a decision is made to go ahead with the planned changes. In some situations, this might be a relatively easy thing to do and will involve some relatively simple financial analysis. However, in other cases it will be much more complex and recourse may be had to the development and use of decision support models to assess the financial and non-financial consequences of the proposed developments and of various alternative options.

Implementation

It is one thing to identify financially related performance improvements and another thing to bring them to fruition. Many examples can be quoted of viable performance improvements which were identified but where the benefits were not properly realised. This might have been through mismanagement or through some form of deliberate sabotage by vested interests that resisted change.

The key tool of financial management here is the budget system of the public service organisation. It is quite common in the public sector for budget systems to incorporate across the board adjustments for efficiency improvements. However, it is also important that where specific performance improvements are identified that the financial aspects of these are incorporated into the budget for the appropriate year.

Monitoring

Finally, it is clearly important to ensure that planned improvements in service performance are actually delivered. The non-financial aspects of this (e.g. quality, access) will be covered elsewhere, but it will be a role for financial managers to monitor improvements in the use of resources and ensure that planned improvements are achieved.

In summary, it can be seen that financial management has a very wide and important role to play in the design and implementation of public service performance improvement.

While many public services have made substantial improvements in performance over a number of years, it does seem likely that further quantum improvements in performance will be necessary in the next few years and much more radical approaches will be required. The need for such performance improvements means that public service organisations will need to *"up their game"* substantially with regard to performance management and performance improvement, and robust financial management approaches will be a major component of this. Perhaps we also need to consider areas where improvements are less necessary from a financial perspective and/or are much more costly to achieve and then devise a system of focusing on low-cost/high-return improvements. This could be a suggestion for a new system of looking at performance?

Given the importance of staffing and staff costs in the delivery of public services, a key aspect of this could well be staff productivity, the various traditional practices of service professionals in public services and the potential for greater use of technology. Also, consideration would be given to looking at models of performance improvement which have been applied in other countries. However, there are often cultural barriers which inhibit the transplantation of practices in one country into another country with a different culture.

Management accounting and risk management in public services

INTRODUCTION

The future is always uncertain and it is inevitable that the further into the future one looks, the more difficult it is to have confidence in the projected information being used for decision making. Consequently, decisions about strategies and actions are often taken on what might be regarded as "soft" data. Hence, a key part of management in any organisation must be to take account of that risk/uncertainty, and identify approaches to managing the inherent risk/uncertainty that exists in life.

Thus, risk management is a key component of corporate governance and management in both private and public sector organisations, in terms of their structures, processes, corporate values, culture and behaviour. It is the bedrock of an organisation's approach for optimising organisational success, in uncertain times, and it needs to fit well as a management process within the overall governance and management framework of the organisation.

This book is about the role of management accounting in decision making in public services. As has been noted above, such decision making very often takes place in an environment where there is limited certainty and thus management accounting approaches must take cognisance of the risk and uncertainty in its application.

The chapter is structured as follows:

- Distinction between risk and uncertainty
- Risk and risk management in public service organisations
- Risk management features in public services
- Importance of organisational resilience
- Management accounting in an environment of risk and uncertainty

DISTINCTION BETWEEN RISK AND UNCERTAINTY

The terms risk and uncertainty are often used synonymously but there is a clear distinction between them which has implications for risk management practices and for which management accounting tools are appropriate. The following definitions illustrate this:

- Risk exists when a *probability* based on *past experience* can be attached to an event. Uncertainty exists when there is no objective way to place a probability on an event (Knight 1921).
- Risk can be defined as imperfect knowledge where the *probabilities* of the possible outcomes are known. Uncertainty exists when these probabilities are not known (Hardaker 2004).

Thus, it can be seen that the difference between risk and uncertainty concerns the issue of whether we have any objective knowledge about the probability of the various outcomes occurring.

Risk and uncertainty have often been classified according to what is sometimes termed knowns and unknowns. These are as follows:

- **Known knowns.** These are things we definitely know about (or should know about) with a fair degree of certainty.
- **Known unknowns.** These are things that although we know of them or have awareness of their existence, we have no details about them or the likelihood of their occurrence.
- **Unknown unknowns.** These are things we do not even know that we do not know about. In other words, we have no idea about their existence or the probability of their occurrence.
- **Unknown knowns.** These are things which we really do know (or should know) but intentionally (or subconsciously) refuse to acknowledge that we know. This can occur for example, where something is seen as "politically incorrect" or "organisationally undesirable" such that there is a conspiracy of silence not to mention it.

An interesting issue which is topical at the moment concerns the huge global impact of the Covid-19 virus on health and the economy. Some may argue that this event was totally unpredictable and that nothing could have been done to forecast its incidence and impact and take actions accordingly. Others will argue that this was laziness or complacency, the danger signs were there and had been there for years (with previous scares such as SARs, swine flu etc.) but these factors were ignored and no remedial actions taken. No doubt, in future, potential pandemics will be factored into risk management strategies of public and private sector organisations but will other risks such as climate change, migration crises considered.

Table 12.1 shows these classes of risk and uncertainty and indicates that different courses of action are required with each class.

> ### TABLE 12.1
>
> #### Classes of risk and uncertainty
>
> | Type | Courses of Action |
> |---|---|
> | • Known knowns | • Incorporate factors involved into risk management plans |
> | • Known unknowns | • Conduct sensitivity analysis on likely outcomes and incorporate into contingency plans |
> | • Unknown unknowns | • Undertake some form of horizon scanning to identify possible trends in this area and act accordingly |
> | • Unknown knowns | • Take actions to break down cultural inhibitions in organisation and encourage free flow of information and views |

RISK AND RISK MANAGEMENT IN PUBLIC SERVICE ORGANISATIONS

This section looks at various aspects of risk and risk management in public service organisations.

Risk factors

What are the risk factors which drive risk and uncertainty in relation to public services? Some of these include

- External risk factors
  - Political and legal
  - Economic and public finance
  - Societal and environmental
  - Reputational
- Internal risk factors
  - Staff
  - Technology

Political and legal

This refers to the complications public service organisations might face as a result of political and/or legal changes. Political changes could involve

- Change of government
- Change of leader (e.g. Prime Minister, Government Minister)
- Change of policies
- All of the above

Such changes might be because of events taking place in one's own country but might also concern events taking place in other countries. With multinational companies, it might be necessary to monitor potential political risks in several countries where the company is operating, but for public service organisations the thrust of this task should focus on political risks in the host country. Having said that, some notice should be taken of political changes in other countries which might inhibit the public service organisation. This could involve issues such as oil shortages consequent on problems in the Middle East or difficulties in recruiting skilled staff from overseas because of restrictions placed by the home countries.

Legal changes could derive from the passing of new legislation or from challenges in court to existing legislation. In either case, there are potential risk factors for public services.

Economic and public finance

Changes in economic circumstances of a country can have implications for public services, most notably:

- They can impact on the demand for public services.
- They can influence the levels of public funding available for public services.

If the economic outlook of a country worsens, it is possible that unemployment will increase with a consequent increase in demands for public services such as social welfare benefits and healthcare services. At the same time, a worsening economy may mean that government revenues contract and hence the level of funds available for public services might need to be reduced. Conversely, if the economic outlook of a country is set to increase, then the opposite impacts may happen.

In looking at economic and public finance risks, public service organisations may wish to look at international, national and regional/local economic trends. International trends may indicate future impacts on the national economy, and regional/local economic trends may be of great relevance to local public services.

Societal and environmental

Changes within society such as ageing populations, behavioural changes, employment patterns, family structures etc. can have considerable implications for public service demands and need to be considered in any risk analysis. However, such changes may take many years to impact on public services. Similarly, changes in the external physical environment such as housing, roads, industries etc. can also have major implications in the longer term.

Reputational

In the same way as private companies, public service organisations can sustain reputational damage as a consequent of certain events. While this might not be thought of as of such importance in public services, it is still a risk. Reputational damage in public services can impact on public confidence and political support for these public services involved. Scandals about hospitals, schools, prisons, police forces are all such examples.

Staffing

At the current time, the majority of public services are labour intensive. Developments in robotics, artificial intelligence may change that situation in years to come but at the moment, staffing is a key resource for public services. Of particular importance are specialist skills which are needed in public services such as doctors, teachers, engineers, scientists, and a major risk to public services would be an inability to recruit or retain such specialist staff.

Technology

In today's world, public service organisations are strongly reliant on the use of modern technology, especially information technology. It seems likely that this degree of reliance will increase as time goes on. Hence there are substantial and increasing risks associated with potential failures of that technology. The impact of such risks depends on the nature of the failures involved.

Responding to these potential risk factors usually involves some kind of change in the organisation and/or its services. The implementation of such changes can themselves then trigger other risks. Austerity has led to waves of transformative change strategies in many public service organisations, with new models for delivering services across functional and political boundaries, unparalleled community engagement and demand management through early intervention. Thus, the risk map for the individual public service organisation has also changed, with new and possibly less manageable risks emerging. Partnerships are now formed between organisations with quite different governance structures and risk profiles, which cannot be ignored when joint decisions are taken. It is therefore important to agree early on how the parties should share the risks of these new service delivery strategies. Public service approaches to risk management need to become more sophisticated and should define early on and review the organisation's appetite for risk, and consider the opportunities and threats associated with each risk.

Nature of risk management

The impact on private sector companies of the economic downturn of 2009 (Prowle et al. 2010) and particularly the corporate failures in the financial sector resulted in a major reconsideration of risk and risk management in companies and especially in relation to company strategy. Similarly, in public services a wide range of changes taking place in the world pose a variety risks to public services and these risks need to be managed.

However, risk management in public services has some significant differences from the private sector. In the private sector, it is generally true that the higher the risk, the higher the potential in the form of higher returns. But in public services this trade-off does not necessarily apply, as public sector strategic objectives are different and complex. For example, local authorities typically have to balance their duties of citizen protection, well-being and prosperity with the imperative to deliver services. Citizens are taxpayers and public bodies have legal obligations for many services, adding further complexity to the risk management balancing act in the public sector. Decisions about existing risks (whether to ignore, address, move or remove them) and taking on new risks have to be made in a complicated and changing context. All the more reason then for a robust risk management process to underpin them.

Barriers to effective risk management

There are serious obstacles to effective risk management. They include the following:

- A lack of integration, where risk management is applied as an add-on rather than being integrated with other management processes, or where there is a "silo" rather than a broad strategic approach which involves staff at all levels.
- A lack of systematic approach, often arising from an incorrect belief that risk management is automatically embedded in day-to-day decisions. An absence of clear reporting to senior management, and the audit committee tends to accompany this weakness.
- A misunderstanding of risk management, its purpose and relevance for the organisation, with some regarding it as just a compliance exercise. Also, poor connectivity concerning risk between the top and bottom levels of an organisation is a further issue.
- An abdication of responsibility, which often arises from individuals' lack of interest in or awareness of risk. This can arise from poorly written job descriptions and a weak risk management process.

RISK MANAGEMENT FEATURES IN PUBLIC SERVICES

To ensure effective risk management in public services, there are two strongly related but important areas to consider, namely risk management environment and risk management frameworks. These are illustrated in Figure 12.1.

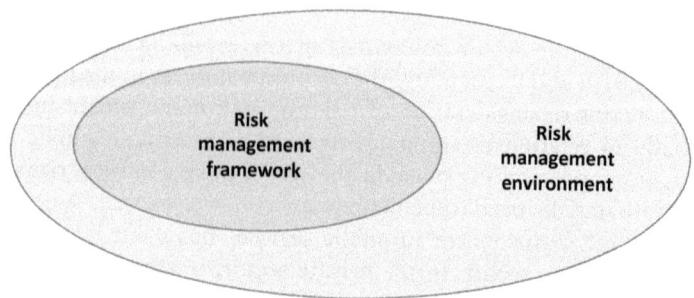

FIGURE 12.1
Risk management approach.

Risk management environment

For any risk management framework to be effective it must exist within an organisational environment and culture which is conducive to its effectiveness. The eight key aspects of this environment are detailed below and are drawn from a well-known and respected risk management approach (COSO 2004).

1. **Internal environment** – management sets a philosophy regarding risk and establishes a risk appetite. The internal environment sets the basis for how risk and control are viewed and addressed by an entity's people. It is critical that senior management express the importance throughout all levels of an entity.
2. **Objective setting** – objectives must exist before management can identify potential events affecting their achievement. Risk management ensures that management has in place a process to set objectives and that the chosen objectives support and align with the entity's mission and are consistent with its risk appetite.
3. **Event identification** – potential events that might have an impact on the entity must be identified. Event identification involves identifying potential events from internal or external sources affecting achievement of objectives. It includes distinguishing between events that represent risks, those that represent opportunities and those that may be both.
4. **Risk assessment** – identified risks are analysed in order to form a basis for determining how they should be managed. Risks are associated with objectives that may be affected. Risks are assessed on both an inherent and residual basis, with the assessment considering both risk likelihood and impact. Risk assessment needs to be done continuously and throughout an entity.
5. **Risk response** – personnel identify and evaluate possible responses to risks, which include avoiding, accepting, reducing and sharing risks. Management selects a set of actions to align risks with the entity's risk tolerances and risk appetite.
6. **Control activities** – policies and procedures are established and executed to help ensure that the risk responses the management selects are effectively carried out.
7. **Information and communication** – relevant information is identified, captured and communicated in a form and timeframe that enables people to carry out their responsibilities. Information is needed at all levels of an entity for identifying, assessing and responding to risk.
8. **Monitoring** – the entirety of risk management is monitored, and modifications are made as necessary. In this way, it can react dynamically, changing as conditions warrant.

If these aspects are not reasonably well fulfilled, then the effectiveness of any risk management framework will be inhibited.

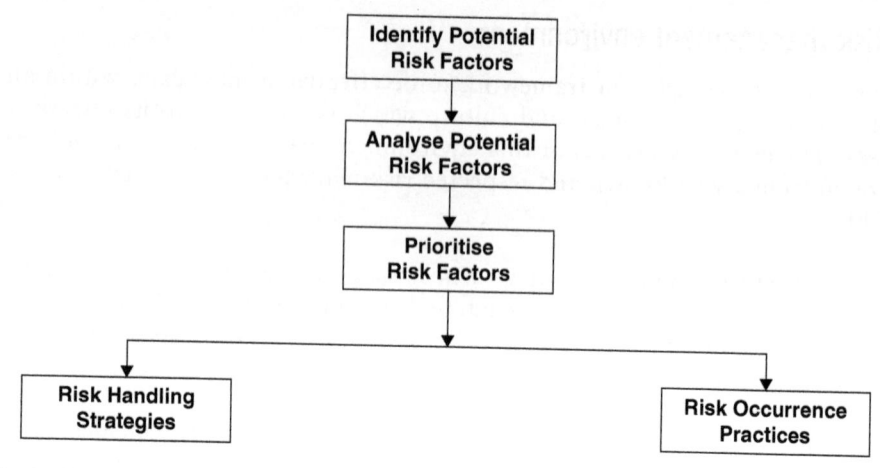

FIGURE 12.2
Risk management framework.

Risk management frameworks

Issues of uncertainty and risk should be addressed systematically according to the stages shown in Figure 12.2.

Identify possible risk factors

The task of identifying possible sources and causes of risk and uncertainty must be undertaken thoroughly and will require considerable thought, brainstorming and critical evaluation. Some questions to be addressed include

- How far ahead in time shall we look?
- How widely shall we look?
- How deeply shall we look?
- How shall we undertake the task?
- How much time and effort shall we spend finding out?

There is no clear-cut answer to these questions and it is a matter of judgement about the balance of time and effort spent looking at risk and uncertainty and the robustness of the analysis.

Analyse potential risk factors

The various risks and uncertainties should be analysed to assess both the

- probability of the risk occurring,
- impact and implications of the risk occurring including possible financial implications.

These tasks must be done thoroughly and objectively since there is much evidence (Economist 2004) to show that people have an inherent tendency to misjudge both probabilities and implications of risks.

Prioritise risk factors

Not all risks can be addressed equally at the same time. Hence, from the above analysis, the organisation should tabulate the risks identified in terms of order of priority to be addressed.

Risk-handling strategies

In the strategic business plan, the organisation has to consider how to respond to the risks it faces. Broadly, there are only four possible actions in relation to each risk factor:

- **Minimise risk** – actions could be taken to minimise the risks faced by, for example, replacing an ineffective manager or an unreliable piece of equipment, providing staff training or developing new procedures or protocols.
- **Transfer/share risk** – risks could be transferred to or shared with another organisation, for example, by the subcontracting of certain activities such as IT management to a third party which would assume many of the IT risks involved.
- **Avoid risk** – the level of risk associated with certain activities may be unacceptably high and the organisation might decide to avoid such risks by not undertaking a particular activity if that is possible (which in the public sector might not be the case) or, more likely, undertaking it in a very different way.
- **Retain risk** – not all risks can be transferred or completely eliminated. Thus, the organisation must be clear about what level of risk it is prepared to retain and accept.

Risk occurrence practices

In view of the residual risks which are inevitably retained within the organisation, it is important to have in place established practices and procedures for coping with such risks should they occur. This could involve effective early-warning monitoring of known risk factors and having in place contingency plans to deal with the impact of retained risks which actually manifest themselves. These could include arrangements to hire contract personnel to replace the loss of specialist staff or arrangements to lease buildings or equipment to replace that lost through breakdown or sabotage. Also, it would involve putting in place financial contingency measures and financial provisions to deal with the impact of risks that might occur.

IMPORTANCE OF ORGANISATIONAL RESILIENCE

Organisational resilience in public services is complementary to risk management. Some authors have argued that resilience is an integrating concept that allows multiple risks, shocks and stresses and their impacts on systems and organisations to be considered together. Organisational resilience can be thought of as the ability of an organisation to anticipate, prepare for, respond and adapt to incremental change and sudden disruptions in order to survive and prosper. It can be considered as involving two sets of measures both of which are important:

- Defensive measures – stopping bad things from happening.
- Progressive measures – making good things happen.

Work done by the British Standards Institution (BSI) suggests that there are 16 main factors of resilience that can be combined into four groups, namely: people, leadership, processes and services. These factors suitably modified for public services are illustrated in Table 12.2.

Thus, public service organisations might consider using these factors of resilience to self-assess their own level of resilience. A number of self-assessment tools exist to facilitate this. They could then compare their level of resilience over time and/or compare with other organisations.

Now the management accountant will probably take an interest in all aspects of resilience, as outlined above, since weaknesses in any aspect of resilience could have severe implications for organisational sustainability.

However, management accountants are bound to have a very strong and specific focus on the financial resilience of their public service organisation. Now financial resilience of an organisation can be assessed in two main ways:

- **Process review** – Item 4 in table 12.2 is termed financial management and this can be broken down into three main processes by asking the following questions:
    - How good is financial planning?
    - How good is financial control?
    - How good is financial governance?

    Thus, financial resilience can be assessed by undertaking a critical review of these processes in a structured manner. The review could be a self-assessment or one conducted by an external party.
- **Data analysis** – Financial data on the organisation could be subject to analysis to assess financial resilience of the organisation. Some key questions to answer would be:
    - How diversified are our income streams?

TABLE 12.2

Resilience factors

Leadership	People	Processes	Services
1. Leadership	6. Culture	10. Governance and accountability	14. Horizon scanning
2. Vision and purpose	7. Community engagement	11. Organisational continuity	15. Innovation
3. Reputational risk	8. Awareness, training, testing	12. Supply chain	16. Adaptive capacity
4. Financial management	9. Alignment	13. Information and knowledge management	
5. Resource management			

- How secure are those income streams?
- What is our debt-to-income ratio?
- How much cash can we access in an emergency?
- How much slack do we have in our budgets?

Once again, various tools are available to do this analysis and the results could be compared over time or against comparable organisations. For example, in relation to English local government, an useful tool is available from CIPFA that allows a local authority to calculate a series of financial resilience ratios for itself and for a selected number of comparable authorities. Key aspects of the tool concern revenue streams, reserves, interest charges, levels of debt etc.

Mention should also be made of the CIPFA Financial Management Code. The code which is aimed at local authorities is designed to support good practice in financial management in demonstrating financial sustainability. The code provides a strong foundation to:

- Financially manage the short-, medium- and long-term finances of a local authority;
- Manage financial resilience to meet foreseen demands on services; and
- Financially manage unexpected shocks in their financial circumstances.

The code is based on a series of principles supported by specific standards and statements of practice.

MANAGEMENT ACCOUNTING IN AN ENVIRONMENT OF RISK AND UNCERTAINTY

Much of management accounting practice, particularly in textbooks, is often presented in a way that suggests there is no uncertainty or risk involved with single-figure cost estimates or single-point multi-year estimates etc. being the norm. Unfortunately, the real world is not like that and management accounting practices must take account of risk and uncertainty.

Management accounting is primarily, although not entirely, concerned with the financial aspects of organisational management. When we consider the financial aspects of risk, we see here are two distinct issues:

- Financial risks which have a direct financial impact (e.g. income shortfalls, fraud, inflation);
- Non-financial risks which have an indirect financial impact (e.g. major IT failure).

Hence, management accountants need to have a strong involvement in all risk management practices in public service organisations. There are three aspects to consider.

Management control systems

All public service organisations require some type of management control system, and management accountants have a key role to play here. A management control system is a system which gathers and uses information to evaluate the performance of different organisational resources like human, physical, financial and also the organisation as a whole in light of the organisational strategies pursued. Leaders of successful organisations have always had some focus on managing risks, but it typically was from a reactive exposure-by-exposure standpoint or a silo approach rather than a proactive, integrated, across-the-organisation perspective. Under a silo approach, individual organisational units deal with their own risks, and often no single group or person in the organisation has a grasp of the entire exposure confronting the organisation.

To correct such a situation, in recent years an approach to risk management was developed which takes an integrated and holistic view of the risks facing the organisation. The model (COSO 2017) has five components broken down into 20 principles and is shown in Table 12.3.

Now we outline a number of techniques and approaches which facilitate the optimisation of these components and these are considered under two headings. These concern

- Risk identification approaches
- Risk assessment approaches

TABLE 12.3

Integrated and holistic view of risks

Components	Principles
Governance and culture	1. Exercises board risk oversight 2. Establishes operating structures 3. Defines desired culture 4. Demonstrates commitment to core values 5. Attracts, develops and retains capable individuals
Strategy and objective setting	6. Analyses business context 7. Defines risk appetite 8. Evaluates alternative strategies 9. Formulates business objectives
Performance	10. Identifies risk 11. Assesses severity of risk 12. Prioritises risks 13. Implements risk responses 14. Develops portfolio view
Review and revision	15. Assesses substantial change 16. Reviews risk and performance 17. Pursues improvement in risk management
Information, communication and reporting	18. Executive leverages information and technology 19. Communicates risk information 20. Reports on risk, culture and performance

Risk identification approaches

The Institute of Management Accountants (IMA 2017) in its recent publication on the implementation of risk management identified a number of approaches which fall under the heading of risk identification. Management accountants can have a strong role in leading and/or participating in these approaches which are outlined briefly:

- **Brainstorming** – when objectives are stated clearly and understood by participants, a brainstorming session drawing on the creativity of the participants can be used to generate a list of risks. In a well-facilitated brainstorming session, the participants are collaborators, comprising a team that works together to articulate the risks that may be known by only some in the group. In the session, risks that are known unknowns may emerge, and, perhaps, even some risks, that were previously unknown unknowns, may become known. Facilitating a brainstorming session takes special leadership skills, and, internal auditors, management accountants and risk management staff may have those skills. Providing participants with some form of stimulation on risks is very important in a brainstorming session. One possibility is to provide a broad list for the sector or a generic set of risks. A general risk classification scheme could be used to start the discussion. In a brainstorming session or facilitated workshop (see later), the goal is to reduce the risk event list to those relevant to the organisation and to define each risk specific to the organisation.
- **Facilitated workshops** – after the information on risks is completed and collected, a cross-functional management team from the unit or several units might participate in a facilitated workshop to discuss it. Again, using voting software, the various risks can be ranked to arrive at a consensus of the top five to ten, for example. As noted previously, using interactive voting software allows the individuals to identify and rank the risks anonymously without fear of reprisal should their superior be a member of the group. Workshops can also be used to review the environment and identify changes from a variety of sources (political, economic, technology and so forth) to identify potential risks.
- **Interviews and self-assessment** – this technique combines two different processes. First, each individual in the organisational or operating units is given a template with instructions to list the key strategies and/or objectives within his or her area of responsibility and the risks that could impede the achievement of the objectives. Each unit group is also asked to assess its risk management capability using practical framework categories which is provided. The completed documents are submitted to the coordinator. That group follows up with interviews to clarify issues. Eventually, the risks for the unit are identified and defined, and a risk management capability score can be determined from a five-point scale.
- **SWOT analysis** – strengths, weaknesses, opportunities and threats (SWOT) analysis was discussed in an earlier chapter in relation to strategy. However, it is also relevant to risk identification. For SWOT analysis to be

effective in risk identification, an appropriate degree of focus must be given to considering and evaluating the organisation's weaknesses and threats. There is sometimes a tendency is to devote more time to strengths and opportunities and give the discussion of weaknesses and threats only cursory consideration. Taking this further and developing a risk map based on consensus will ensure that this side of the discussion gets a robust analysis.

- **Risk questionnaires and risk surveys** – a risk questionnaire that includes a series of questions on both internal and external events can also be used, effectively, to identify risks. For the external area, questions might be directed at political and social risk, reputation risks, regulatory risks, industry risk, economic risk, environmental risk, competition risk and so forth. Questions on the internal perspective might address risks relating to customers, creditors, suppliers, services, operational processes, facilities, information systems etc. Questionnaires are valuable because they can help an organisation think through its own risks by providing a list of questions around certain risks. The disadvantage of questionnaires is that they usually are not linked to strategy. Rather than a lengthy questionnaire, a risk survey can be used. In one organisation, surveys were sent to both lower- and senior-level management. The survey for lower management asked respondents to "list the five most important risks to achieving your unit's goals/objectives". The survey to senior management asked participants to "list the five most important risks to achieving the organisation's strategic objectives". The survey instruments included a column for respondents to rank the effectiveness of management for each of the five risks listed, using a range of 1 (ineffective) to 10 (highly effective).

- **Scenario analysis** – this is a particularly useful technique in identifying strategic risks where risks are less defined and "what-if" questions should be explored. Essentially, this technique is one way to uncover risks where the event is high impact/low probability on the grid referred to above. Using this technique, a cross-functional team could consider the long-term effects resulting from a major shift in the pattern of need for public services and/or lack of capacity and capability to provide those services.

- **Using technology** – the risk identification process can also utilise the organisations' existing technology infrastructure. For example, most organisations utilise an intranet in their management processes. Examples of best risk practices can be placed on the intranet to encourage managers to think about risk in their unit and to take actions. Also, tools that have been found particularly useful to various units can be catalogued. Use can potentially be made of modern technologies such as big data analytics and artificial intelligence to help the organisation identify possible risks (see Chapter 13).

- **Other techniques** – many organisations calibrate their identified risks by comparing their risks to external sources of risks. Another method for calibration is to try and benchmark with a peer organisation in the same sector and compare what each has identified. The organisation might also have an approach which aims to identify and record emerging risks separately from long-standing risks in order to highlight their lack of experience in managing such risks. Finally, there can be a separate focus within the organisation on strategic risk analysis. Strategic risks can derive from an organisation having its actual strategy being misaligned from its chosen strategy, and from the actual risks to implementing the strategy. This perspective, along with a lot of big changes in data, operational models, innovation and disruption has led to a new emphasis on strategic risk identification.

After a risk is identified, the temptation to quantify it before further analysis is completed should be avoided. Additional understanding of the risk's potential causes is required before its impact can be quantified. Working with the various units of the organisation that own parts of the risk, risk management team should drill into the risk to uncover what is beneath the surface and to get a better understanding of the potential risk drivers.

Risk assessment approaches

Risks must be identified correctly before an organisation can take the next step. Assessing the wrong list of risks or an incomplete list of risks is futile. The act of identifying risks is itself a step to effective risk assessment. Any risks identified, almost by default, have some probability of influencing the organisation. Once risks are identified, it may be helpful to categorise them. This may be a necessity if the risk identification process produces hundreds of risks, which can be unmanageable. Risk categories include hazard, operational, financial and strategic. Knowing the risk categories is sometimes a step towards understanding risk interconnectedness.

Risk assessment techniques can vary from qualitative to quantitative. The qualitative techniques can be a simple list of all risks, risk rankings or risk maps. Even though no quantitative analysis or formal assessment has been applied to the initial list of risks, the list and accompanying knowledge is valuable. Some risks on the list may just not be quantifiable. For these risks, identifying them and adding them to a priority list may be the only quantification possible. Organisations should not be concerned that they cannot apply sophisticated statistical modelling to every risk.

Once again, a number of risk assessment techniques can be identified (IMA 2017) which can be utilised by management accountants in public services.

- **Risk rankings** – once an organisation has created its list of risks, it can begin to rank them. Ranking requires the prioritisation of the risks on a scale of importance, such as low, moderate and high. Although this seems unsophisticated, the results can be dramatic. Organisations find considerable value in having conversations about the importance of a risk. The conversations usually lead to questions about why one group believes the risk is important and why others disagree. Again, this process should use a cross-functional risk team so that perspectives from people across the entire organisation are factored into the rankings. This is a critical task requiring open debate, candid discussion and data.
- **Impact and probability assessment: risk maps** – when considering particular future events which may affect public services, it is almost inevitable that the risks associated with such events will be considered to some extent. However, in considering these risk issues it is also important to

recognise that there are two dimensions of risk which need to be considered and evaluated.

- The probability of the particular event happening;
- The likely impact on the organisation and its services should that particular event be manifested.

The magnitude of these two dimensions needs to be measured or assessed and the results can be expressed in the form of a risk map as shown in Figure 12.3.

Looking at this, it can be seen that this sort of analysis identifies those events (A) which have a high likelihood of occurring and have likely high impact. Therefore, these are the ones which need closest analysis and careful consideration about actions that need to be taken in relation to the risks involved. At the other extreme, those events which have a low likelihood of occurring and have likely low impact (B) might only be given very cursory attention. The response to other combinations of likelihood/impact need careful consideration of the following:

- **Analyse risk by departments or objectives** – identifying risks by organisational objective gives the option to map risks against those objectives. This is very important in public service organisations where there are usually a multiplicity of objectives to work with. A risk map by objective captures all the risks related to a single objective, helping the organisation understand the broad spectrum of risks facing that objective. Similarly, risks can also be identified by departments of the organisation which may be more informative for departmental managers.
- **Residual risk** – after organisations assess risks, they should also ascertain that any residual risk is known. A residual risk is the remaining risk after mitigation efforts and controls are in place to address the initially identified inherent risks that threaten the achievement of objectives. Understanding residual risk can provide major benefits because organisations do not want to over- or under-manage a risk that may be deemed to be "tolerable" or acceptable relative to stated objectives.
- **Sensitivity analysis** – at the outset, it is important to recognise that a sensitivity analysis is not the same as a scenario analysis. A sensitivity analysis is the study of how the uncertainty in the output of a quantitative model can be divided and allocated to different sources of uncertainty in its

Probability of risk event occurrence

		HIGH	MEDIUM	LOW
Likely impact of risk event occurrence	HIGH	A		
	MEDIUM			
	LOW			B

FIGURE 12.3
Risk map.

inputs. A sensitivity analysis is often referred to as "what-if" and is a way to predict the outcome of a decision given a certain range of variables. By creating a given set of variables, an analyst can determine how changes in one variable will affect the output of the model. Hence, sensitivity analysis can be used to assess and quantify the impact on the organisation of different levels of risks occurring.

- **Expected values** – this is a fairly simple statistical technique for dealing with uncertainty over financial estimates. Where the outcome of a particular course of action is not known with certainty, it may, nevertheless, be possible (perhaps based on previous experience) to assign probabilities to alternative possible outcomes. An "expected value" of the alternative outcomes can then be calculated and the optimal course of action identified as the one with the highest expected value. This is illustrated simply in Table 12.4.

In the last couple of decades, risk management has become of increasing importance in both public and private sectors and often a significant proportion of organisational resources are devoted to the functions. However, it is suggested that in public services it is often the case that risk management has the following features:

- A disproportional emphasis on operational risks to the detriment of strategic risks.
- Risk management is seen as just a set of processes to go through driven by a large volume of paperwork to be completed.
- Having a risk focus is not always something inculcated into the culture of the organisation apart from areas affecting professional liability.
- Management accountants have only a limited involvement in risk management.

This chapter tries to suggest that management accountants should have a stronger role in all aspects of risk management but need to acquire the skills necessary to fulfil that role.

TABLE 12.4

Expected values

Estimated Cost (£)	Probability	Expected Value (£)
1,000	10%	100
1,100	55%	605
1,200	35%	420
Total expected value		1,125

Contemporary aspects of management accounting in public services

INTRODUCTION

This chapter summarises a number of aspects of management accounting which may not necessarily be seen as current mainstream activities, in all situations, but which may have considerable potential in public services in the future.

The topics covered are

- Modern costing developments
- Interorganisational cost management (IOCM)
- Environmental management accounting (EMA)
- Management accounting and modern operational processes
- Technology and management accounting
- Impact on management accounting

MODERN COSTING DEVELOPMENTS

Under this heading are considered the following modern costing developments:

- Target costing
- Life-cycle costing (LCC)
- Quality costing

Target costing

Traditionally, in the commercial sector, unit product costs have been ascertained in order to (among other things) facilitate pricing decisions. Target costing, which is largely of Japanese origin, puts this into reverse by starting with the "right price" (given market conditions and competitors' prices) and deriving from this a unit product cost which will generate an acceptable level of profit. This approach, known as target costing, has many definitions but, perhaps, the clearest is as follows.

> A cost management tool for reducing the overall cost of a product over its entire life-cycle with the help of production, engineering, research and design.

Thus, a target cost is the maximum amount of cost that can be incurred on a product such that the organisation can still earn the required profit margin from selling that product at the market price.

The target cost for a product is calculated by subtracting the target profit from a predetermined selling price based on customers' views about willingness to pay. Once this cost is established, the organisation needs to be able manufacture the product for that amount.

One option available to the manufacturer would be to conduct a value engineering exercise in order to redesign the product so that its value to the customer is enhanced, while its costs are reduced. Value engineering is a complete audit of a product or service that takes place while that product or service is *still on the drawing board*. In some cases, it could lead to a complete redesign. At the same time cognisance would need to be taken of any statutory requirements or customer preferences in undertaking this exercise.

A well-known example of target costing being used in this way concerned the manufacture of the low-priced automobile, the Tata Nano in India. The initial objective of the company was to develop a product for people who want to move from two-wheeler to four-wheeler at affordable price – this implied being able to supply a car at around 1,000,000 Indian rupees. The car was to be developed in relation to three main factors: cost, safety and compliance with regulatory requirements. Thus, the car had to be developed on the basis of low cost, safety, low on emissions and fuel efficient and needed to be seen as a truly people's car.

At first thought target costing might not seem appropriate to public services since most public services do not have a market price let alone deduct a profit margin to get a target price. However, this is not necessarily true for a number of reasons.

First, in some situations, public service organisations do work in a competitive market where there is a ruling price and so target pricing can be as applicable here as in the commercial sector. Take for example the delivery of a programme of short courses at a college. Using a form of target costing, the following approach could be applied:

- Identify or estimate the likely price the client is prepared to pay for the programme.
- Identify the target cost envelope for the course programme taking account of the financial surplus required.
- Identify the current costs of delivering such courses at the college.
- Make changes to current approaches to course delivery to get inside the cost envelope. In doing this, client requirements and professional standards need to be maintained.

Second, even where there is no competitive market, public service organisations do have to deliver services in an environment of scarce resources, particularly during a period of austerity. In Chapter 2 on operations management, it was noted that a key aspect of operations management, which precedes service delivery, was that of service design. Thus, a form of target costing could be used to design (or redesign) services that will fit the resources available rather than the other way around.

There are many situations where the same public services show large-scale cost variations across different providers with no obvious reason for the differences. One example of this concerns imaging services in hospitals (Prowle 2007) which suggested large-scale variations in imaging procedure costs between different hospitals for the same type of imaging scan (e.g. CT, X-ray, ultrasound). In this situation a target costing approach might be used in order to reduce imaging costs:

- Establish the costs of delivering imaging activities at different hospitals.
- Establish the quality of imaging work being achieved.
- Choose a target cost in line with comparable hospitals but with some efficiency savings.
- Review existing operational processes (stages, staffing, timing etc.) applied in undertaking imaging scans.
- Identify process changes which would reduce costs while maintaining quality standards.
- Implement and monitor the revised changes.

Target costing would probably be seen as alien to many public service professionals as normal practice is to identify client needs and then use the resources available to meet those needs, probably using what might be seen as traditional approaches. Target costing turns this on its side by first identifying the resources that should be spent delivering a service (based on comparisons with others etc.) and designing a service to meet client needs based around this cost envelope.

Life-cycle costing (LCC)

In the commercial sector, conventional product costing methods such as absorption costing or activity-based costing were designed to ascertain the cost of manufacturing a product or providing a service. However, many other costs which are involved in developing, launching and supporting a product or service during its life cycle are ignored. Some costs, such as design, development and setting up the production/delivery process, are incurred prior to manufacture. Other costs are incurred after manufacture, such as distribution and after-sales service. There may also be costs involved in the eventual dropping of the product at the end of its life cycle.

Conventional accounting systems account for such costs on a calendar/time basis to which they relate, they are treated as expenses in the income and expenditure account of the period in which they are incurred. In order to understand the true costs of a product or service, however, such costs should be tracked and assigned to the product/service from the beginning to end of its life.

Revenues earned during its life cycle can also be tracked and, by comparing these with the accumulated costs, the true longer-term profitability of the product can be evaluated.

With regard to public services, incorporating LCC into decision making will provide public service organisations with the opportunity to demonstrate the best value for money across the asset life cycle. Key cost aspects concern:

- Acquisition
- Use
- Maintenance
- End-of-life disposal

Life-cycle costing in public services can be defined as an assessment which considers all agreed projected significant and relevant cost flows over a period of analysis. The projected costs are those needed to achieve defined levels of performance, including reliability, safety and availability. The use of LCC is essential to demonstrate that decisions have moved beyond just considering the initial cost of a service which does not reflect the financial and non-financial gains that are offered by using environmentally and socially preferable assets as they accrue during the operations and use phases of the life cycle.

Typical LCC analyses are therefore are based on:

- purchasing costs and all associated costs such as delivery, installation, commissioning and insurance;
- operating costs, including utility costs such as energy and water use and maintenance costs;
- end-of-life costs such as removal, recycling or refurbishment and decommissioning.

Now LCC methods have been well known in the public sector for many years, but such life-cycle approaches may often be seen as clashing with the short-term funding approaches of many public services which force short-term considerations. For example, the pressure to minimise initial capital costs of a new building in spite of the fact that higher capital costs may generate lower LCCs through factors such as improved energy utilisation. The current emphasis on slowing climate change and achieving sustainability demands much stronger consideration should be given, in future, to costing on a life-cycle basis than has been traditionally the case. Hence, LCC has been incorporated into this chapter as a contemporary management accounting issue.

Quality costing

In recent years, the quality of products and services has been of increasing strategic importance to companies. With the increased emphasis on quality, however, has come the need to manage the costs of achieving quality. This applies to public services as well as the commercial sector, and public service organisations may wish to address this issue.

Albright and Roth (1992) developed a framework for managing quality costs, based on their observation that "Quality costs are incurred to ensure that quality standards are met or because quality standards are not met". Accordingly, they proposed a framework for analysing quality costs, which can inform management of the problem areas and action priorities through the regular provision of a cost of quality report. In the cost of quality report, costs are analysed into four distinct categories as shown below.

- **Prevention costs** – costs associated with personnel engaged in designing, implementing and maintaining the quality system. Subcategories include quality engineering, design and development of equipment, quality training, quality planning, quality reporting, supplier evaluation and selection, quality audits.
- **Appraisal costs** – costs associated with measuring and evaluating products, components and purchased materials to assure conformance with quality standards and performance requirements. Subcategories include inspection and testing of incoming materials and of finished products before despatch.
- **Internal failure costs** – these occur when products, components and materials fail to meet quality requirements prior to transfer of ownership to the customer or client. Subcategories include scrap, rework, failure analysis, re-inspection and machine down time due to defects and so on.
- **External failure costs** – these occur when the product does not perform satisfactorily after the transfer of ownership to the customer/client. Subcategories include complaints, rejects and returns, repairs, warranty costs and ultimately the loss of customer goodwill, and sales and market share that may result (adapted from Hoque 2006).

Ultimately, money invested in prevention and appraisal activities should reduce internal and external failure costs by an amount that significantly exceeds this investment. The cost of quality report should, over time, inform management whether this trend is occurring so that they can assess the overall effectiveness of their quality programme.

Quality costing is often thought of in relation to material goods but it also has applicability in relation to services and by extension also has potential applicability in relation to public services. Quality has many dimensions in relation to public services but the costs of delivering that quality just cannot be ignored. With information on quality costing, it is possible to consider a number of key issues such as:

- Can the costs associated with quality assurance be reduced without having any major impact on quality levels?
- If quality levels are a problem in the organisation, should we be enhancing quality assurance approaches? How should that be done and what would be the associated costs?

INTER-ORGANISATIONAL COST MANAGEMENT (IOCM)

As emphasised throughout this book, cost management involves initiating and making decisions which will improve the cost-effectiveness of an organisation. A topic of increasing importance in recent years is that of interorganisational

of environment-related information mainly for external readers. It focuses on reports required for shareholders and other stakeholders. EMA is a subset of environmental accounting which focuses on information required for decision making by managers within the organisation.

The International Federation of Accountants (IFAC 2005) defined EMA as:

> The management of environmental and economic performance, through the development and implementation of appropriate environment-related accounting systems and practices. While this may include reporting and auditing in some companies, environmental management accounting typically involves lifecycle costing, full cost accounting, benefits assessment, and strategic planning for environmental management.

Traditional management accounting practice focusses on providing information, both financial and non-financial, on the activities of an organisation in order to assist with strategic and operational decisions. EMA goes beyond that and is a part of management accounting that focuses on matters such as the cost of energy and water, the disposal of waste and effluent, the consumption of materials, transportation costs and carbon footprint. It is important to note, at this point, that the focus of EMA is not purely on financial costs. It includes consideration of matters such as the costs versus benefits of buying from suppliers who are more environmentally aware, or the effect on the public image of the organisation of failure to comply with environmental regulations etc.

Such management information requirements could include the following:

- Identifying and estimating the costs of environment-related activities
- Identifying and monitoring the use and cost of resources such as water, electricity and fuel, so that such costs can be reduced
- Making sure environmental considerations form part of capital investment decisions
- Assessing the likelihood and impact of environmental risks
- Including environment-related indicators as part of routine performance monitoring
- Benchmarking activities against environmental best practice

Thus, EMA involves the identification, collection, analysis and use of two types of management information for internal decision making:

- Physical information on the use, flows and rates of energy, water and materials (including wastes)
- Monetary information on the environment-related costs, earnings and savings

Defining environmental costs

Organisations will vary considerably in the way they define their environmental costs, as their cost structures will vary between sectors and organisations. Hence, it is difficult to come up with a standard definition. In broad terms, a useful over-arching approach to defining organisational costs is that provided by the US Environmental Protection Agency (EPA 1998). Their approach was to consider the way in which an organisation intended to use the information. They made a distinction between four types of costs:

- **Conventional costs** – raw material and energy costs having environmental relevance
- **Potentially hidden costs** – costs captured by accounting systems but then losing their "environmental" identity in general overheads
- **Contingent environmental costs** – costs to be incurred at a future date – for example, clean-up costs
- **Image and relationship costs** – costs that, by their nature, are intangible, for example, the costs of preparing environmental reports

Other models may be available but in public services it is for each sector to come up with its own approach to categorising environmental costs.

Identifying environmental costs

Much of the information needed to prepare environmental management accounts can be found in the financial systems of a public service organisation. A review should reveal the costs of materials, utilities and waste disposal. However, many costs with environmental impacts will be found within the category of "general overheads". Identifying them could be a lengthy process, particularly in a large organisation, but some attempt needs to be undertaken possibly by a sampling exercise. If this is not done, then the fact that environmental costs are often "hidden" in this way makes it difficult to identify opportunities to cut environmental costs and yet it is crucial that to try to do so. It is equally important to allocate environmental costs to the activities, processes, products or services which give rise to them. Only by doing this can an organisation make well-informed decisions. Possible approaches are discussed in the next section.

Accounting for environmental costs

A number of accounting techniques have been identified by the United Nations Division for Sustainable Development (UNDSD 2003) as being appropriate for the process of accounting for environmental costs. These are discussed below:

- **Inflow/outflow analysis** – this technique records and contrasts material inflows with outflows and, on the basis that what comes in must go out the causes of any differences are analysed. For example, if 500 kg of materials have been issued for production and only 400 kg have been used in production, then the 100 kg difference must be accounted for in some way. Some of it might be scrap and the rest might be waste. By accounting for outputs in this way, both in terms of physical quantities and, at the end of the process, in monetary terms, organisations are forced to focus on environmental costs.
- **Flow cost accounting** – this technique links material flows to the organisational structure. It looks at the physical quantities, the costs and the value of these flows and divides them into three categories: material, system and

delivery/disposal. The values and costs of each of these three flow categories are then calculated and examined. This makes material flows more transparent. The aim of flow cost accounting is to reduce the quantity of materials which, as well as having a positive effect on the environment, should have a positive effect on an organisation's total costs in the long run.

- **Activity-based costing** – the activity-based costing approach has already been discussed, at length in Chapter 7. In an environmental accounting context, activity-based costing distinguishes between environment-related costs, which can be attributed to joint cost centres, and environment driven costs, which tend to be hidden in general overheads.
- **Life-cycle costing** – this approach has already been discussed earlier in this chapter and is a technique which requires the full environmental consequences, and, therefore, costs arising from production of a product to be taken account across its whole life cycle, literally "from cradle to grave".

Controlling environmental costs

Once environmental costs have been defined, identified and accounted for, organisations can consider the vital task of identifying how to control them.

The size and mix of environmental costs will vary substantially from sector to sector and so it is difficult to be prescriptive about how this should be approached. Key items in public services are

- Energy and utilities
- Transport and travel
- Consumables

Each of these costs is considered in turn below.

- **Energy and utilities** – these are often a huge cost in many public service organisations. They are also major contributors to global warming. Such costs can often be reduced significantly at very little cost by identifying inefficiencies and wasteful practices in the organisation. Environmental management accountants may help to identify opportunities in this area.
- **Transport and travel** – transport (and especially air travel) is also one of the major contributors to global warming. Transport can involve people and goods. Public sector organisations need to examine the number of journeys made by staff, the travel mode and the degree of necessity of the journeys. In the Internet age, it may be easy to utilise social media applications (e.g. Skype, Zoom) or home working for many activities rather than making physical journeys. Similarly, public service organisations need to analyse their pattern of purchases for physical goods and where these goods were sourced from. Consideration might be given to reducing their carbon footprint by sourcing goods more proximate to their base. Again, EMA can often help in doing this. A particular issue in purchasing considerations is whether the public authority can set off savings in environmental costs against a possibly higher purchase price.

- Consumables – public services do not generally produce goods and so there are not usually large amounts of raw materials, work in progress etc. associated with production. However, there will be large financial and environmental costs associated with consumable items such as stationery, foodstuffs, clothing, building materials, medications etc. The key mantras in relation to these items are the three Rs of reduce, reuse and recycle, and many public service organisations now have various policies and procedures in place to implement these matters. These involve designated responsibilities for environmental matters, procedures for reducing environmental costs, measurement devices and frequent reports on progress.

MANAGEMENT ACCOUNTING AND MODERN OPERATIONAL PROCESSES

As already seen, management accounting has a major role to play improving information about the operational processes used in the organisation to produce goods and/or services. In recent years, two particular approaches that have become increasingly popular in many types of organisations (including public services) are those of lean and theory of constraints (TOC).

Lean

Lean is an approach to operations management that focuses on cutting out waste whilst ensuring quality. This approach can be applied to all aspects of an organisation from design through production to distribution. It originated in the manufacturing plants of Japan (particularly Toyota) but has now been adopted well beyond that in many large and sophisticated manufacturing activities. Many public services have also attempted to adopt lean practices most notably the NHS.

Lean aims to cut costs by making the organisation more efficient and responsive to external needs. The lean approach sets out to remove or minimise activities that do not add value to the operational process, such as holding of stock, repairing faulty product and unnecessary movement of people and product around the organisation.

Some key aspects of waste to be looked at include

1. **Over-production** – making more than is needed which leads to excess volumes of finished goods.
2. **Waiting time** – equipment and people standing idle waiting for a production process to be completed or resources to arrive.
3. **Transport** – moving resources (people, materials) around unnecessarily often due to poor layout.
4. **Stocks** – often held as an acceptable buffer but should not be excessive.
5. **Motion** – a worker who appears busy but is not actually adding any value.
6. **Defects** – output that does not reach the required quality standard – often a significant cost to an uncompetitive business.

The concept of lean is an incredibly powerful one for any organisation. Why? Because waste = cost. Less waste therefore means lower costs.

A big problem is that lean is often seen, merely, as a collection of techniques to be utilised including:

* Time-based management
* Simultaneous engineering
* Just-in-time production
* Cell production
* Kaizen (continuous improvement)
* Quality improvement and management

However, this is a serious error. Experience shows that the successful implementation of lean requires a major cultural change in the organisation which encourages employees, at all levels, to focus on identifying waste and taking remedial actions. The various tools shown above assist in this process.

The lean approach to managing operations is really about:

* Doing the simple things well
* Doing things better
* Involving employees in the continuous process of improvement and as a result, avoiding waste

Lean approaches have been employed in many parts of the public sector and in many countries in the world including defence, healthcare, police, higher education, central government and local government. Much has also been written about how lean should be applied in public services and how successful it is seen as being. It is probably true to say that the degree of success of lean in public services is mixed and that the reasons for this are debatable. It is beyond the scope of this book to address these matters in any detail, but it seems one main reason for the failure of lean in public services is that, as quoted earlier, there was a too strong focus on the use of techniques and a weaker focus on developing a lean culture.

Theory of constraints (TOC)

The theory of constraints (TOC) is a management philosophy that was introduced in 1984 with the publication of *The Goal* by Eli Goldratt, an Israeli academic and business management expert. Basically, TOC says that a small number of constraints prevent any production system from achieving more of its goals. There is always at least one constraint, and the TOC uses what is called a focusing process to identify that constraint, and then restructuring in order to address it. Think of it like the old axiom, "A chain is no stronger than its weakest link". The TOC works to find that link and lessen its vulnerability. That applies to processes, organisation, individual team members, whatever or whoever is a risk to the successful completion of the project.

The TOC was initially developed and applied in manufacturing industry where product production involved the flow of raw materials and work in progress through various manufacturing stages leading to a final product. Within

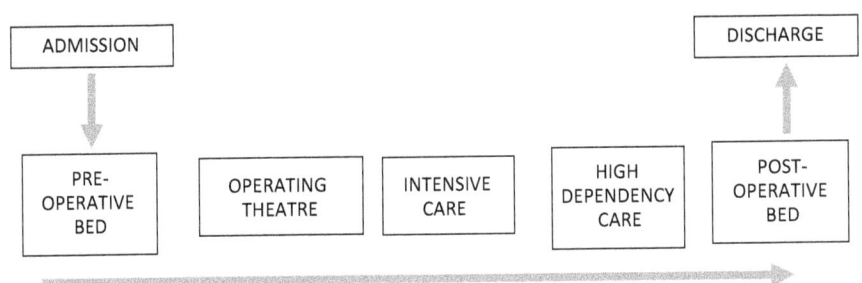

FIGURE 13.1
Example of flow in public services delivery.

these production processes, bottlenecks would occur at various stages in the process leading to the production of finished goods being held up. The TOC is concerned with identifying those bottlenecks and optimising the whole production process.

However, TOC also has great applicability in relation to a wide variety of service industries where the provision of services involves a flow through various stages in the service delivery process and where bottlenecks can occur. Indeed, the TOC creator Eli Goldratt simply defined it as, "A thinking process that enables people to invent simple solutions to complex problems". The TOC has also had a lot of applicability in public services where the process of delivering the service might suffer a bottleneck which inhibits service delivery. One example of this shown in Figure 13.1 concerns planned hospital surgery and shows how the patient might flow through the system.

Clearly the aim of the hospital is to treat as many patients as possible. However, in a flow system like the above, it is often the case that a bottleneck is caused by insufficiency of capacity, in one of the above stages, meaning that a patient transfer cannot take place and so the operation cannot commence until the bottleneck is cleared. This inhibits the total number of operations that can take place.

Management accounting aspects

There are some similarities between lean and TOC but a considerable difference in the main focus of each. Also, there are approaches to TOC which involve linkages to the six-sigma methodology.

However, there are some management accounting approaches which have been developed associated with these operational process developments and these are outlined below.

Kaizen costing

Kaizen costing is closely aligned to lean manufacturing, whose main aim is to eliminate waste through continuous improvement. This is achieved by identifying the best resources and most efficient procedures to remove waste from production.

Improving performance through eliminating bottlenecks

The cardiac surgery department of the Bromford Hospital is under severe pressure. Although its level of resourcing seems reasonable, the department has long waiting lists of patients who require surgical treatment. Hospital management suspects that the problem is that the available resources are not being utilised in the most optimal manner resulting in bottlenecks in the system which are inhibiting patient throughput. Consequently, they have initiated a review of the department.

Basically, cardiac surgery involves a linear flow process whereby patients move through the following stages:

- Admission
- Pre-operative bed
- Operating theatre
- Intensive therapy unit
- High-dependency unit (HDU)
- Post-operative bed
- Discharge

The review team constructed a dynamic simulation model designed to simulate the flow of patients through the surgical system. The model was populated using actual data about the resources of the department and actual data on patient flows (e.g. number of patients, length of stay at each stage in the process).

The modelling exercise showed that there was insufficient bed capacity in the HDU to cope with the flow of patients. This was creating a bottleneck in the system which held back the flow of patients from earlier stages in the process. The model showed that the addition of one more HDU bed would free up the blockage and improve the flow of patients thus resulting in increased patient throughput. Also, it was possible to identify how resources could be moved around the department in such a way as to provide much of the funds required for the additional HDU bed without impacting on the rest of the system.

The necessary changes were implemented and found to work well. Thus, the department had obtained significant increases in throughput at little additional system cost. Clearly, however, there would be marginal costs associated with the increases in patient throughput.

Kaizen is a Japanese term for continuous improvement in every aspect of an organisation's performance and forms part of the lean approach. When the organisation has reached an accepted product design (with changed methods, materials etc.) manufacturing can start. This is where "kaizen" costing comes in. Whereas target costing relates to a product that is not yet in production, kaizen aims to obtain incremental cost reductions in the production phase, as opposed to achieving big improvements at longer intervals. There are two approaches to kaizen costing:

- **Broad based** – improvement activities are focussed on a specific asset or resource in the organisation irrespective of which organisational activities it supports.
- **Specific** – improvement activities are related to the different resources related to one activity or service.

Kaizen costing is based on a philosophy that nothing is ever perfect and improvements are always possible. Kaizen costing utilises the following basic principles.

1. Continuous improvements in the present situation.
2. There are no limits to the improvement level that can be achieved subject to the avoidance of negative effects on quality, staff, safety, etc.
3. Advocates collective decision making and knowledge application.
4. Concentrates on waste or loss elimination, system and productivity improvement – the wastes are the six items described earlier.
5. Establishes standards and then continually works on improving them.
6. Participation of all employees and covering every business area, that is, all the levels, departments and units.

Like lean itself, kaizen costing is strongly cultural in nature and becomes part of the culture of the organisation and everyone is encouraged to make suggestions, however small, that could lead to a reduction in the variable costs.

There seems only to have been limited attempts at applying kaizen costing in public services, although there is clearly much work done on the theme of continuous performance improvement of which kaizen is an element. There would seem to be scope in applying kaizen costing in many public services although it is likely that, in the same manner as for lean in general, the main difficulty is that of developing a culture where employees focus on costs and cost reduction. Public service employees are trained, quite correctly, to deliver high-quality public services and in the absence of commercial pressures it is often difficult to get them to focus on cost issues rather than service issues. Indeed many public service employees on the front line will often say something like "I don't do money". This illustrates the scale of the problem.

Throughput accounting

As we have seen earlier, various approaches to cost accounting usually try to establish the total costs of a product or activity through the allocation or apportionment of the various costs involved to that product or activity. Throughput

Like TOC itself, TA is generally thought of as having main applicability to the production of goods but it is easy to see how it can also be applied to the service sector including banking, public transport, call centres, healthcare etc. One difference in public services which would impact on the relevance of TA is the lack of a distinct revenue stream for specific services being delivered. However, it may have applicability in those public services where charges are levied on clients for the service provided. Also, for services (such as hospital services) where remuneration for the delivery of a range of healthcare services is provided by government based on some sort of national tariff for each service type.

Overall, a full TA system might be thought to be not something a public service would want to adopt. However, the thinking behind the bottleneck resource concept is a useful one which may have applicability in some public services.

Further information about TA can be found in Galloway and Waldron (1988a, 1988b, 1989a, 1989b).

TECHNOLOGY AND MANAGEMENT ACCOUNTING

New technology is set to have a big impact on the practice of accounting in the future. Many themes are talked about including blockchain, the cloud, Internet of things etc. However, in this section, I consider three themes concerning technological developments which will have implications for management accounting in the future.

- Big data analytics (BDA)
- Artificial intelligence and machine learning (AI and ML)
- Implications of technology for management accounting

Big data analytics

In recent years the approach known as BDA has become of increasing importance in all organisations. Big data is a field that involves analysing and systematically extracting information from large datasets that are too large or complex to be dealt with by traditional data-processing application software.

The importance now given to BDA has come about because of two main causes:

- **Amount of data** – the huge proliferation in the amount of data actually being collected largely as a consequence of the digitisation of data making it easy to collect. This can be further considered as:
  - *Volume* – the overall quantity of generated and stored data.
  - *Variety* – the variety of data including text, images, audio, video.
  - *Velocity* – the speed at which the data are generated and processed.
- **Processing power** – the availability of advanced software to analyse large volumes of data.

Basically, BDA involves utilising this advanced software to analyse, in a reasonable period of time, the massive volumes and variety of data (which is now available through the digital revolution) available in order to derive information about the issues being studied. Now organisations of any reasonable size will already hold a wide variety of financial and non-financial data within its data banks. However, BDA goes beyond this and also utilises the much larger pool of data which can be found in external repositories.

BDA can be seen as having three main functions in an organisation:

- **Descriptive** – this involves converting past and current data into usable information in the form of reports, charts, pivot tables and graphs. The idea is to identify patterns by using statistical measures (e.g. the mean, correlation, range, standard deviation) to make informed decisions. Visualising tools may also be used here such as different types of charts, scorecards, frequency distributions, clustering, Pareto analysis.
- **Predictive** – this involves going beyond merely descriptive characteristics of data, by using data from the past and current performance to be able to make relevant predictions for the future. It analyses past performance and makes it possible to come up with relevant forecasts for the future by examining historical data in detail, detecting patterns or relationships and then extrapolating these relations forward in time. Items such as cause-and-effect relationships, the balancing of financial and non-financial, of internal and external measures can be considered. However, the most important assumptions are that data must be relevant, reliable and timely for decision-makers to be able to use. Such forecasts will inevitably be wrong, but it is better to make some prediction knowing the risks of error than to make no forecast at all.
- **Prescriptive** – this involves using experimental design and optimisation to identify the best possible alternative courses of action given different scenarios, criteria and objectives. Many problems simply involve too many choices or alternatives for a human decision-maker to effectively consider (bounded rationality). Prescriptive analytics uses optimisation to identify the best – and most likely – alternatives to minimise or maximise some objective.

Big data and public services

Just a few of the many examples, which can be quoted, about the use of BDA in public services are as follows:

- **Traffic management** – data from traffic sensors can be mapped to time and other metrics to determine traffic patterns as part of planning to alleviate traffic congestion.
- **Regulatory compliance** – big data can be useful for managing natural resources such as soil, forests and water. For example, environmental managers use big data to track if facilities meet environmental regulations.
- **Health services** – data from hospitals, accident reports, disease monitoring, social services and other sources can provide a comprehensive picture of community health trends. For example, a specific area may be seeing more incidents of cancer or sickness due to unknown toxins, or big data can be used to track an epidemic or advise distribution of vaccines.
- **Law enforcement** – big data can prove valuable for law enforcement. Police forces can analyse arrest records, crime statistics and social media to identify hot spots that require additional coverage.

- **Tax fraud** – a huge amount of money is lost from government coffers as a consequence of uncollected taxes and fraudulent claims being recovered. Big data can be used to detect fraudulent refunds and match tax information against billions of personal records.
- **Social services** – big data are having an impact on social security and child care. In Los Angeles County, for example, fraud for low-income child care is on the rise. Data mining has made it easier to identify suspicious cases, resulting in 408 fraud referrals for prosecution. It also has made it easier to identify families in need of social services.

Artificial intelligence and machine learning

Artificial intelligence (AI) is the branch of computer sciences that emphasises the development of intelligent machines that think and work like humans. For example, some current aspects of AI include speech recognition, problem-solving, learning and planning. However, AI is not limited to just IT or technology industry but is being extensively used in other areas such as medical, business, education, law and manufacturing.

Machine learning (ML) is an application of AI that involves systems with the ability to automatically learn and improve from experience without being explicitly programmed to do so. ML focuses on the development of computer programs that can access data and use it to learn for themselves. The process of learning begins with observations or data, such as examples, direct experience or instruction, in order to look for patterns in data and make better decisions for the future based on the examples provided. The primary aim is to allow the computers learn automatically without human intervention or assistance and adjust actions accordingly.

The implications of technology for management accounting

There are many aspects of management accounting practices in public services where AI, ML and BDA can and will have a significant impact, including

- More accurate costing of service activities as a consequence of using a wider variety of cost drivers and a larger data pool;
- Improved cost allocation procedures through using ML algorithms to decide the best approaches;
- Improved financial forecasting by taking account of errors in previous forecasts;
- More accurate budget setting by taking account of errors made in previous budget setting exercises;
- Improved budget variance analysis by taking account of a wider variety of factors than has traditionally been the case;
- Improved forecasting of future demands for public services;
- More sophisticated performance analysis and reporting.

Now these impacts will take place at different speeds within different organisations but they will eventually happen. They will, clearly, have a major impact on the role and work of the management accountant.

A major transformation is taking place in public and private sector organisations, regarding the role of the finance department and its staff. This is illustrated diagrammatically in Figure 13.2.

This implies that, in the future, the roles and focus of management accountants will increasingly be on the provision of analytical services to the organisation. Transactional services will have a reduced focus as a consequence of outsourcing and/or the use of shared services as a delivery medium. While the pace of change will vary from place to place, technological developments mean that such change is inevitable.

In future, public service organisations will expect its management accountants to be champions of evidence-based decision making, translating analytical insights into public service insights and ensuring these are used to improve future prospects and performance. This provides a huge opportunity for public service management accountants to use their combination of accounting and analysis skills with an understanding of the organisation and the services it delivers. Consequently, these technologies will hugely impact on the role and work of the management accountant. If we turn to the role of the public service management accountant of the future, four possible roles can be delineated:

- **Data scientist** – management accountants could evolve into data scientists directly involved in the design and utilisation of new technologies. However, to become a data scientist they must be prepared to invest (and many do) in extensive professional development to complement their accounting skill set with greater expertise in advanced analytical techniques.

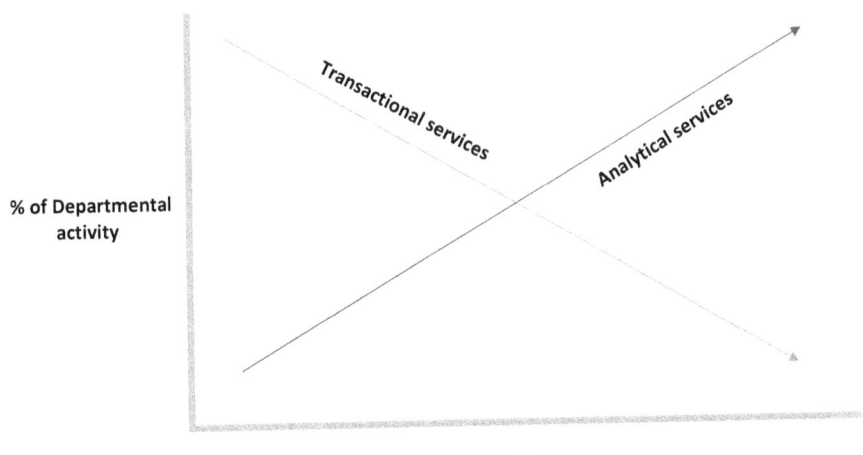

FIGURE 13.2
Change in management accounting activities.

agers, service professionals, IT professionals and data scientists, experts to support value creation in the organisation. This involves participation in data analytics exercises and the interpretation and communication of their findings to interested parties.

At the very least we can be confident that management accountants will need

- An awareness of these technologies.
- An understanding of their capabilities.
- Expertise to interrogate them.

REFERENCES

Albright, T.L. and Roth, H. (1992), The measurement of quality costs: An alternative paradigm. Accounting Horizons (June).

Armstrong, J.S., Green, K.C., and Graefe, A. (2010), *Forecasting Principles*. Wharton School, University of Pennsylvania, Philadelphia.

Baumol, W. (1982), *Contestable Markets and the Theory of Industry Structure*. Harcourt Brace Jovanovich. San Diego, CA.

Birnberg, J.G. and Nath, R. (1967), Implications of Behavioral Science for Managerial Accounting. *The Accounting Review*, Vol. 42, No. 3, pp. 468–479.

Boettke, P.J. and Leeson, P.T. (2002), Hayek, Arrow, and the Problems of Democratic Decision-Making. *Journal of Public Finance and Public Choice*, Vol. 20.

CaPRI (2015), Public Sector Reforms in Jamaica.

Chase, R. B. and Tansik, D. A. (1983), The Customer Contact Model for Organizational Design, Management Science, *INFORMS*, vol. 29(9), pp. 1037–1050, September.

CIPFA, A guide to forecasting in public services.

CIPFA, Financial Management Code, https://www.cipfa.org/policy-and-guidance/publications/f/financial-management-code.

CIPFA, Financial Resilience Index, https://www.cipfa.org/services/financial-resilience-index.

CIPFA, Having a Value-focused Culture: Continually Improving to Face the Challenges of Austerity.

Colgan, A., Rochford, S., and Burke, K. (2016), *Implementing Public Service Reform – Messages from the Literature*. Centre for Effective Services, Dublin.

Collinson, T. (2012), Why is the public sector so complex?, Public Net 16 May 2012.

Colville, I. (1981), Reconstructing Behavioural Accounting. *Accounting, Organisations and Society*, Vol. 6, pp. 119–132.

COSO (2004), Enterprise Risk Management — Integrated Framework, Committee of Sponsoring Organisations of the Treadway Commission.

COSO (2017), Enterprise Risk Management — Integrated Framework, Committee of Sponsoring Organisations of the Treadway Commission.

Cox, S. (2019), An examination the negotiated order of NHS Commissioning: Decisions in the absence of objectivity, unpublished PhD thesis, Nottingham Trent University.

Dilworth, J. (1993), Production and Operations Management, chapter 10, McGraw-Hill.

Drury, C. (2004), *Management and Cost Accounting*. Cengage Learning.

Economist (1993), Nobody knows what strategy is, 20 March 1993.

Economist (2004), Be prepared: What companies must do to face a much-increased range of risks, 24 January 2004.

Elcock, H. (1996), "Strategic management'", in Farnham, D. and Horton, S. (Eds), *Managing the New Public Services*, 2nd ed., Macmillan, London.

EPA (1998), An Introduction to Environmental Accounting as Business Management Tool: Key Concepts And Terms, Environmental Protection Agency.

Freeman, R.E. (1984), *Strategic Management: A Stakeholder Approach*. Cambridge University Press.

Galloway, D. and Waldron, D. (1988a), Throughput accounting – 1: The need for a new language for manufacturing. Management Accounting, November 1988, pp. 34–35.

Galloway, D. and Waldron, D. (1988b), Throughput accounting – 2: ranking products profitably. Management Accounting, December 1988, pp. 34–35.

Galloway, D. and Waldron, D. (1989a), Throughput accounting – 3: a better way to control labour costs. Management Accounting, January 1989, pp. 32–33.

Galloway, D. and Waldron, D. (1989b), Throughput accounting – 4: moving on to complex products. Management Accounting, February 1989, pp. 40–41.

Goldratt, E.M. (1984), *The Goal*, North River Press.

Gray, M. and Barford, A. (November 2018), The Depths of the Cuts: The Uneven Geography of Local Government Austerity. *Cambridge Journal of Regions, Economy and Society*, Volume 11, Issue 3.

Hanover Research (2010), Programe costing models at institutions of higher education, https://pdf4pro.com/view/program-costing-models-at-institutions-of-higher-education-5a46f2.html

Hardaker, J.B. (2004), *Coping with Risk in Agriculture*. CABI Publishing.

Heintzman, R. and Marson, B. (2005), People, service and trust: is there a public sector service value chain?, International Review of Administrative Sciences, December 2005.

HM Treasury (2003), The Green Book: Central Government Guidance on Appraisal and Evaluation, latest update 19 March 2019.

Hofstede, G. (1976), *The Game of Budget Control*. Tavistock.

Holmes, D. (February 2013), Mid-Staffordshire Scandal Highlights NHS Cultural Crisis, *The Lancet*.

Hope, J. and Fraser, R. (1993), *Beyond Budgeting: How Managers Can Break Free from the Annual Performance Trap*, Harvard Business Press, Boston, MA.

Hopwood, A.G. (1972), An Empirical Study of the Role of Accounting Data in Performance Evaluation. *Empirical Research in Accounting, Supplement to Journal of Accounting Research*, Vol. 10, pp. 156–182.

Hoque, Z. (2006), *Strategic Management Accounting*. Pearsons.

Hudson, R. (2019), Why policy failure is so common in the UK, https://blogs.lse.ac.uk/businessreview/2019/01/26/why-policy-failure-is-so-common-in-the-uk/.

IFAC (2005), *Environmental Management Accounting*. International Federation of Accountants.

IMA (2017), Enterprise Risk Management: Tools and Techniques for Effective Implementation, Institute of Management Accountants.

Institute of Management Accountants (2008), Definition of management accounting, https://www.imanet.org/-/media/6c984e4d7c854c2fb40b96bfbe991884.ashx?as=1&mh.

Kaplan, R.S. and Anderson, S.R. (2004), *Time Driven Activity Based Costing*, Harvard Business Review, November 2004.

Kaplan, R.S. and Atkinson, A.A. (1998), *Advanced Management Accounting*, third edition, Prentice Hall, Upper Saddle River, NJ.

Kaplan, R.S. and Bruns, W. (1987), *Accounting and Management: A Field Study Perspective*. Harvard Business School Press, Cambridge, MA, ISBN 0-87584-186-4.

Kaplan, R.S. and Norton, D.P. (1996), *Balanced Scorecard: Translating Strategy into Action*. Harvard Business School Press, Boston, MA.

King, A. and Crewe, I. (2013), *The Blunders of our Governments*. One World.

Kluvers, R. (2001), An Analysis of Introducing Program Budgeting in Local Government. *Public Budgeting & Finance* Vol. 21, No. 2 pp. 29–45.

Knight, F. (1921), Risk, Uncertainty, and Profit, in Hart, Schaffner and Marx (Eds.), Houghton Mifflin Company.

Kotter, J. (2012), *Leading Change*. Harvard Business Review Press.

Leite, H. R. and Vieria, G. E. (2015), Lean Philosophy and Its Applications in the Service Industry: A Review of the Current Knowledge, *Production*, September 2015.

Markides, C. (2004), What Is Strategy and How Do You Know if You Have One?. *Business Strategy Review*, Vol. 15, No. 2.

Mazlan, Y. (2008), Strategic management in the public sector: An interpretive study of the application of strategic management practices in the local authorities in Malaysia, unpublished PhD thesis, University of hull.

Mintzberg, H. (Fall 1987), The Strategy Concept 1: Five Ps for Strategy. *California Management Review*, Vol. 30, No. 1 pp. 11–24.

Mitchell, R.K., Bradley, R.A., and Wood, D.J. (Oct. 1997), Toward a Theory of Stakeholder Identification and Salience: Defining the Principle of Who and What Really Counts. *The Academy of Management Review*, Vol. 22, No. 4 pp. 853–886.

Moullin, M. (2017), "Improving and Evaluating Performance with the Public Sector Scorecard", *International Journal of Productivity and Performance Management*, Vol. 66, No. 4.

NAO (2018), Rolling Out Universal Credit. National Audit Office.

OECD (2019), OECD survey reveals many people unhappy with public services and benefits, https://www.oecd.org/newsroom/oecd-survey-reveals-many-people-unhappy-with-public-services-and-benefits.htm

Parasuramam, A. et al. (1988), SERVQUAL: A Multiple Item Scale for Measuring Customer Perceptions of Service Quality. *Journal of Retailing*.

Porter, M.E. (1985), *Competitive Advantage*. Free Press, New York.

Porter, M.E. (1985), *Competitive Strategy*. Free Press.

Porter, M.E. (1996), What is strategy?, Harvard Business Review, November-December 1996.

Prowle, M.J. (1981), Beyond Specialty Costing: Patient Costing. *Public Finance and Accountancy*, Vol. 8 pp. 47–49.

Prowle, M.J. (June 2007), Radiation Vibes, Healthcare Finance.

Prowle, M.J. (August 2008), Developing Contestability in the Delivery of Public Services. *Public Money & Management*, Vol. 28, No. 4 pp. 255–260.

Prowle, M.J. (2018), Mergers in public services: A panacea?, https://www.linkedin.com/pulse/mergers-public-services-panacea-professor-malcolm-prowle/

Prowle, M.J. and Harradine, D. (2012), Service Line Reporting in a National Health Service Foundation Trust: An Initial Assessment of Its Relevance and Applicability. *Public Money & Management*, Vol. 32, No. 3.

Prowle, M.J. and Lucas, M. (2016), *Management accounting in the contemporary business world*. Palgrave Macmillan, London.

Prowle, M.J., Harradine, D., Latham, R., Lowth, G., Murphy, P., and Orford, K. (2013), *The Importance of Strategic Financial Leadership in the UK Public Sector in a Time of Financial Austerity.* Association of Chartered Certified Accountants (ACCA), London.

Prowle, M.J., Lowth, G., and Zhang, M. (2010), *The Impact of Economic Recession on Business Strategy Planning in UK Companies.* CIMA, London.

Radnor, Z.J., Bateman, N., Esain, A., Kumar, M., Williams, S.J., and Upton, D.M. (2016), *Public Services, Operations Management.* Chapter 1, Routledge.

Reiter, R. and Klenk, T. (May 2018), The Manifold Meanings of 'Post-New Public Management' – A Systematic Literature Review. *International Review of Administrative Sciences.*

Simon, H. (1991), Bounded Rationality and Organisational Learning. *Organisation Science*, Vol. 2, No. 1.

Slack, N., Chambers, S., and Johnson, R. (2001), Operations Management, chapter 4, Pearson Strategic financial leadership in the UK public sector, ACCA London.

Ugyel, L. (2013), *Dynamics of Public Sector Reforms in Bhutan: Interaction of Values within a Hybrid Administration.* Crawford School of Public Policy.

UN ECOSOC (2006), United Nations Economic and Social Council, Definition of basic concepts and terminologies in governance and public administration, New York.

UNDSD (2003), Environmental Management Accounting Procedures and Principles, (EMARIC Environmental Management Accounting Research and Information Centre, United Nations Division for Sustainable Development.

Uzonwanne, F.C. (2016), Rational model of decision making, https://www.researchgate.net/publication/311761486_Rational_Model_of_Decision_Making

Valix, C.T., Peralta, J.F., and Valix, M. (2009), *Financial Accounting.* Volume 1, GIC Enterprises & co.

Welsh Government, 2019, NHS Expenditure Programme Budgets, 2017–18 https://gov.wales/sites/default/files/statistics-and-research/2019-04/nhs-expenditure-programme-budgets-april-2017-to-march-2018-168.pdf

INDEX

Lightning Source UK Ltd.
Milton Keynes UK
UKHW021937260921
391240UK00012B/77